BIG BOOTS TO FILL

DAVID MICHAEL NOLAN

BIG BOOTS TO FILL

The New Maradona, Riquelme, Messi and Beyond

First published by Pitch Publishing, 2023

Pitch Publishing
9 Donnington Park,
85 Birdham Road,
Chichester,
West Sussex,
PO20 7AJ
www.pitchpublishing.co.uk
info@pitchpublishing.co.uk

A CIP catalogue record is available for this book from the British Library.

ISBN 978 1 80150 172 9

Typesetting and origination by Pitch Publishing

Printed and bound in Great Britain by TJ Books Limited, Padstow

Contents

Mexico, 1986 7

Prologue: The Number 10 in Argentina before Maradona 11

1. Diego Maradona, 'El Pibe de Oro' 24
2. Claudio Borghi, 'El Bichi' 55
   Diego Latorre, 'El Gambetita'
3. Ariel Ortega, 'El Burrito' 74
   Marcelo Gallardo, 'El Muneco'
   Fernando Redondo, 'El Principe'
4. Juan Román Riquelme, 'El Último 10' 98
5. Pablo Aimar, 'El Payaso' 125
   Javier Saviola, 'El Conejo'
6. Carlos Marinelli, 'Dieguito'. 146
   Cristian Colusso, 'El Chiri'
7. Andrés D'Alessandro, 'El Cabezón' 166
   Darío Conca, 'El Mago'
   Walter Montillo
8. Carlos Tevez, 'El Apache'. 183
9. Lionel Messi, 'La Pulga' 209
10. Ezequiel Lavezzi, 'El Pocho' 283
   Angel Di María, 'Fideo'
   Sergio Agüero, 'Kun'
11. Javier Pastore, 'El Flaco' 304
   Maximiliano Moralez, 'Frasquito'
12. Franco Di Santo, 'Crespito' 323
   Mauro Zárate, 'El Pibe de Haedo'
   Diego Buonanotte, 'El Enano'
13. Paulo Dybala, 'La Joya' 337
   Diego Valeri, 'El Maestro'

Mexico, 1986

THE 1986 World Cup in Mexico was a tournament dominated by playmakers as never before. In an era before sports science, nutritionists and the unfeasible riches that became part of the game in the first two decades of the next century, football was played at a slightly slower pace.

Not every player was a grass-covering physical beast, not every team played a pressing game designed to deny the opposition space and set up rapid transitions, not every game was played at 100mph. There was more time on the pitch, more space – and in that time and space a playmaker could thrive.

In the 1986 World Cup, played in the heat and humidity of Mexico, so many great players, many bearing the number ten on their backs, orchestrated the attacks of their teams.

From Europe, an ageing Michel Platini attempted to use his sublime vision and consistent goalscoring feats to add a World Cup to the European Championship he claimed with France in 1984.

Denmark fed impressive veteran striker Preben Elkjær with the clever promptings and genius flicks of a young Michael Laudrup. Belgium allowed their own young tyro, Enzo Scifo, the freedom of their attack and he responded with some exhilarating performances. Even the more pragmatic football nations of England and Germany arrived at the tournament with high-profile playmakers in their squads in the shape of Glenn Hoddle and Felix Magath.

South America, perhaps the spiritual home of the number ten due to the wonder of the likes of Pelé, Rivellino and Teófilo Cubillas during the previous two decades, contributed most. Brazil were still dominated by the mature class of midfielders who had made their 1982 side such a wonder – the elegance and goals of Zico behind the strikers with the languid artfulness of Socrates deeper.

Copa América champions Uruguay were built around the guile and creativity of Enzo Francescoli. Julio César Romero, meanwhile, helped surprise package Paraguay escape the group stage with his performances in a team otherwise short of stars. One South American playmaker in particular came to dominate the tournament, however: Argentina's diminutive Diego Maradona.

Maradona was seen as potentially the world's greatest player at the time but, while his talent was never in doubt, he had yet to fully express it on a major stage. After early success in Argentina, where he won the 1981 Primera title with Boca Juniors in his only year at the club, his expensive and high-profile transfer to Barcelona was deemed a failure.

Maradona had won a few cups but injury and scandal had tainted his spell at Camp Nou. His expensive move to Napoli appeared to be a step down at the time, although the success he went on to enjoy has altered that view.

Maradona had arrived at the 1982 World Cup as the star of a strong team sent by defending champions Argentina but he endured a frustrating tournament. The Argentina squad was fractious while Maradona was fouled heavily and persistently in every game – most notably by Italy's limpet-like and efficiently cynical Claudio Gentile and a revolving cast of Brazilians in a game in which the little Argentinian finally snapped and was sent off for retaliation. Argentina went out and Maradona's reputation took a hit, so 1986 provided an opportunity for redemption – an opportunity Maradona embraced. In an Argentina team built around his talents and stuffed with good professionals, he rose to the occasion in every game. As captain, he scored five goals and contributed five assists, including braces against England in the quarter-final and Belgium in the semi-final. In the tightest of circumstances, he also found an assist for the winner against West Germany in the final.

Maradona's performances at the tournament led to him being commonly regarded as the greatest player in world football, and his subsequent trophy-laden years at Napoli only added to his legend. More than that, Maradona gave the number 10 shirt and the playmaker role a mystique it had always flirted with. After him, the '10' on the back of a shirt had more meaning, more magic – especially in Argentina.

Once Maradona had retired, wearing the number 10 shirt for Argentina became both an honour and a burden, and one that came to dominate and define careers. Being labelled the 'new Maradona' was a recognition of potential but also a stamp of impossible expectation. For decades, a series of otherwise fine footballers were regarded as having underperformed, until another little genius, by the name of Lionel Messi, also playing at Barcelona, emerged to make the number 10 shirt and the Argentina side his own.

PROLOGUE:

The Number 10 in Argentina before Maradona

THERE WAS a tradition of garlanded playmakers in Argentina before Diego Armando Maradona was even born.

In the 1940s, when the legendary River Plate team 'La Máquina' (the machine) were thrilling Buenos Aires with their beautiful attacking play, football was a very different game in tactical terms. In the 1920s and 1930s, Argentinian teams were generally set up in a British-style 2-3-5.

By the 1940s, South American coaches had started tweaking their tactics to accommodate the types of players produced by teeming cities such as Buenos Aires and São Paulo. Argentinian footballers already had a style to match the character of the Buenos Aires street urchin thanks to playing the game on rough ground in the city's many barrios – it was impudent, thrilling and fearless.

Argentinian players loved the 'gambeta' (the dance); dribbling endlessly and beating opponents through guile and trickery. This suited the physical character of the youths of Buenos Aires, Córdoba and Rosario, who were often short and slight, the combination of a low centre of gravity, agility and speed compensating for a lack of size and strength.

The mythology of Argentinian football allies with the tango and its combination of elegance and beauty, and the country is famous for both the dance and its football style. Another concept that developed in Argentinian football in the middle years of the 20th century was that of the 'pausa' (pause), the moment when the music of an attack stopped for an instant, allowing somebody to see the gaps, feel the rhythm and exploit both. That 'somebody' was the playmaker, known in Argentina as the 'enganche' (hook), who linked midfield and attack. At that time, what we now call a playmaker was an inside-forward playing on the right or left side of the pitch.

By the 1940s, some Argentinian sides played in a 3-2-2-3 formation in which the inside-forwards tucked in behind the actual forward line, similar to the WM formation popular in Britain and Europe at the time. The number 10 shirt, therefore, which had been typically worn by the left-sided inside-forward, was now worn by one of the two players positioned in the attacking zone at the opposition end of the midfield – what would now be termed 'between the lines' or 'the hole'. Those players needed the vision to find forwards with through balls, the touch and dribbling ability to make use of the tighter marking around the opposition area, and the understanding of space to be able to play as part of a five-man attack.

Before Maradona arrived on the scene, probably the two most famous Argentinian players in that position played together for La Máquina. José Manuel Moreno and Adolfo Pedernera had markedly different characters and playing styles, but both orchestrated and controlled the attack.

Moreno was often compared to Maradona for his chaotic personal life and the many apocryphal stories about his approach to training and fitness. He thought the tango was the best training method for football, drank and smoked to excess, and met pitch invaders with his fists up as befits someone who had been a boxer before he played football. He also sported a rakish moustache and played with an explosive combination of physical power and sneaky creativity that meant Argentinian football fans loved him. His success at River meant he went on to spend seasons in Chile with Universidad Católica, in Uruguay with Defensor, and in Colombia with Independiente Medellín.

Pedernera was more cerebral and controlled than his volatile team-mate. Nicknamed El Maestro, he also spent a few years playing in Colombia after the Máquina era. A players' strike in Argentina in 1948 coincided with a time when money was pouring into the Colombian game, with a huge amount spent by clubs to lure Argentina's stars to travel north.

Pedernera, Alfredo Di Stéfano and Néstor Rossi followed the trail of money to power Millonarios of Bogotá to success. In the early 1950s, the 'Ballet Azul' (Blue Ballet) were widely claimed to be the best club side in the world.

Players such as Huracán's Norberto 'Tucho' Mendéz and San Lorenzo's Rinaldo Martino were figures who definitively established the enganche role as key to Argentina's attacking football style popularly known as 'la nuestra' (our style). It was a source of pride in the nation as it was viewed as beautiful, skilful and intrinsically Argentinian.

La nuestra was a style based on short passing, close control, trickery in the gambeta, and deceptive moves such as the caños (nutmeg) and sombrero (flick). It was also characterised by a certain openness in defence – sides were more focused on scoring goals than anything else. In this system a talented, cunning enganche was crucial. The role required a player who knew how and when to engage la pausa, when to play the key pass, and when to keep a passing move ticking over. An embryonic version of the modern playmaker, perhaps?

* * *

All this may indicate the peculiarity of Argentina as a country and the complexity of its identity. Self-consciously the most European of South American countries, Argentina has always been torn between disdain for the Old World, which spewed hundreds of thousands of working-class immigrants from the cities of Italy to fill the slums of Buenos Aires, and an inferiority complex about its own position in relation to the motherland of Spain and the quasi-colonial power of Britain, which built much of Argentina's infrastructure and whose sailors introduced football to the country by playing it on the docks.

Buenos Aires often feels like a Mediterranean city and porteños (port city people) speak Spanish with the rhythm and musicality of Italians. German and Jewish influences are also evident in many of the country's institutions and cultural assumptions. Then there is an enormous Irish diaspora – the fourth-largest on Earth – and the historic Welsh communities in Patagonia, mingling with persistent economic migration from Paraguay and Bolivia.

While regarding itself as better than the rest of South America, which is a common source of jokes to its neighbours, Argentina has always struggled with how it feels about Europe. However, one area where there was no inferiority whatsoever was football. La nuestra was an obvious expression of that confidence and self-assurance and gave it an importance rare in any modern nation.

By the time Diego Armando Maradona was born on 30 October 1960, Argentinian football had entered a dark period that had started in the late 1950s. President Juan Perón believed in the power of football and politicised it to a degree hitherto unseen in South America. As such, he reportedly refused to allow Argentina to play in the 1949 Copa América – where they would have been defending champions – or the 1950 World Cup in Brazil.

In retrospect this might seem a baffling decision – Argentina had a huge pool of talent playing at or near their peak and could easily have won both tournaments – but Perón was fearful of a similar situation to that which befell Brazil, whose failure to win their home tournament in 1950 after they were beaten by Uruguay in the final saw the country plunge into depression.

The exodus of footballers from Argentina to Colombia and Europe in the late 1940s had started to hurt the nation's game and Perón was heavily dependent on the support of football fans – he had a particular relationship with the masses at Boca Juniors, who famously sang: 'Boca! Perón! Un solo corazón' (Boca! Perón! A single heart). Perón thought defeat for the national team at either tournament could have disastrous social and political consequences similar to the ones Brazil went on to suffer.

Argentina's snub of the 1950 World Cup set off a long-running feud between the Argentinian and Brazilian football associations, which spiked when Brazil refused to support Argentina's bid to host the 1954 tournament. When the honour went to Switzerland instead, Argentina petulantly refused to attend.

In 1957, a young Argentina side won the Copa América, based around the win-at-any-cost ethos of 'los angeles con caras sucias' (angels with dirty faces). The main contributors to the ethos were the attacking trio of Humberto Maschio, Antonio Angelillo and the superb Omar Sívori, of River Plate, who combined goalscoring forward play with unmistakable enganche elements, linking play from the hole with trademark caños and through balls to his strike partners.

When all three players moved to Italy in 1958, the Argentinian Football Association (AFA) banned them from playing for the national team. Sívori and Maschio would go on to represent Italy at the 1962 World Cup, while Angelillo also made a couple of appearances for the Azzurri. That hysterical example of Argentinian isolationism helped create the disaster of the 1958 World Cup in Sweden, where a much-weakened side was overrun and humiliated by West Germany and Czechoslovakia, suffering 3-1 and 6-1 defeats respectively.

That 6-1 loss to the Czechs in Helsingborg has taken on a retrospective importance and is now seen as the death of la nuestra. It rocked Argentina's self-image of a nation that saw its perceived superiority reflected in the quality of its football. That image had been shattered by the Czechs. The golden age of Argentine football was over and it would be two decades before free-flowing attacking play returned to the national team.

The dynamic approach and athleticism of the European sides in 1958 surprised Argentina, who spent another decade or so attempting to catch up. In doing so, the traditionally aesthetic strengths of Argentinian football were neglected in favour of other, less savoury aspects.

If today respect and appreciation for the beauty of Argentinian football's skill and creativity is widespread, it is perhaps balanced by a different attitude to the country's undoubted excellence at the 'dark arts'. Much of that comes from the memory of the 'anti-fútbol' often attributed to coach Victorio Spinetto at Vélez Sarsfield and adopted by the Argentina side at the 1959 Copa. In reality, Spinetto was a pragmatist who had reservations about la nuestra.

He encouraged his own number ten, Osvaldo Zubeldía, to play more like a box-to-box midfielder and prized what Argentinians generally refer to as 'garra' (grit and spirit). Uruguayans place even more value on this and refer to it more specifically as 'garra charrúa' (claw of the Charrúa, an indigenous people). Spinetto called it 'fibra' (fibre) and used it to help his sides win games. He believed winning was all that mattered in football.

In time, Zubeldía retired as a player and adopted many of his mentor's beliefs about tactics and fitness. He became coach of Estudiantes de La Plata and transformed a provincial side into champions when he led them to success in the Copa Libertadores, South America's continental club competition. It also reflected a shift in the emphasis of football throughout Argentina.

In the 1966 World Cup, Argentina were eliminated after a bad-tempered encounter with hosts England in which their number ten and captain Antonio Rattín was controversially sent off.

That had been presaged by an even more fractious game with West Germany, full of gamesmanship, tactical fouling and whining to the referee, all elements of the game we have become accustomed to but little seen on such a grand stage in northern Europe at the time. Argentina's behaviour was blisteringly criticised by the British press, and the elimination of the team in a match the nation deemed a 'fix' was taken as evidence European sides had it in for Argentina, which only encouraged the trend for anti-fútbol.

Racing Club de Avellaneda were the first to showcase the blend of brutality and cynicism that had become ascendent in Argentine football when they beat Glasgow Celtic in the 1967 Intercontinental Cup. Each side won their home leg so the tie was decided via a play-off that became known as the Battle of Montevideo. Celtic, by now accustomed to the violence and trickery of the Argentines, responded in kind and the game was seen as a new nadir for the sport. That youthful Racing side has been otherwise remembered as a team capable of beautiful football and it is perhaps evidence that new insecurity had crept into Argentinian football as the side felt the need to resort to a different approach against the assumed superiority of European opposition.

Zubeldía's Estudiantes sank even lower when they beat Matt Busby's acclaimed Manchester United side in 1968. Both games were tainted by spitting, head-butts, elbows, punches and time-wasting. Despite an influential offside trap and impressive athleticism, the Argentinian team were destroyed once more by the international football media.

If, in previous decades, Argentinian sides had been famed for their style, sparkling skill and the imagination of its players, the world was now seeing teams notable for their ability to provoke and injure the opposition and, crucially, doing just enough to win games.

The playmaker for that Estudiantes team was Juan Ramón Verón, father of Juan Sebastián, and his elegance and skill was counterbalanced by players such as Carlos Bilardo, who has since admitted to carrying a pin on the pitch to prick opposition players in an attempt to provoke a violent response to get them sent off.

Bilardo, Verón and Estudiantes defended their Intercontinental title against AC Milan in 1969. After a 3-0 defeat in Italy, Estudiantes' 2-1 win at La Bombonera in Buenos Aires was overshadowed by the manner of their play. Assaults, head-butts, the punching of Italian golden boy Gianni Rivera and the fact Argentina-born Milan player Néstor Combin was stretchered off (and subsequently arrested) led to bans for several Estudiantes players, general condemnation even in the Argentine press, and a boycott of the competition by European clubs.

* * *

Something needed to change in Argentinian football and that something was prompted by the arrival of César Luis Menotti. The coach, who had been an elegant journeyman midfielder known as 'El Flaco' (skinny one), loved the stylish, all-conquering Brazil side that had won the 1970 World Cup. It featured his old Santos team-mate Pelé and the dashing Rivellino as twin playmakers in a free-flowing, artistically expressive team.

Menotti set about introducing something equally beguiling but along more stylistically Argentinian lines when he took over at Huracán. The coach was a romantic, a liberal, a philosopher, and he viewed football as a team game that should be played with lots of short passes, many tricks and feints, and positional interplay.

Huracán, nicknamed 'El Globo', had enjoyed success in the pre-professional era of Argentine football but had been overshadowed by their giant Buenos Aires neighbours in the decades since. Menotti's arrival changed that overnight. His Huracán side featured a line-up of stylish, clever attacking players who used flicks, dribbles, caños and sombreros. They switched positions fluidly to create space and scored lots of goals. Crucially, they played a brand of football that was obviously la nuestra but, where the Argentinian teams of the late 1950s and 1960s found their play was made to appear ponderous by more dynamic European opposition, Menotti's side played la nuestra with the ability to shift gears. They moved the ball slowly when they could but quickly when it hurt the opposition, generally around the penalty area.

Menotti employed a 4-3-3 system with a 'cinco' (number five) in the form of Francisco Russo. By that point, Argentine shirt numbers reflected roles and expectations. If the number ten was worn by the most creative player or enganche, the number eight was also a creative midfielder, but generally one who played in a more shuttling, box-to-box role. They were expected to track back and link both ends of midfield. The number nine was a centre-forward, often a tall, powerful striker who could lead the line. The number five not only disrupted opposition attacks and provided protection for the defence, they generally began attacks from their own half. Not in the way of modern quarterback-style holding midfielders with sprayed long passes but in a way befitting the nation of la nuestra – short passes and one-twos, dribbling and moving the ball upfield.

There were some dazzling attacking players ahead of Russo, most notably the mercurial René 'El Loco' Houseman. He was a fantastic dribbler, possessed dizzying pace and trickery, and his dissolute lifestyle recalled that of Moreno and foreshadowed that of Maradona.

He was not alone in bringing flair to the team. Miguel Angel Brindisi would go on to star alongside a young Maradona at Boca Juniors but was a devastating goalscoring midfielder at that point, capable of setting up team-mates or scoring himself. They were allied with the equally prolific Carlos 'El Inglés' Babington. 'The Englishman' was another who was deadly in combination play around the box; dribbling, misdirecting and dinking the ball to team-mates.

Omar Larrosa was the final attacking midfielder in that famous line-up and this surfeit of offensive talent created a team that seemed to be a living repudiation of everything anti-fútbol stood for. They were a team who famously attracted the fans of other clubs to watch them play, such was the pleasure they gave.

They – together with the continued success of a devastatingly talented, old-fashioned enganche at Independiente by the name of Ricardo Bochini, who prodded and prompted the Buenos Aires giants to four successive Copa Libertadores in the early 1970s – also suggested the time was right for a new breed of Argentine playmaker to redefine the number ten role.

Having won the 1973 Metropolitano Championship with his Huracán side, Menotti was handed the biggest job in Argentinian football. The 1974 World Cup had been another disaster. Again, a talented Argentina squad that included the likes of Houseman and Babington alongside younger stars such as Mario Kempes were humiliated by a European side playing football that seemed on another level. The 4-0 pasting at the hands of Rinus Michels's Netherlands was based around the talents of a more modern kind of playmaker – one Johan Cruyff.

Menotti got the job in the aftermath and set about transporting the kind of football his Huracán side played to the national team. In a way, he was lucky. He had a bunch of highly receptive players, including hungry younger stars such as Mario Kempes and Daniel Passarella, who would accept his ideas. And although his liberality meant Menotti abhorred the military dictatorship that was tearing Argentina apart, its focus on impressing at and winning the 1978 World Cup – to be played in Argentina – meant the coach's demands for his team were accommodated.

Perhaps his most baffling and controversial decision was to exclude the most exciting young prospect in Argentinian football from his squad but Menotti thought Maradona could upset the balance and chemistry of his team. The risk paid off and Argentina won the World Cup playing some magnificent, exhilaratingly attacking football.

Menotti used Valencia's Kempes, nominally a prolific line-leading striker, as an unorthodox playmaker, dropping into the hole to harass opposition defences with his aggressive, pacy dribbling and ability to score from anywhere.

The cult of 'Menottismo', born during his time at Huracán, was enshrined and became one of the guiding principles in the way football is seen in Argentina. Menotti stayed on to guide his nation's defence of their title at the 1982 World Cup in Spain and, this time, he could no longer ignore Diego Maradona.

ONE

Diego Maradona, 'El Pibe de Oro'

THE CULT of Maradona means the story of his early years is a familiar one. Born in Avellaneda, his parents had moved from Corrientes in the northeast of the country, where they had been brought up in huts made from clay, manure and reeds. Diego was named after his father and both his parents worked the kind of jobs that had not changed for a century. In Buenos Aires, his father found a job as a factory worker, while his mother became a maid.

As well as a name, Diego also inherited something of his father's build – short, squat and powerful, with a large head due to the mix of his father's Guaraní and Italian heritage.

Diego was raised in Villa Fiorito, a shanty town to the south of Buenos Aires, where his father built their house using bricks and sheet metal.

Years later, Maradona would claim in interviews that Villa Fiorito had made him who he was – an archetypal 'pibe' (kid) of Argentinian folklore, playing football with a bundle of rags in a 'potrero' or area of waste ground, living on his wits and trickery, always fighting to survive.

And he would have had to fight to survive in Villa Fiorito – it had no police station. It was ruled by criminal gangs and suffered from the kind of violence and poverty that would have been shocking in most of Europe or the US at that time.

Given a football by his uncle, Maradona's honest and hardworking parents quickly realised that their son's talent was their best chance to escape poverty. Diego went from scraping a living as a street urchin in central Buenos Aires to local fame for his ball-juggling skills. Archive footage reveals his magical control of the football, and it wasn't long before he was signed up by 'Los Cebollitas' (the little onions), the youth team of Argentinos Juniors.

The Buenos Aires club had been one of the founding fathers of Argentinian professional football but spent most seasons fighting relegation and had dropped a division and returned without ever winning a championship. They did, however, have a reputation for being a great nursery for football talent, a reputation that the discovery of Maradona would firmly fix as a key to the club's DNA.

Maradona was signed at the age of eight and his coach immediately took him to see a doctor who treated boxers. Diego was prescribed a course of pills and injections to aid his growth and physical development. It would not be the last time Maradona accepted medical aid to compete as an equal on the pitch, even if later on it would be painkilling injections to deal with the consequences of the absurd number of fouls he suffered during his career.

Maradona made his debut for Argentinos Juniors' senior side on 20 October 1976, ten days before he turned 16. This made him the youngest player in Argentine league history and he became a legend within minutes, after nutmegging Juan Domingo Cabrera. With his blend of cocksure impudence and sublime skill, Maradona arrived more or less fully formed.

He spent five years at Argentinos Juniors, scoring 115 goals in 167 games, while soaring to fame in his homeland and growing a personal fortune bolstered by the clever guidance of Maradona Productions, a company that profited from the commercial use of his image.

Even as a young player, Maradona had a sponsorship tie with Puma to wear the company's kit and boots, a deal that lasted his entire career and proved extremely fruitful for both parties. It was also a hint of Maradona's potential and the way the corporate structure around football was ready to exploit it. Puma had established a strategy based around signing only the most talented and iconic stars to wear its Puma King boots. Pelé had worn a custom pair at the 1970 World Cup and famously delayed a kick-off so he could tie his laces, giving the boot and brand immense exposure, for which Puma paid him a significant bonus. George Best also wore the boots, as did Johan Cruyff in the 1974 World Cup and Mario Kempes in 1978.

When Puma saw Maradona, the company saw the future and there was huge pressure on Menotti to select him for the 1978 World Cup. Menotti stuck to his guns, however, and although Maradona was selected for the preliminary Argentina squad, Menotti told him he had missed the final cut due to inexperience. Maradona wrote and spoke of his heartache at missing out, which was increased by the fact he had already made his senior debut against Hungary in February 1977 and been acclaimed the best youngster in the country, with two full seasons at Argentinos Juniors behind him. Maradona wept but later acknowledged the negative energy he felt became a motivation, something that became a theme in his career.

He was already a terrible loser, having been indulged by coaches and team-mates, and had an agent and the beginnings of a group of hangers-on surrounding him. Maradona talked about his paranoia about Menotti, believing the coach was jealous of him. Even as a 19-year-old, Maradona spoke about the pressure his newfound fame had brought to his life and family.

Instead of taking him to the World Cup, Menotti selected Maradona to represent Argentina at the 1979 World Youth Championship in Japan, a tournament that served as an international unveiling of the little playmaker's incredible gifts. Playing in a free-attacking role in and around the hole alongside another talented number ten, River Plate star Ramón Díaz, Maradona wowed observers with his performances at the tournament. Díaz scored eight goals and won the Golden Boot, while Maradona scored six and won the best player award.

Aside from an easy 5-0 win over minnows Indonesia, Argentina faced tough opposition. They shaded a tight match against one of the only nations with a comparably rich factory of young players, Yugoslavia, wiped out a Poland side that would be the basis for the senior team that reached the semi-finals of the 1982 World Cup with a 4-1 victory, then obliterated Algeria 5-0 in the quarter-finals. That set up a heavyweight semi-final clash with Rioplatense rivals Uruguay, driven by their own star playmaker Rubén Paz. Argentina won 2-0, then defeated USSR 3-1 in the final, a match settled by a beautiful Maradona free kick.

Maradona's gifts were evident at this point in his career. He possessed staggering close control, arguably the best seen in elite-level football. His low centre of gravity and thick, short legs allowed him to surge and pivot at will, and he could accelerate explosively when required. The ball always seemed under his control. This was the gambeta of Argentine football culture and Maradona did it like no one else in the modern era, setting off on slaloming runs from midfield at pace, dragging defenders with him, shedding them in his wake, twisting and turning, rolling and prodding the ball wherever he needed it to go.

That meant, however, that from the start of his career he was targeted with wild tackles while playing with heavy footballs on surfaces that were often terrible. Argentinian dark arts included knee-high, studs-up challenges as well as sly trips and barging slides. Maradona came of age as a flair player in an era when referees often turned a blind eye to rough play and in a country where defenders were expected to do anything they could to stop the opposition. He began to suffer injuries around the time of his transfer to Boca Juniors and, in a way, his career would be seriously affected by them from that time on.

Dribbling was not all Diego offered, he had an eye for goal too. He could score from distance and tended to take free kicks as if he was stroking a pass, placing the ball precisely in the corner of the net. He also made late runs into the box to meet crosses and in one other way was a typical Argentinian enganche – his passing was stupendous.

If the modern memory of Maradona – fuelled by highlight reels of the famous goals and a seminal and deceptive photograph from the 1982 World Cup in which he seemingly dribbles towards a mass of Belgium players – is of a player taking on defences alone, rewatching his performances reminds you Maradona was a team player with many dimensions to his game.

He often used his dribbling proficiency to draw the opposition towards him so he could play a perfectly timed through ball and free a team-mate in front of goal. So many of his alternately direct and mazy runs became beautiful assists because of his gift for la pausa and incredible vision. Later in his career, after injury, age and a lifetime of pain-killing injections had robbed him of much of his pace and dynamism, he still retained that ability. He played deeper, prompting and cueing up younger players around him who were there to do his running.

In that, he resembled the most classical examples of the Argentinian number ten – such as the idol of his teens, Ricardo Bochini, and his eventual successor at Boca Juniors, Juan Román Riquelme. Even without pace, Bochini and Riquelme were players capable of dominating a game by setting their own rhythm and forcing the game to conform to it. Bochini saw every run, every inch of space before him, and he had a genius for slowing and then slipping the ball through gaps invisible to all except him. Maradona claimed that, after an early devotion to Boca's legendary forward Angel Clemente Rojas, he 'caught the Bochini bug'.

His heroes undoubtedly resemble Maradona's footballing fathers. Rojas was a famously stylish player in the era of anti-fútbol, adept at the gambeta, a dribbling goalscorer adored by the Boca faithful. Bochini, on the other hand, was calm and cerebral, allowing the ball to do the work. Maradona took the gifts of each and improved them. Added to that was Maradona's unique personality; a rage, passion and energy forged in the wastelands of Villa Fiorito and a childhood warped by his own genius.

His 1981 transfer to Boca Juniors, the team he supported, saw a thrilling season that included two goals on debut, a trademark dribbled goal in the Superclásico win over River Plate, and his solitary league title in Argentinian football. However, his transfer fee to Boca almost bankrupted the club and, following numerous rows with coach Silvio Marzolini, Maradona was transferred to Barcelona in 1982 for a then-world record fee of £5m.

* * *

By that point the pattern of his career was becoming established. Everywhere he went, Maradona's fame and talent attracted attention. He caused trouble; or trouble found him. His entourage indulged him and he fell out with team-mates, club and football association officials and reporters. Tales of his personal life and excesses began to spread, even as he was trying to establish a reputation as a family man. Despite all that, even on a bad day, Maradona's singular genius was evident when he played football.

At the 1982 World Cup he was singled out by the opposition and systematically fouled to an extent that recalled the treatment of Pelé in various tournaments for Brazil. Maradona's legend was already so powerful it even made the players who fouled him famous.

Claudio Gentile, the uncompromising Juventus defender who man-marked Maradona in Argentina's loss to eventual champions Italy, fouled him six times in total in that game, yet stuck at his side throughout, niggling and jostling in a relentless way that, in modern football, would earn him a red card to go with the yellow he received for his third foul on Maradona.

In Argentina's clash with a Brazil side that was arguably the most beautiful to grace that tournament, the Brazilians showed another side to their game. Brazil's respect for the talent of Argentina's number ten saw them queue up to kick and trip Maradona whenever he had the ball. The golden boy from Villa Fiorito, so used to getting his own way on the field, eventually snapped and kicked out in retaliation, getting himself sent off.

The tournament was a miserable experience for the World Cup holders. The squad was split along generational lines, with the veterans of 1978 and the younger players clashing repeatedly as Menotti proved unable to solve those problems. The team had also arrived in Spain from an Argentina that found itself amid a deepening crisis after years of junta rule.

The military dictatorship, by this point reviled internationally for 'disappearing' thousands of its own citizens while it struggled to cope with huge economic problems, had declared martial law and invaded the Falkland Islands – known in Argentina as Islas Malvinas – seemingly as a patriotic distraction from domestic issues.

The media, cowed by the government, spewed the official line that the Falklands war was being won. In Spain, the players who were still based in Argentina saw the truth on television and many, still feeling distaste at the way the junta used the 1978 and 1979 victories as propaganda, were disgusted.

For his part, Maradona did not play badly and he and Osvaldo Ardiles had a good understanding in midfield, but it was already obvious that, to really thrive, he needed a team built around his talents. He needed that indulgence and, even at that young age, expected it. But in a team with huge stars such as Passarella and Kempes, Maradona was just another famous player, not yet the talisman his genius demanded.

* * *

The story in Barcelona had similarities with that of Argentina's national team. On the pitch, Maradona's price tag and growing celebrity made him a target. He dazzled in some performances but Barcelona, even then, were expected to challenge for and win titles, and a variety of factors conspired to prevent that. For Barcelona fans, this stretched the drought since they last won the Spanish league to a decade and, in an era when Basque sides Athletic Club and Real Sociedad rose to claim titles, many wondered whether the vast sums spent on Maradona's transfer and wages had been wasted.

One of the factors in the fans' unrest was the number of Maradona's absences from the team at key stages. In his first season he spent 12 weeks out after contracting viral hepatitis. In his second, an ankle injury caused by a terrible tackle ruled him out for three months. Maradona did not help himself, either. Despite scoring a famous goal against Real Madrid, forging unlikely on-field chemistry with rival playmaker Bernd Schuster, and enjoying success in cup competitions, he also alienated many supporters through his extended battles with club president Josep Lluís Nuñéz and gossip that raged around the city about his personal life.

Maradona had been rewarded, praised and celebrated so consistently he could barely accept any authority and his relationship with Barça coach Udo Lattek was strained from the off.

Partly in order to handle Maradona, Barcelona replaced Lattek with Menotti, who moved training sessions from mornings to afternoons to avoid forcing the Argentinian to get out of bed early after another late-night session in town.

Timekeeping was becoming a recurring issue – Lattek reportedly left him behind at an away game after growing sick of waiting for him to board the team coach – as was Maradona's attitude to the demands on him to play in friendlies on top of so many fixtures. His body was already worn despite his young age, from the many kicks and trips he had received and the painkilling injections that allowed him to play in games he should have sat out. Yet he could not or would not change his style of play. His style was what made him Diego Maradona, and his bravery in persistently taking the ball and running at and past defenders who wanted to stop him was part of that.

Yet it was already evident his body would eventually stop him from playing like that particular version of Diego Maradona. In the run-up to a Cup Winners' Cup tie against English giants Manchester United, Maradona had been suffering from back problems for days. He received a series of injections to help him play but his body appeared to react to the medication – his reflexes were off and he did not seem himself. Menotti substituted him and, although Barcelona won the home leg 2-0, Maradona was criticised for his anonymity.

He had left the pitch and gone straight to the dressing room, where his mood swung between fury and self-pitying paranoia about his perception the Catalans were trying to destroy him. At that point, the expectation on Maradona was he would always make the magic happen. Anything less was a disappointment.

In the second leg, he was again muted and a United team inspired by the dynamic – if equally injury-prone – Bryan Robson beat Barcelona 3-0 and eliminated them from the competition.

At the same time, it was also reported Barcelona were unhappy at not receiving money for Maradona's image having paid so much for his services. Maradona, always ready to respond to any rebuke or insinuation in the press with his own juicy quotes, made his displeasure clear.

* * *

The injury that would basically end Maradona's time at Barcelona once again made the defender who was responsible for it famous. At the time, Barcelona and Athletic Bilbao were genuine rivals; the Basque club played more functional, British-style football than the aesthetically pleasing Catalans and games between the clubs were always tense and frequently dirty affairs.

The battle felt sporting but also ideological and almost political. Barcelona's snooty superiority complex about their classier attitude could have been designed to enrage a Basque support still living off the enmity of years of struggle against a Francoist-Spanish state it accused of crushing their culture and nation. They saw their football – tough, pragmatic, winning – as inherently Basque.

Athletic centre-back Andoni Goikoetxea was already infamous in Barcelona for a horrendous tackle on Schuster in 1982 that left the German with a cruciate ligament injury that sidelined him for nine months, forcing him to miss a World Cup where his presence may genuinely have changed the course of the final.

In truth, he never fully recovered, and in a 1984 game was determined to exact revenge. He hunted down Goikoetxea and brutally fouled him but the 6ft 1in defender was unhurt and took his own vengeance the only way he knew how. He charged into midfield and hacked a dribbling Maradona down from behind, snapping an ankle bone and rupturing several ligaments. Goikoetxea's infamy was sealed as the 'Butcher of Bilbao'.

Coaches and clubs traded barbs for months. Goikoetxea, who had only received a yellow card in the match, was banned for 18 games, reduced to seven on appeal. Meanwhile, Maradona began his lengthy recovery. In 2018, *The Sun* reported Goikoetxea kept the boot he wore that day on display in a glass case at home, just another sign of the legendary status already accorded to Maradona.

The climax to the entire affair only served to further add to the legend. Although Maradona had showcased his sublime gifts and immense force of personality by masterminding a 2-1 win for Barça in a Super Copa Final at the San Mamés in Bilbao, scoring both his team's goals in a game marred by a then-record 50 fouls, his final game for Barcelona would also come against his Basque nemeses.

The final of the Copa del Rey, before almost 100,000 fans at the Bernabéu in Madrid, was recorded as a 1-0 win for Clemente's Athletic, who claimed a historic league and cup double. But it is remembered chiefly for the riot that broke out after full time, when Maradona responded to goading by Athletic's Miguel Sóla with a knee to the face.

An instant melee broke out, with players from both teams, officials and substitutes wading in as Maradona aimed kicks and elbows at anybody in Athletic red and white. Goikoetxea proved unsurprisingly adept at hand-to-hand combat, leaving his stud marks on Maradona's thigh and chest.

The universal condemnation that followed that battle only added to the controversy surrounding the Argentine in Barcelona. There were rumours of drug use, later confirmed by Maradona, who admitted using cocaine for the first time while living in Barcelona. Menotti reportedly told the board his Barcelona team could win the title in 1985 without the distraction and provocation of his countryman.

Nevertheless, footage of a tousle-haired Maradona fearlessly fighting bigger Athletic players, pumped up and every inch a warrior, merely added to his mystique. Few players who followed him and vied to be seen as the world's best could ever have done something like that but, with Maradona, who never shied from excess in any part of his life, it seemed entirely fitting. He thrived on 'bronca' (aggro), feeding off that mix of anger and frustration that often seemed to fuel his brilliance in a way so many of his successors at number ten for Argentina, Boca and Barcelona could not.

His next destination, Napoli, seemed a much better fit than Barcelona. SSC Napoli were easily the biggest club in southern Italy but had endured decades of relative underperformance. Numerous spells as a solid top-five side, one second-place finish, a few appearances in the UEFA Cup and Cup Winners' Cup, and Coppa Italia triumphs in 1962 and 1976 were counterbalanced by relegations. They were as likely to be fighting to stay up as they were competing for a place in Europe.

Given the passion for football in the historically and enduringly working-class city of Naples and the fact

Napoli have consistently had the fourth-highest number of supporters in Italian football – behind northern giants Juventus, AC Milan and Internazionale – made the club a sleeping giant. The city of Naples could have been custom-made for Maradona, too. The working-class identity and sense of struggle against the snobbery of the wealthy northern industrial elite was perfect.

Maradona's transfer was a statement of intent. He cost a then-world record £6.9m and, within a few years, had been joined by more leading players in a massive rebuilding job that made Napoli a genuine Serie A force. The team was set up to allow Maradona to express himself. The purchase of Fernando De Napoli to play alongside Salvatore Bagni gave Napoli a powerful defensive base in midfield, while Maradona combined beautifully with the skill and athleticism of striker Bruno Giordano and the cold-eyed precision of another forward, Andrea Carnevale.

Maradona wowed Napoli supporters in his first season. Serie A was renowned for the tightness of defences that had spent a couple of decades honing 'catenaccio', a system that emphasised tightness of marking and – in the version perfected by Argentinian coach Helenio Herrera at Inter Milan in the 1960s – used a sweeper to pick up any loose balls or stray attackers.

By the 1980s, despite the defensive discipline of the Italian national side, many Serie A sides embraced only elements of the style after it had been rocked by Dutch total football in the 1970s. Those elements were generally enough to win, however, and teams facing Italian clubs in European competition knew goals would be hard to come by. Maradona turned catenaccio into a myth. He played with a freedom and imagination that showed how constricted he felt at Barça, so corporate and cold in comparison with the passion and liberty he found in Naples.

Italy appeared to suit him – the fans' frenzy, the play-acting, arguing with the referee – the Maradona who emerged at Napoli was recognisably the same player who had made Argentinian football his own, perhaps because Italian football had some resemblance to the football culture he grew up in.

* * *

Maradona, emboldened by his performances at the World Cup and comfortable in the city and at the club, inspired Napoli to a double in 1986/87 and, with that, became more than a footballer in Naples. Today the city is full of images of the Argentine, on par with a religious cult. He delivered the city's first league title, in style, and felt at one with the fans – a working-class warrior taking on the north.

He was now the best player in the world – perhaps the greatest player to grace the game – and he played for Napoli. Following that amazing season, Napoli recruited another star in the form of Careca from São Paulo. The Brazil forward and Maradona struck up an instant understanding and became close off the pitch, too. On it, Careca's pace, power and explosiveness were intuitively served by Maradona's probing and ability to create space.

Together with Bruno Giordano, the trio became known as Ma-Gi-Ca and, alongside another Brazilian in the form of the rugged, skilful Alemão, the club won the 1989 UEFA Cup for their first European trophy and another Scudetto in 1990.

Napoli is Maradona's crowning achievement in his club career. The success the club enjoyed is unimaginable without his presence, and he is inextricably linked to the club. This is recognised by Napoli, who are not shy of exploiting Maradona's fame to enhance the club's legacy. After Maradona's death in 2020, Napoli renamed their stadium Stadio Diego Armando Maradona and launched a shirt that featured Argentinian-style sky-blue-and-white stripes. They also retired the number 10 shirt. Who, after all, could live up to that number? His image and retro football shirts from the 1980s are now omnipresent in the city on matchdays.

Despite the success, his time at Napoli followed the established pattern – Maradona attracted trouble. It was chaotic from the start – 85,000 fans turned up for his unveiling but he complained Napoli had failed to meet his needs in terms of the home and car they provided. In Barcelona he had been isolated and unhappy but in Naples his family arrived from Argentina, and his entourage became immense. Maradona's drug problem, which he claimed started during his lonely period recovering from injury in Catalonia, was not helped by the easy availability of drugs amid a busy social life.

In a way, Napoli fans did not care. As long as Maradona delivered on the pitch, the tabloid claims and gossip about his nocturnal habits were tolerated. But other clubs were sniffing around the superstar. His contract was due to expire in 1987 and Napoli soon realised that contract would need to be renegotiated and extended or the player could be lured by a wealthier rival. As a case in point, Maradona admitted to meeting with AC Milan chairman Silvio Berlusconi about a possible move. Maradona judged the Italian politician a 'gentleman'.

Maradona later claimed he could never have played for another team in Italy. The crucial reason was his fear of the Napoli fans – whose love became another addiction – would despise him. Maradona joked he might be murdered if he joined another Italian club and, in reality, rumours of connections with the Camorra – a Mafia-type criminal organisation operating in Campania – added spice to his jest. Regardless, by 1989 the situation at Napoli was becoming increasingly disagreeable for both player and club. With his drug problem becoming more serious, leading to more compromises, Maradona was set for a move to Marseille.

Napoli had done much to accommodate Maradona's hedonism. He stayed out late partying and missed training, even though, as at Barcelona, it was moved to allow him to sleep into the afternoon. Club owner Corrado Ferlaino had promised Maradona he could leave at the end of the 1988/89 season and Olympique Marseille, then France's biggest club, seemed the perfect fit for the Argentinian. Like Buenos Aires and Naples, Marseille is a working-class port city and the fans are passionate, fervent and obsessive. At the time, club owner Bernard Tapie was sparing no expense to transform the team into a winning machine, bringing stars such as Maradona's friend and rival Enzo Francescoli and England international Chris Waddle to the South of France. They played explosive, exciting football.

That dream didn't last long. On the pitch, just minutes after lifting the UEFA Cup in 1989, Ferlaino told Maradona he was going nowhere. In his autobiography, *El Diego*, Maradona wrote he wanted to hit Napoli's owner over the head with the trophy. And Maradona – so pampered and proud – could bear a grudge. Once Napoli had crossed him, his rebellious nature turned against the club itself. His behaviour worsened. He would do it for the team, for the fans, but not for the club. His natural inclinations were to rebel against authority but he failed to consider just how much protection Napoli offered him. In the 2019 *Diego Maradona* documentary directed by British filmmaker Asif Kapadia, the star admitted passing drugs tests by using a fake penis filled with somone else's urine. Maradona was coddled in his bubble of superstardom, which protected him from repercussions.

Yet Maradona's talent was so great, he still delivered. He was not one to let supporters or team-mates down if he could help it. Even when alienated and angry and constantly sniping at club directors and the Italian FA, he was the driving force behind the 1990 Scudetto, contributing goals and assists in key games and lending the team his immense aura.

His talent did seem to be fading, though, and he was increasingly injured. His idiosyncratic training regime – which would aim to have him in shape for the 1990 World Cup in Italy – did not always make him seem as dynamic as he once had been. All those kicks, knocks and injections – and cocaine – started to affect his body. Players such as the young Gianfranco Zola were learning the playmaker role at his feet, and increasingly replacing him on the pitch. Indeed, Maradona insisted on Zola wearing his number 10 shirt in a February game at Pisa, while he wore the number 9, telling reporters Zola was 'the future' of Napoli.

* * *

The problems reached a nadir with Napoli's elimination from the European Cup in 1990/91. Maradona was already more disaffected with life in Italy that season after his World Cup experience with Argentina, when they lost to West Germany in the final. He took an extra-long holiday to get over the disappointment, missing the first four games of the season because he was hunting in Argentina with some of his entourage. On his return, he partied more and played less – but the magic was still there when he was fit.

In the European Cup home leg against Spartak Moscow in November, he was electric. Napoli hit the post three times and Maradona was uncontainable. But, for the return leg, he failed to show up for the coach or at the airport. A group of players arrived at his house to plead with him only to find Maradona asleep after another hellacious bender and his tearful wife, childhood sweetheart Claudia Villafañe, telling them he wasn't coming on the trip.

On awakening, however, Maradona hired a private jet. The European Cup was the only major trophy he had yet to win – indeed, he had only played in five games – and Maradona flew to Moscow to take a nocturnal stroll around Red Square in a characteristically enormous fur coat before joining his team-mates. The club was furious, with Maradona consigned to the bench. In a move rife with symbolism, Zola wore the number 10 shirt – the future had arrived, and Maradona had been left behind.

Maradona, wearing number 16, came on in the second half but was powerless to prevent a terrible game from going to penalties. He scored his but Napoli lost and exited the competition. Infamous club administrator Luciano Moggi and Ferlaino were incensed and Maradona's time at Napoli was all but over. They could not sell him out of fear of the fans but his lifestyle meant it would be easy for them to engineer his exit in other ways. Just as at Barcelona, a steady drip of stories in the media accelerated to a flood. Maradona's personal life, his many indiscretions, his friendships with criminals, his own complaints about

Napoli, his personal training programme were all topics of conversation. The *Guardian* reporter Ed Vulliamy claimed that during an investigation into the Camorra in Naples in 1991, he heard Maradona's voice on wiretaps.

Worse was to follow. After a game at Bari in March 1991, Maradona failed a random drug test. Traces of cocaine were found in his urine. Napoli virtually disowned him. He received a 15-month ban and left Italy at night to avoid the paparazzi who followed his every step.

He would return to Europe for a season at Sevilla in 1992/93, where he played well under his former Argentina coach Carlos Bilardo, but it was obvious the pace that had made him so unstoppable as a dribbler had evaporated, except over short distances and in occasional bursts. His range of passing and understanding of space and movement remained, however. Maradona's physical gifts were undeniably waning but he was still special, and evolving.

* * *

His last three seasons as a professional footballer were spent back home in Argentina. He played a few games for Rosario giants Newell's Old Boys in 1993/94 and, while a talented Argentina side under Alfio 'Coco' Basile toiled to qualify for the World Cup, notably losing 5-0 to a Colombia inspired by another number ten in the vivid shape of Carlos Valderrama, Maradona merely watched on as a fan.

The public obviously turned to their hero, the living legend who had won them a World Cup, and Maradona answered the call, playing in the play-off games against Australia in 1993. It was a good version of the new Maradona in the Sydney leg, contributing an assist as Argentina drew 1-1. The turgid return was settled by a deflected Argentina goal but they had qualified. Diego had delivered for his country again – in a World Cup tournament, he was capable of anything.

The enormous pressure he had been under for most of his life would not go away, however, driving him to declare in February 1994 he would not play at the tournament. He relented but the constant media attention in Argentina only exacerbated the pressure as journalists camped outside his home. Maradona snapped, shooting at the group with an air rifle, injuring four and adding to his many legal worries.

The tournament started off like a dream, however. That Argentina side was probably the most gifted Maradona ever played in; beautifully balanced and with some extraordinary talent. The combined gifts of Fernando Redondo, Gabriel Batistuta, Abel Balbo and Maradona's old friend Claudio Caniggia took much of the creative burden off his shoulders, and the snapping presence of Diego Simeone alongside Redondo seemed to liberate him.

Maradona played well in the first two games of the tournament, scoring against Greece and creating two against Nigeria. His style at that age was beautifully efficient. He was far less mobile – the toll of those injuries evident to anyone who had watched him in his prime – but he could still do it in bursts. Closed down, he could send a defender one way while his body seemed to pump a jackknife and the ball went another. His passing was one-touch; a dazzling spectrum of flicks and redirected play, the ball stroked and caressed, chipped and spun. He dictated the game with the minimum of touches.

His goal against Greece and insanely passionate celebration were the last iconic images he was to contribute on the pitch at a FIFA tournament. The goal was a blindingly rapid series of one-touch passes around the edge of the Greek area, awakening memories of Menotti's version of la nuestra, and finished with a beautifully precise Maradona placement into the top corner. The celebration had him charging at a camera, eyes bulging, face contorted into a Hulk-like snarl.

People were already speculating about his mental state or perceived chemical consumption and perhaps few were surprised when he failed a drugs test for ephedrine. He argued it was due to a mix-up with energy drinks but the world had become used to Maradona arguing and used to his excuses. He was ejected from the tournament and a weakened, stunned Argentina, who replaced their star with Ariel Ortega, one of the many 'new Maradona' candidates that Argentine football was already producing, went out to Romania.

All that was left were two final seasons back at Boca Juniors and there his magical talent was on fitful display. The range of passing was undiminished. He pinged raking balls around the pitch, played no-look backheels and sent flicks around defenders with the casual artistry that made it look so easy. His promptings and vision made his team-mates look better than they were.

Again, he was playing with players who had been compared to him. Diego Latorre was also approaching the end of his career and had moved from a number ten role to more of a dedicated second striker, but he had the awareness and skill to play profitably off Maradona. Meanwhile, a youngster named Juan Román Riquelme was rising through the ranks and played alongside the veterans on a few notable occasions.

However, Maradona's swansong ended in yet another failed drugs test. After an August 1997 game against Argentinos Juniors – in which Maradona and Riquelme both started – Maradona tested positive for cocaine. On 25 October, in another hugely symbolic moment, Riquelme replaced Maradona at half-time during the Superclásico at River Plate's Estadio Monumental. It was Maradona's last professional game.

* * *

So many great Argentinian players – many of them number tens and possessing some of his characteristics – have followed in the footsteps of Maradona, it is reasonable to ask what made him better than all of them.

Talent is unquantifiable and certainly subjective but Maradona's achievements are singular. Beyond his spell at Napoli, there was his peak period with the Argentina side between 1986 and 1990, when he inspired his country to one World Cup triumph and another final. The impact of that in Argentina cannot be overstated. Nor can the manner of it. The dominant performances in 1986 have never really been matched by any player in a subsequent tournament. Players have scored more goals and been as devastating in single games but Maradona did it repeatedly. And his team won the trophy.

When coach Carlos Bilardo, he of anti-fútbol Estudiantes fame, decided to set up his side to get the best out of the number ten, he took the leash off a player who until then had always been constrained in the national team. But now he had a strong, compact, disciplined side around him. Batista protected the defence. The classy Valdano stretched the opposition. Runners moved in space around Maradona.

He could surge on the ball if he chose. He could pick passes into channels. He could play one-touch give-and-go, moving, agile, unpredictable. Maradona was the ultimate team-mate and captain; a leader, vocal, charismatic, supportive but also a one-man team. If the side was in trouble, they all knew if they gave the ball to Diego he would get them out of it. As he did in 1986, scoring two against England and two against Belgium. Those goals are legendary, and probably the best examples of his talent. His dribbling, explosive pace and close control against England were like nothing seen in a modern game of such magnitude. To do it again against Belgium seemed supernatural.

The other side of his personality was evident too; however, the 'Hand of God' goal was Maradona at his most cunning and impish. His later pride in his trickery only served to enhance his cult status – outside of England – but his performance in the final was just as important. In that game, in front of 115,600 people at the Azteca Stadium and millions watching worldwide, West Germany shackled him as well as any team had at that tournament. Followed around the pitch by a young Lothar Matthäus, Maradona faced two players whenever he took possession. Matthäus was swiftly joined by whichever German player was closest, showing how much the Germans feared Maradona's ability to hurt them.

If you watched a lot of Maradona, you'll know one of his typical moves when tightly marked was to dribble into the narrow space between two opponents, turning one or both. With his markers chasing or leaning on him, he squeezed his squat little frame between them, all three heading in the same direction. Then, with a deft suddenness made possible by his low centre of gravity, Maradona would shift direction. Stopping, shrugging, twisting; he was away and the area occupied only an instant before by two opponents was now space. Maradona knew what to do with space.

But the German players stuck to their roles well. Maradona was relatively stifled and repeatedly smothered. When he did manage to break free, he was fouled. Yet still he created moments of genius; one characteristic gambeta through the middle was ended by a double challenge by goalkeeper and defender that could have been deemed a penalty – and would be in this century of football. The referee's decision may have been affected by Maradona's trademark way of selling a foul – a leap upwards, arms aloft, head thrown back in apparent agony followed by a roll which, such was its extravagant, Italian theatricality, seemed to convince some referees he was diving.

He also pulled off roulettes and shimmies and elaborate flicks during the final but the lack of space forced him to mainly use his beautiful, deft vision and range of passing to dictate the game – and that would settle the final. Argentina had dominated but, with customary determination, West Germany had come back from 2-0 down to equalise in the 80th minute.

Three minutes later, Maradona found himself receiving a return ball just inside his own half in the centre circle. Instantly, two German players converged at speed and another two approached to stifle that sublime ability to wriggle free, as had been the case all game.

That was the moment Maradona exploited all the attention he had been getting to play in team-mates as he explored space around the edges of the game.

This time, the tiring German defence was slack and Jorge Burruchaga, a tidy attacking midfielder playing at Nantes in France, whose understanding with Maradona had thrived in the tournament, was already running. Maradona turned as the ball fell, opening his body and playing a one-touch through ball with his divine left foot – a volley, chipped delicately just before the ball was about to bounce. Maradona barely seemed to look up.

The German defence was made irrelevant by the perfect pace and spin on the pass and Burruchaga, loping clear into the other half, took four touches as a German defender bust a gut in pursuit. The Argentinian prodded the ball through goalkeeper Harald Schumacher's legs for the winner.

Maradona was universally acclaimed after lifting the World Cup. No player had ever made a tournament their own in such a way: the unbelievable talent he consistently displayed, the fighting spirit to lead such a surprise package through the tournament, the bravery in the face of persistently brutal methods employed by opponents to stop him, and the beauty of the football.

Maradona's legendary status was sealed. His second goal against England, that accelerating slalom from the halfway line past five hapless opponents, would go on to be voted goal of the century. The first, the handball, made him a villain in England but a hero to anybody who loves an underdog. Images of him from the tournament have become as iconic and recognisable as any in football history – leaping to beat England goalkeeper Peter Shilton (7in taller) to the ball with his hand; in the middle of his dribble in the lead up to the second goal, the ball apparently glued to his foot; holding the trophy aloft, face contorted in ecstasy, the triumphant superstar and captain.

That World Cup win meant the tainted 1978 victory could be relegated in significance. There were no awkward questions about this tournament, no allegations of corruption. Argentina were world champions because the best player in the world played for Argentina.

In the years between 1986 and 1990, Maradona's success at Napoli only underlined that he was unquestionably the best player in world football. Old rivals such as Platini and Zico faded towards retirement, while youngsters who had arrived at the 1986 tournament like Denmark's Michael Laudrup and Belgium's Enzo Scifo proved their quality without approaching Maradona's rarefied heights.

However, after the euphoric high of Mexico, the Argentina team stumbled. They were beaten by eternal rivals Uruguay in the semi-finals of the 1987 Copa América, a competition Maradona would never win – he was still in self-imposed international exile when Argentina won the tournament in 1993 – and arrived in Italy in summer 1990 in awful shape. Numerous key players, including Jorge Valdano and José Luis Brown from the 1986 team, were out injured. Maradona was no different. A toe injury, compounded by an ankle problem he picked up in the group stage, would limit his impact for the entire tournament.

His ankles were a constant issue at this point. Years of being kicked while playing for Argentinos, Boca, Barcelona, Napoli and Argentina had left a terrible imprint on his legs. The cortisone injections that helped him carry on had created their own long-term damage, while the referees who allowed the brutality during the 1980s had not helped the little number ten.

He was not himself but he was still important to his country, team-mates and football as a whole and this was a Bilardo team, led by the anti-authoritarian rebel that was Diego Maradona. If Argentina could not play their way to the 1990 World Cup Final with skill and finesse, they would growl and battle every inch of the way instead.

Becoming the pantomime villains every big tournament requires, Argentina ground out win after win. Caniggia and goalkeeper Sergio Goycochea – who only played after Nery Pumpido broke his leg in a collision with his own defender Julio Olarticoechea – were the team's standout players.

Maradona was anonymous, save for suffering some astonishingly brutal, blatant fouls by Cameroon in the tournament's opening game in a shock loss and using his hand to block a goal-bound shot in the second game against Russia, which Argentina won 2-0.

In their homeland, the public loved the spirit their players were showing; their grit, cunning and determination. Maradona's chief contribution came in attempts to antagonise the Italian authorities and players.

After the Cameroon game he spoke about his satisfaction that in booing him and his team-mates, Milanese football fans had at last ceased to be racist, because they were supporting an African team. And he knew how to needle Italy; he had been doing it on behalf of Naples fans for a while. Northern Italy, and the snobbish and withering way it regarded Naples, were a constant theme but his sarcasm and scorn were undoubtedly fuelled by the worsening experience he was enduring in Naples and perhaps frustration with his own play.

Argentina drew 1-1 with Romania to squeak through the group only to face arch-rivals Brazil in what looked likely to be a classic. As it was, Brazil battered Argentina. Goycochea's heroics and the woodwork kept them alive in the game but Maradona was invisible until, ten minutes from time, he seized another defining moment and reshaped it to his will.

Receiving the ball in the centre circle with four Brazilians in attendance, Maradona threw one of his patented wriggling hip feints and surged away. Ahead of him were four more Brazilians. Maradona dribbled at pace for goal as a defender jostled him, another moving to cut him off. That low centre of gravity, surprising muscle and unerringly amazing balance kept him up, the ball at his toes, until at the last instant he angled a little out towards the wing. Going over under the impact of a shoulder-barge, Maradona finally played the pass, putting it through the legs of one Brazilian, eliminating four opponents, and into the stride of Caniggia, who threw his own feint on the goalkeeper before finishing coolly into the empty net. It felt as though only Maradona could have created such a moment. So anonymous and disappointing so far, he settled a game with one moment of genius – and not just any game but a derby of fearsome proportions. That was the legend of Maradona.

After that 1-0 win, he never matched it on the pitch for the rest of the tournament. Argentina fought their way to the final with a siege mentality and without Maradona's inspirational gifts, often carrying a passenger, albeit an iconic, great leader. They were playing some grim football but you got the feeling Bilardo was loving it and it seemed they were destined to win the trophy.

Argentina beat a superior, ten-man Yugoslavia side on penalties in a dreadful game in Florence despite the most talented players on the pitch, Maradona and little Serbian number ten Dragan Stojković, missing their spot-kicks.

The semi-final, played in Naples against a talented Italian team featuring Franco Baresi and Giuseppe Bergomi in defence alongside the youthful zest of Roberto Baggio, Paolo Maldini and Gianluca Vialli, went the same way. Argentina clung on, came back from a goal down to equalise through Caniggia, had a man sent off, and won on penalties.

Maradona's football was uninspiring but his trash-talking enhanced his legendary status once more when he reminded Neapolitans before the game that the rest of the country hated them most of the year so they should support Argentina.

For the first time in the tournament, at the Stadio San Paolo, the Argentina national anthem was not booed, the catcalls and loathing that had met Maradona and his team elsewhere were absent. Instead, banners attested that Naples loved Maradona but supported Italy. It also meant the final in Rome against West Germany saw the Italians in the crowd standing squarely against Argentina and Maradona. Throughout the tournament, the tension between the star player and the country where he made his living had been building. Eliminating Italy and his comments about Italians guaranteed Rome would let him know how it felt.

The tension and incidents began before the game. Maradona's brother, driving Diego's Ferrari, was pulled over by Roman police, an Argentina flag was vandalised at their training ground and, when the team emerged into the night at the Stadio Olimpico, the wall of noise that greeted them was thunderous. Maradona took it personally. During the national anthem, buried beneath a wave of jeers, as the camera tracked along the Argentina team, a scowling

Maradona clearly mouthed at the camera: 'Hijos de puta (sons of whores).

Again, his team were dreadful. Cynical and negative, Argentina lost two men to red cards and were defeated by a questionable penalty. Maradona was a shadow of himself and wept as old rival Lothar Matthäus held the trophy aloft but the little genius had contributed another moment to his legend. Only Maradona could begin a World Cup Final hurling insults at the home nation's supporters. He was a genius but he was also a boy from a Buenos Aires barrio, and both things made him special.

If he had already entered a rarefied pantheon of elite players in his youth, after the 1986 World Cup Maradona was in a bracket with only a handful of contemporaries. Perhaps only Pelé was truly seen as a rival but, for all his extended achievement and skill, the Brazilian lacked Maradona's abundance of personality. He was sporting, diplomatic, reserved and dignified; Maradona was none of those things.

The choice between them for who is the greatest player in history depends on how you view football itself. Both were blessed with divine talent. Both achieved great things. But Maradona was a divisive character; controversial and often unlikeable. In contrast, Pelé could seem boring. In their homelands, any young player who had any passing similarity to either was haunted by comparisons and, due to the size of Maradona's personality and cultural prominence, that was a heavy burden on generations of Argentinian players.

TWO

Claudio Borghi, 'El Bichi'
Diego Latorre, 'El Gambetita'

IT MUST be like being the cleverest pupil at school. You always get the highest marks in tests and receive never-ending praise from your teacher. But then you have to leave for another school, one for older children. Maybe you're not the cleverest pupil any more. Maybe someone else – another who was best in their class – is smarter, does better in tests, and gets more praise. Maybe, for the first time, they make you feel inferior.

Or maybe not. Maybe you're the one making the others feel inferior, all the way through school through every grade and age. But then you reach university – and you don't stand out at all. There, everyone was the cleverest at their school; a thousand people who have always made others feel inferior.

Now imagine you're a young footballer. You play as the link between the forwards and midfield, in the hole. Your passing is beautiful – visionary, incisive, perfectly timed. You can dribble too, able to swerve and turn at speed past dumbfounded defenders, and you score your fair share of goals. You have been a phenomenon at your club. A golden boy of whom great things are expected. You are called up to the national team, hoping to play a major role in the World Cup, but another player who plays in your position has also been called up and is, there can be no denying it, better than you. He is the best player in the world, maybe the best player of all time. He leads your country to victory at that World Cup, scoring unforgettable goals, and you are lost in his wake.

You never play for your country again. Your career, while continuing in a variety of countries for a multitude of clubs, flounders and you never live up to those early expectations. You are Claudio Borghi. You are a nearly man.

* * *

Maradona was so significant in Argentinian football that the hunt for the 'new Maradona' began while he was in his prime. Borghi was a contemporary of Maradona's, born four years later in 1964 on the outskirts of Buenos Aires.

Like Maradona, he was developed from a young age at Argentinos Juniors and its growing reputation as a finishing school for what Argentinians call 'cracks' (star players) gave his talent and potential a glow it might not have received at any other club. Taller than Maradona, Borghi played a similar role. He liked to pick up the ball and run at defences, while his range of passing – often one-touch – opened up his side's attacking across the forward line.

Even though they played together in the youth team before Maradona's ascent to the senior squad, comparisons between the two were inevitable and, in a sense, Borghi was lucky he was being compared on the basis of the young

Diego's early career, before the World Cup win and heroics at Napoli.

Borghi's talent tended to suggest he would go on to enjoy his own great career, although even Maradona expressed retrospective reservations about him in one of his autobiographies, claiming Borghi was always telling him to pass more as he thought dribbling endlessly was pointless without an end product.

Borghi was emerging at the perfect time. In 1984, Argentinos Juniors claimed their first Argentinian title after a thrilling final day when they won and rivals Ferro Carril Oeste lost. That victorious Argentinos team was a strong blend of youth and experience, with international centre-back Jorge Olguín playing behind future 1986 World Cup mainstay Sergio Batista, who anchored the midfield. That base allowed attacking talents such as Mario Videla – bought with some of the money the club made from the sale of Maradona to Barcelona – and veteran midfielder Emilio Commisso to flourish. That meant a 20-year-old Borghi could be used by coach Roberto Saporiti as an exciting substitute, injecting pace and invention.

By the following season, under new coach José Yudica, who had worked wonders when winning a title with Quilmes in 1978, Borghi was playing more and with growing confidence and acclaim as Argentinos claimed a second title in a row. The club – enjoying the greatest period in its history – would go on to contest its first Copa Libertadores Final in 1985. In that era, Copa Libertadores finals were two-legged affairs, with a play-off at a neutral venue as a decider in the event of an aggregate draw. Borghi played in both legs, each a 1-0 win for the home side, before appearing in the play-off in Asunción, Paraguay. That game was also tied, 1-1, with Argentinos winning 5-4 on penalties. Borghi scored his.

Next came the final of the Copa Interamericana, which was played on a sporadic basis between 1968 and 1998 between the winners of the South American CONMEBOL Copa Libertadores and the North American CONCACAF Champions Cup. The logic behind it was the refusal of UEFA and CONMEBOL to consider allowing other confederations to compete in the more prestigious Intercontinental Cup.

Unsurprisingly, the giant clubs from South America who qualified for that 'final' generally beat the sides from North and Central America. Independiente, Nacional of Montevideo and Atlético Nacional all won two or more titles, with only Mexico City superclubs UNAM and Club Ameríca bucking that trend before DC United won the last such game in 1998.

Argentinos Juniors beat Defence Force of Trinidad and Tobago 1-0 in Port of Spain to claim their title and, for a club that had only won the equivalent of the Argentinian third division before 1984, any trophy was a big deal. Borghi missed that match but arrived on the international stage with the next final the club contested.

The Intercontinental Cup had always been a bigger deal in South America than it was in Europe. Winning it held prestige – beating the wealth and strength of Europe counted for a lot in South America, particularly in Argentina, with its enduring insecurities about the Old World. In the 1985 Intercontinental Cup Final, often referred to as the greatest in the competition's history, Argentinos would face an all-conquering Juventus under the legendary and long-serving Giovanni Trapattoni.

Juve were Italy's most successful and well-supported club, and under Trapattoni were a strong and disciplined outfit who entrusted their elite playmaker, three-time Ballon d'Or winner Michel Platini, with responsibility for creating and scoring goals.

Platini was one of Maradona's rivals for the title of best player on Earth; elegant and cerebral, his passing was wonderful, he had an almost artistically perfect first touch, and he scored a bewildering number of goals for a player who was stationed behind the forward line – managing to notch 25-plus in each season between 1982 and 1985. In that time, he also starred in the phenomenal France team that won the 1984 European Championship on home soil.

To complement his gifts, Juventus brought in another number ten. Michael Laudrup was a young Dane who had emerged at Brøndby in Copenhagen and transferred to Lazio in 1983. His development there drove Juve to buy him in 1985, with the long-term aim of replacing an ageing Platini. Short term, he replaced dynamic Polish striker Zbigniew Boniek and, playing as more of a pure second striker than a playmaker, he and Platini composed a beautifully imaginative and dangerous forward line alongside the prolific wandering Italian international striker Aldo Serena.

It was something of a shock, then, when 20-year-old Claudio Borghi outshone the two celebrated Juventus maestros in a final played in Tokyo in December 1985. Borghi repeatedly surged forward on the ball, unafraid to take on the stubborn Italian defence. He drew fouls from cynical trips and the more rugged chops Maradona had grown accustomed to in Europe. He played impudent flicks around Juventus' markers, first-time through balls, and more composed lofted passes.

Borghi looked the finished article; another talented, deadly Argentine number ten – although he wore nine in that game – and big European clubs began to pay attention. He was the first 'new Maradona' before the term 'new Maradona' was even a thing and his subsequent career, while successful by most metrics, showed the dangers of that tag.

Despite the quality of their exciting performance and Borghi's energy and potential, Argentinos Juniors lost that final. The game ended a 2-2 draw, with Borghi contributing a spectacularly Maradona-esque dribble and assist for the second goal, putting Argentinos in the lead before Platini created and Laudrup scored a late Juventus equaliser. Juventus won the ensuing penalty shoot-out 4-2 and Platini the man-of-the-match award – he had scored a breathtaking disallowed goal – but Borghi's emergence was the story of the game for any European scouts.

His talent and impact was recognised by a place in the Argentina squad at the 1986 World Cup, where he jostled with legendary Independiente playmaker Ricardo Bochini for the role of Maradona's chief understudy. Borghi started two of the group games, playing as a second striker alongside Valdano and in front of Maradona, a nervy 1-1 draw with then-champions Italy and a 2-0 win over Bulgaria.

Part of Borghi's problem – even at that stage – was that, while talented, he wasn't quite mature enough to work around Maradona. And his talent wasn't unequivocal; when he had somebody truly special in his team, Maradona found a way to accommodate them, to make his talent dovetail with theirs. He did it with Careca for Napoli and later with Caniggia for Argentina.

Borghi did not demand that consideration from Maradona. He was unpredictable and scintillating in tight spaces yet he already had a habit of disappearing from games. This fault would become more marked over his long, strange career, and is a huge part of what many see as his wasted talent. So Diego did his thing and Borghi was largely anonymous.

The Italy game was tight and unkind to creative players but, in the Bulgaria game, Argentina took an early lead through a fourth-minute Jorge Valdano goal. Bilardo, typically, hooked Borghi at half-time, replacing him with the defensively minded Olarticoechea, and that was the end of Borghi's participation in the tournament. Argentina played their way into more consistent form without him, Maradona came into his own, and Borghi was forgotten.

When Bilardo wanted to waste time by bringing on a sub in midfield near the end of the semi-final against Belgium with Argentina 2-0 ahead, he was always going to reward the legend that was Bochini instead of the youngster from Argentinos, who could be thrilling but was also a risk. Still, Borghi won the World Cup while virtually a kid with his whole future ahead of him. His career was off to an excellent start.

* * *

Borghi spent another year in Argentina before being brought to Italy by a newly wealthy, resurgent AC Milan in 1987. Milan had been perhaps Italy's most glamorous club in the 1950s and 1960s, with scudettos and European trophies regularly won by a stylish side epitomised by the cool of playmaker Gianni Rivera. The 1970s and early 1980s were less kind, featuring a single league title and even relegation.

Their recovery was partly funded by the wealth of new chairman Silvio Berlusconi, who wanted foreign stars to drive his team to success. Here was the Maradona route from Argentina to a giant European club, the same route taken by the likes of Sívori and Kempes in the past, but Borghi was one of the first to take it with an expectation of success and flair created by Maradona hanging over him.

In his book about the Milan side he crafted, visionary coach Arrigo Sacchi refers to Borghi as a player wanted by Berlusconi and acknowledges he was 'not the new Maradona' after all, before claiming his later career was anonymous. In truth, his timing was unfortunate. So much of a career at that bewilderingly high level can come down to fortune; be that in the guise of injuries, signings or performances.

In that era, the 'two foreigners' rule applied throughout much of European football. In the same year Milan bought Borghi, they bought a duo of talented Dutchmen – Ruud Gullit and Marco van Basten. The Ajax products were unveiled alongside Borghi at the San Siro but, behind the smiles, they must have known they were competing for two places in what was otherwise a very strong and entirely Italian team.

Borghi was still developing but had shown flashes of what might be possible, against Juventus in the Intercontinental Cup. On arriving at Milan he delivered a man-of-the-match performance and a goal for Milan in the Mundialito tournament against Porto, where he looked very much the classic Argentinian enganche, directing the attacking football played by his team with a dangerous variety of passes, flicks and shimmies. But perhaps he was not quite ready for the mean defences or disciplined approach he would find week in, week out in Serie A.

His style was unpredictable and could be dazzling – he loved to dribble and could beat a defender from a standing start – but he was inconsistent and a bit of a rebel. If Argentinos Juniors produced beautiful footballers, it also seemed to breed footballers with strong characters. Maradona and the forthright Fernando Redondo are both examples but Borghi was never shy of giving his views, and never afraid of going his own way.

In terms of football, Borghi's direct rivals for places were intimidating. Gullit was already a muscular, dynamic and intelligent presence all around the pitch, while Van Basten has a good claim to be the most complete striker in European football during the past half-century. Both hit the ground running and Borghi was loaned to nearby Como, then a mid-table Serie A outfit, to allow him to acclimatise to Italian football.

Como coach Aldo Agroppi was defensively minded and he and Borghi had entirely different visions of how football should be played. Hence, Borghi rarely started and, when he got to play, he often played badly. He has since suggested he and Sacchi did not get along either, based on Borghi's disgust at the Italian's strident demands for running drills in training. Sacchi's glib dismissal of Borghi suggests there might be some truth to that. It was not an expected part of the Maradona route, and Borghi struggled. Still, the 'two foreigners' rule was to be altered to a 'three foreigners' rule in 1988, so there was hope Borghi might be recalled to Milan for the next season.

After the Netherlands swaggered their way to the 1988 European Championship that hope receded. Sacchi persuaded Berlusconi to add another Dutchman to the Milan squad in the shape of Frank Rijkaard. Borghi, frustrated and annoyed at Sacchi, moved to Swiss champions Neuchâtel Xamax. He played little there and was soon back in Argentina with a much-hyped move to River Plate, who had a policy of bringing in big names under their new coach, the legendary César Menotti.

His 1978 World Cup-winning captain Daniel Passarella was probably the biggest signing, returning after six successful years in Italy with Fiorentina and Inter, but there were others. Borghi's 1986 Argentina team-mate Sergio Batista was brought in; Uruguayan striker Jorge da Silva returned from years in Spain with Valladolid and Atlético Madrid; and prolific midfielder Omar Palma had been lured from Rosario Central alongside the young and exciting Abel Balbo from Newell's Old Boys.

Borghi's signing excited River fans perhaps more than any other. He seemed a player born for River, whose supporters pride themselves on the style and beauty of their side's play. But it did not work, Menotti's team struggled and Borghi was characteristically inconsistent, mixing moments of individual brilliance with passages of anonymity.

After one goal in 21 games, Borghi was gone and the pattern of a journeyman half-genius was established. He still garnered attention from some of the biggest clubs in the South American game, attracted by his name and the gifts he sporadically displayed. Borghi would spend a season at a club, six months perhaps, then move on. He had developed a niggling knee injury that would confine him to the bench or stand for periods each season, and eventually ended his career a mite prematurely.

He moved from Brazilian behemoths Flamengo back to Argentina for a while, completing spells with Independiente before moving on to Unión de Santa Fe and then Huracán. From there he went to Chile's biggest club, Colo-Colo, where he won another Copa Interamericana and a Recopa Sudamericana in 1992.

His time there was Borghi's most successful since he left Argentinos Juniors. He scored five goals in 18 games, something of an indication of how expectations around him had changed during the past few years. Again he moved on – a few months back in Argentina with Platense, then a spell with Correcaminos from Victoria in Mexico. His time with the national team was over, and he was now a confirmed footballing itinerant.

Borghi was drawn back to Chile, where he would spend the rest of his career. In 1995 he did well at O'Higgins, then had a three-year period at Audax Italiano, where he was loved by fans for his artistry and flair and helped the team achieve a third-place finish in the league while reaching a cup final. His knee problem had become a more regular worry, though, and it contributed to him finishing his career with a season at Santiago Wanderers.

In the few years between his retirement and the start of what would be an excellent coaching career, taking in league titles in Chile and Argentina and spells coaching giants such as Colo-Colo, Boca Juniors and the impossible task of replacing Marcelo Bielsa at the Chilean national side, Borghi spoke of the idea of living up to Maradona. He knew what he was talking about. He had played with Diego and admitted there could be no new Maradona, no heir.

Claudio Borghi, for all his talent, had shown how heavy a burden any comparison with Diego Maradona could be for a player. He was to be the first of many.

* * *

Although he had spent more time in his playing career at Argentinos Juniors, Maradona has come to be associated with Boca Juniors. They are seen as 'his' club. The fact he always professed his love for them helped create this impression. After his second spell there, he attended games and wore Boca shirts, showing he shared the passion of the ordinary fans. Boca's image as the club of the working class of Buenos Aires was a perfect fit for Maradona's own image – the people's player, one of them. For the players who came after him at Boca, that meant there was an added pressure. They were playing in Maradona's position, at Maradona's club, wearing Maradona's number on the back of Maradona's jersey.

Diego Latorre was really the first Boca player to endure that process and is popularly seen as the first 'new Maradona'. There were numerous similarities. Latorre, born in Buenos Aires in 1969, was short and agile, and an exciting exponent of the gambeta. His 5ft 7in frame was slighter than Maradona's but, as a youngster, he had a similarly electric burst of pace.

Latorre emerged through Boca's youth teams in the 1980s and made his debut against Platense in 1987, scoring a goal. Fans were excited by his dribbling prowess. He had the ability to surf over challenges due to a Maradona-like sense of balance allied with a natural confidence that gave him the bravery to try the unlikely. He was a precocious talent and the comparisons had already begun.

Latorre found himself starting his career during one of Boca's regular downturns of financial and executive chaos, generally reflected in some shocking results including beatings at the hands of more humble Argentinian clubs. But he was also lucky – as a youngster he found himself under less pressure than some of the more experienced players. Fans were excited by his potential and matters improved during his first spell at the Bombonera.

In one of CONMEBOL's regular attempts to devise competitions to create new interest and make more money, the Supercopa Libertadores was created in 1988. That put all past winners of the Copa Libertadores – the South American equivalent of the European Cup, so basically a list of the grandest, oldest clubs on the continent – into a tournament played on a single-elimination basis over two-legged ties. That allowed Boca to compete in a bizarrely prestigious competition without necessarily deserving to based on recent history, and in 1989 they beat fellow Argentinian side Independiente on penalties to win the title. That, in turn, allowed Boca to compete in the Recopa Sudamericana, a final between the current Copa Libertadores champions and the winners of the Supercopa.

Boca were paired with Atlético Nacional of Medellín. Security fears over the situation in Colombia at the time and the understandable fixture congestion caused by an eye-watering number of tournaments in South American football meant the final was played as a one-off game at a neutral ground. Only 9,000 fans watched at the Orange Bowl in Miami, Florida, as Latorre rounded René Higuita and angled a lithe finish into the net to score the only goal of the game and bag another trophy for Boca.

Those trophies kept the passionate Boca fans quiet while one of the regular rebuilding jobs most big South American clubs were being forced to mount took place. The economics of football were shifting again. European football was rising in wealth and prestige, and the global success of the 1990 World Cup ushered in new eras in Italy – where Serie A became the world's leading league – and England, where the creation of the Premier League allowed the first steps to the eventual financial explosion it would enjoy.

South America could not keep up. If, in the 1980s and even early 1990s, players could make a good living staying at their hometown clubs in Argentina or Brazil, as the 1990s progressed it quickly became apparent there were fortunes to be made for decent professionals in Europe.

Argentina and Brazil began losing their good players to European leagues, a process that became accepted and part of the life cycle of the game. South American clubs, deprived of the mammoth television contracts enjoyed by even mid-table clubs in the Premier League or La Liga, were resigned to depending on European transfer payments for financial boosts. It wasn't only the leading leagues, either; players were now likely to move to Russia, Greece or Turkey as well as the established routes to England, Italy, Spain, Germany and the Netherlands. It was not only the football factories in Buenos Aires, Rosario, São Paulo and Rio that suffered this – European clubs had scouts in Colombia, Montevideo, Lima and Asunción, too. South American football flair was a prized commodity.

The situation had been foreshadowed by Maradona's move from Boca to Barcelona in 1982. But Maradona's talent had been exceptional, and many hoped his transfer would be too. Nevertheless, Boca fans allowed themselves to get excited about their young players. They were still excited by a maturing, evolving Latorre, who was becoming more of a second striker than an enganche, although he had the talent and vision to drop deeper and play raking passes. They were also excited by the partnership he struck with a classic Argentinian number nine by the name of Gabriel Batistuta after the latter was bought from River Plate in 1990.

Under the guidance of experienced, cerebral Uruguayan coach Óscar Tabárez, Latorre and Batistuta formed a devastating partnership. Tabárez had done well within the Uruguayan football structure, winning a Copa Libertadores with powerhouses Peñarol and refining a generation of young players in various underage sides before guiding the senior side to the 1990 World Cup.

He saw Batistuta had been misused at River Plate and in his early months at Boca as he had been played on the wing due to his pace and running power. Tabárez moved him to centre-forward, and he exploded. His dynamism, mobility, monstrous shooting power with either foot, work rate and aerial prowess made him a terrifying prospect for a central defender, and with the dribbling menace of Latorre alongside, Boca became contenders again. They were to win the 1991 Clausura title and in 19 games scored 20 goals between them, with Batistuta taking 11 to Latorre's nine. That form earned both players spots in Alfio Basile's Argentina squad for the 1991 Copa América.

* * *

At that time, a broken squad was recovering from the trauma of defeat in the final of Italia 90. Under Carlos

Bilardo, for all the fighting spirit and defiance shown by the team and its supporters, Argentina had disgraced themselves. The nation of la nuestra had played deplorably negative football and earned 22 bookings and the most red cards at the tournament. It was time for a fresh start.

Bilardo and Maradona both went into exile and Coco Basile was given the job. Basile was a proponent of a more Menotti-esque possession game, and his Racing Club side had won plaudits and favour for their stylish football. Basile brought some youngsters into the national side to play with a few carefully chosen veterans. Alongside Latorre and Batistuta there was a dominant, energetic central midfielder who had come through at Vélez Sarsfield who was now impressing in Europe, despite playing in a weak side at Pisa. His name was Diego Simeone.

There was also prolific Huracán striker Antonio Mohamed; River midfielder Leonardo Astrada; peripatetic midfielder Leonardo Rodríguez; and defenders Darío Franco and Fabián Basualdo from Newell's and River Plate respectively. Ruggeri, Goycochea and Caniggia were the veterans chosen to lend some experience and seasoned know-how to this team of youth and energy.

It worked. Argentina won the 1991 Copa in Chile, Batistuta was top scorer with six goals in seven games, and Latorre impressed alongside him. Latorre's reputation had attracted interest from European clubs but, watching him, scouts' eyes were quickly drawn to the dashing striker rifling in unstoppable drives with his right foot from all angles. In 1991, Fiorentina made a triple swoop, taking Batistuta and Latorre from Boca and Antonio Mohamed from Huracán. While the newly nicknamed 'Batigol' would go on to become a Fiorentina legend, scoring 167 goals for the club and winning a pair of cups before moving to Roma for his only Serie A title, neither of the other two Argentines would succeed.

Mohamed never even played for 'I Viola'. Instead, he was instantly loaned back to Boca Juniors. Latorre, meanwhile, endured a horrendous start to his European experience. Because of a legal issue with an agent involved in a web of complex transfers of Argentinian players in Italy, Latorre was taken to a hotel in Rome when he arrived where he had to wait in legal limbo while his contract was sorted.

Although there were other players there at first – including Simeone and Caniggia – soon it was just Latorre and he could not train with his new team-mates, play games or speak Italian. From the glory of the Bombonera and Argentina to a hotel room in a foreign city, Latorre's mental health suffered and he became depressed. He rang Boca pleading with them to take him back but the situation was beyond their control.

Eventually, the intervention of Batistuta, already a success for his new club, prompted a solution and Latorre joined his new club. He had been brought in as a replacement for Fiorentina golden boy Roberto Baggio and, for the first time after the trauma of those months in limbo, the 'new Maradona' tag weighed heavily on his shoulders. He only played twice in Florence and when Carlos Valdano, newly installed as coach of Spanish side CD Tenerife, contacted him to join him in the Canary Islands, Latorre went. On such decisions are legacies defined; Latorre had failed in Serie A. He was obviously not the new Maradona.

What he was, however, was a gifted second striker with exceptional dribbling ability and an eye for goal. Under Valdano, Latorre starred in what is remembered as

Tenerife's greatest-ever side. He scored 15 goals in 69 games over two thrilling seasons, helping the club to achieve its highest league finish, fifth in 1995.

The Argentinian contingent was key to that success. Alongside Valdano and Latorre there was also Fernando Redondo, a sublimely gifted defensive midfielder who had also been compared to Maradona, and strikers Juan Antonio Pizzi from Toluca and Oscar Dertycia from Cadiz, famed for losing all his hair, reportedly in dismay at missing out on the 1990 World Cup squad.

Twice in two seasons, Tenerife denied Real Madrid a title win by beating them in their final game in the Heliodoro. Latorre's personal highlight against Madrid was scoring two goals to eliminate them from the Copa del Rey. That fifth-place finish gave Tenerife a UEFA Cup spot but Latorre would not be around to play in it, moving to UD Salamanca in 1995. The team struggled, however, and were relegated in 1996, with Latorre returning to Argentina and Boca Juniors.

By that point, the Maradona comparisons were little more than a footnote and the players were now team-mates at Boca. Latorre played further forward and plundered 12 goals in the 1997 Apertura, reclaiming some of his old stardust. As Maradona retired, Latorre moved on, and his career began to bear more of a resemblance to Borghi's. He criticised Boca in the Argentinian media and forced a move to rivals Racing, where again he had a good season.

He was a good example of a new phenomenon: a player who was good enough for a mid-table European club but not up to the elite level of the superclubs already dominating the European game. When he returned to Argentina, he found a league where the greatest talents had already emigrated and what was left was a football with a hole in the middle. The high-quality players at their peak had all gone to Europe, Mexico or the MLS. What was left were the young players, soon to leave themselves; the solid players without the necessary quality but who had enough to make a living in the Argentinian leagues; and the returning veterans, possibly financially secure after years abroad but still craving the acclaim of a crowd and the buzz of competition.

Latorre left Racing after a year to play for Mexican club Cruz Azul and from then on he bounced between Argentina and Mexico until his retirement in 2006. His reputation as a crack in Argentina meant he had stints at big clubs such as Rosario Central and Chacarita Juniors, but his Mexican sides began to dwindle in prestige and popularity. He had a spell with Comunicaciones in Guatemala before a final season with Alacranes de Durango before he retired. He would go on to become a prominent television commentator.

His spell as the new Maradona had basically ended with a whimper at Fiorentina. For all his subsequent mid-level success at Tenerife and back at Boca, the fact he was never again selected for Argentina provides a telling picture of the landscape of Argentinian football at the time. Younger, more exciting talents were coming for Maradona's number 10 shirt. The next in line would be Ariel Ortega.

THREE

Ariel Ortega, 'El Burrito'
Marcelo Gallardo, 'El Muneco'
Fernando Redondo, 'El Principe'

MARADONA'S LEGEND was already established enough by the early 1990s that players from other countries, in other positions, were anointed with his name. It made sense for a few other South Americans to be compared to him, although Brazil, Uruguay and Colombia had their own distinctive football cultures so players playing in the number ten role in those nations usually avoided the comparisons.

Many of them were Maradona's contemporaries and rivals in any case. In Colombia, Carlos Valderrama was nicknamed 'El Pibe' and his style recalled the elegant Argentinian enganches of old more than it did Maradona. He was a conductor; a hypnotic passing playmaker with phenomenal vision, awareness and touch.

Valderrama was capable of tricks and flicks but really it was all about gaining an extra yard or second to deliver a killing pass. He had his own trademark look, too, which was even more distinctive than Maradona's. Valderrama played with his blond cloud of hair shading his eyes and his shirt and shorts appearing too large for his lean frame as his lazy tread took him around the centre of the pitch.

Enzo Francescoli and Maradona were friendly rivals – Maradona was Boca while the Uruguayan Francescoli was River. He was more of a second striker than a number ten, although he did take much of his side's creative responsibility. For River Plate, that was eased by a more classical Argentine number ten, Norberto Alonso, who had lost his place in the national side to Maradona prior to the 1986 World Cup.

The sheer weight of other 'new Maradonas' started to become ridiculous around the mid-1990s. Some earned the title because they were mazy dribblers, others because they were imaginative passers. Some scored goals, while others played in the hole as a number ten. Some emerged as gifted teenagers; some were short and stocky with dark hair; and some were rebellious and outspoken. At least one managed to score a goal with a handball, in which case the title may have been somewhat tongue-in-cheek, but others had virtually nothing in common with Maradona besides being good at football.

Gheorghe Hagi, a Romanian legend and great player in his own right, was the 'Maradona of the Carpathians'. At least he was similar in stature to the real thing, was immensely skilled, and had the charisma to lead his country during a World Cup. Austria Vienna's 6ft playmaker Andi Herzog was the 'Maradona of the Alps', mainly down to his dribbling ability, although he enjoyed a fine career.

Vasilis Hatzipanagis was the 'Maradona of the Balkans' or the 'Greek Maradona', although few outside the Soviet

Union or Greece enjoyed him near his peak. His love of dribbling prompted the comparisons. Other contenders for the title of 'Maradona of the Balkans' included Dejan Savićević and Zvonimir Vukić.

The following list gives an idea of just how widespread the custom of saddling a player with a comparison to the Argentine great became:

Saeed Al-Owairan: 'Maradona of the Arabs'
Georgi Kinkladze: 'Maradona of the Caucausus'
Krishanu Dey: 'The Indian Maradona'
Emre Belözoğlu: 'Maradona of the Bosphorus'
Joe Cole: 'Maradona of the East End'
Hidetoshi Nakata: 'Maradona of the Orient'
There are at least a few dozen more.

What this reveals is how Maradona had transcended his own life and achievements and become, for better or worse, an ideal. 'Maradona' meant something more than Diego Maradona. It meant an outstanding player; potential; skill; passion; victory; charisma; athleticism; personality; dribbling and goals. It meant football. That was an easy concept to understand, and it crossed borders and cultures.

But in Argentina it meant something more specific – Argentinian football greatness, in a package, playing in the number ten role. If River Plate, with Alfredo Di Stéfano, Pedernera, Moreno and Sívori, had once been more prominent for producing great Argentinian creative players, the rise of Maradona and even the coming of Latorre meant Boca Juniors had usurped 'El Mas Grande' in this respect.

During the next few decades, however, River seemed to churn out an endless stream of exciting attackers, including numerous 'new Maradonas'. Ariel Ortega was the first and, in one regard, was very much in the mould of Maradona. Ortega was what the football media euphemistically refer to as a 'maverick'. He had disciplinary issues from early on in his career, increasingly serious substance-abuse problems as his powers waned, and a volatile, fragile temperament that would affect the passage of his life as a footballer. For all that, the Argentinian public loved him. He was a fascinating, manifestly flawed figure but one who could create genuine wonder on the pitch. With his fights and binges, tantrums and scandals, Ortega was the closest Argentina got to the new Maradona.

* * *

Ortega was born in Ledesma in Jujuy in 1974, a remote province bordering Bolivia. Spotted by a River Plate scout at a local tournament, his talent was already apparent. Like many others compared to Maradona, 'Orteguita' was a magician when he dribbled. He could throw feints, fakes and dummies at speed and had the ability to surge and shift direction that recalled Maradona, together with an impeccably balanced ability to stay up as he moved the ball, even under heavy challenges.

Ortega seemed to sway with his body over the ball, as if he could not get it out of his feet. Then his hips would shift, the ball would be manipulated in a blink, and both he and it would be away. His pace was fine when he needed to burn past an opponent on the wing – especially as a young tyro – but it was almost as if he did not need pace.

To watch Ortega was to see a player dazzle and intimidate the opposition with his skill. He often appeared to dribble past defenders at a relaxed speed, two or three of them in succession, never really bursting clear, clearly enjoying himself. After an initial brush with the kind of talent that can make a ball do the things he could, defenders would back off, afraid of it happening again. That gave him more space and made it more likely he would draw fouls – and from set pieces, Ortega could be deadly.

A year after being spotted, he was playing for River Plate's first team under coach Daniel Passarella. He managed an assist on his debut and, as a raw youngster, found himself playing alongside River legend Ramón Díaz at the tail end of an era of huge success, which included the club's first Copa Libertadores and Intercontinental titles.

Ortega was shy in his youth but fearless and even impish in the application of his talent. The crowds at River's huge El Monumental stadium were thrilled by him from the start. His dribbling style left defenders perplexed and even embarrassed, and against the calibre of players he was facing in Argentina, a frequently unplayable Ortega resembled a genius.

Although Passarella usually played him on the flank, Ortega tended to drift infield with the ball and his rapidly developed passing range and vision marked him out as an enganche. He could score, too, with a particular eye for a lob or chip. Throughout his career he would humiliate a string of goalkeepers by stroking balls into the precise space between their highest dive and the crossbar, always making it look casual and cheeky. But chiefly there was the dribbling. Endless dribbling, showcasing caños and flip-flops, leaving opponents floundering in his wake.

With his mop of dark hair and powerful 5ft 7in frame, the comparisons to Maradona had already begun. Ortega won the Primera four times with River Plate in that initial spell as his star shone in the sky above Argentinian football.

By 1996, River had installed the club legend that was Ramón Díaz as coach, who assembled one of the greatest teams Argentine football has ever seen. Ortega was abetted in attack by Uruguayan icon Enzo Francescoli, who proved frighteningly prolific in front of goal after his 1994 return from Europe. Alongside them were several other exciting youngsters: striker Hernán Crespo, with movement and the surgical finishing of a veteran centre-forward in the sprightly form of a 21-year old; defensive midfielder Matías Almeyda, offering grit and muscle allied to calm precision on the ball; and a classic, artistic number ten in the form of Marcelo Gallardo. That side won River a second Copa Libertadores with a 2-1 aggregate win over América de Cali of Colombia in 1996.

Ortega was 22 then, much more confident after his years of trophies and adoration from the fans of 'Los Millonarios'. He knew what his gifts were, and he wasn't much good at trying to do anything beyond those gifts. But those gifts – and his role with the national team – had been attracting suitors from Europe for years.

* * *

In 1996 he moved to Valencia for £9.18m, then the highest fee paid for an Argentinian. Moving to Spain for a record fee again evoked memories of Maradona but Ortega's struggles at 'Los Che' were largely without the highlights and glory of Maradona's spell at Barcelona. Even at that point in his career, Ortega was the kind of player you might watch for a single game and come away thinking he was the greatest player in the world. The element of fantasy, of attempting and achieving the improbable, was always close to the surface. But perhaps he had spent too long in his comfort zone in Argentina, adored and coddled at River Plate where there was a value inherent in being the new Maradona, even if everybody already knew he would fall short.

European football was hard, it was professional, it was corporate. Players ran more, worked harder, and demanded more. There might be fewer idiosyncratic geniuses around but every solid pro would have something to offer. Unless he could change his attitude, Ortega was bound to struggle and an inability to change his attitude would become a memorable theme in Ortega's career. His nickname, 'El Burrito', means little donkey, after all. It was given to him because of his mule-like stubborn streak, on the pitch and in life. Changing was not something Ortega seemed capable of.

Jorge Valdano, who knew more than most about Argentine playmakers, was the Valencia coach who pushed for Ortega's purchase as part of his vision of a scintillating South American attack. Valdano wanted to unite Ortega with Brazilian striker Romário, who had been on Valencia's books for a year even though he had been exiled by his former coach, the disciplinarian Luis Aragonés, who had been disgusted by Romário's Dionysian lifestyle.

Romário had spent a year on loan at Flamengo in Brazil, partying and doing what he wanted. He told reporters that there was a clause in his Valencia contract that allowed him to go nightclubbing whenever he pleased. Valdano accepted that and knew Ortega had similar habits but perhaps his experiences alongside Maradona had shown him that sometimes genius needs to be indulged.

Ortega arrived in March and his debut for Valencia suggested the money had been well spent. That unplayable genius from River had arrived; he tormented a Sevilla defence all game to the extent they resorted to cynical fouls and late tackles. That only resulted in a penalty for a trip on him inside the box, which he calmly dispatched to give him a brace in his first game.

Romário returned to Spain in the summer and in pre-season Valencia looked magical with the two South Americans leading their attack. Then Romário got injured. Ortega played well in the first few weeks of the season – he scored nine goals in 29 games for a team that was generally struggling during his spell there – but the team was losing. Valdano was sacked and replaced by young Italian coach Claudio Ranieri, who had more authoritarian ideas about lifestyle and fitness.

Romário, who bragged about his nightclubbing, clashed with Ranieri early on, while Ortega was dropped for lack of application, which led him to copy a move straight from the Maradona manual. During a spell on international duty, he criticised Ranieri's coaching and formation to the Argentinian media, who lapped up that kind of talk. Then he stayed on longer than he should have, partying and generally living it up with his friends before returning to Spain.

There, he often missed training and, when he did show up, he was singled out for not trying. Ranieri speculated Ortega was missing so much training because he was trying to ensure he made it to that summer's World Cup 'well rested'. At the end of the season, Ortega again followed Maradona's example by moving to Serie A. First, though, he had an Argentina team to lead into the 1998 World Cup in France.

* * *

The new Maradona tag had really stuck to Ortega because of his experiences with Argentina. The early 1990s were a brief, odd golden period for the side. Following the 1991 Copa América triumph, they won the 1992 King Fahd Cup in Saudi Arabia after beating the hosts, USA and Nigeria. In 1993 they beat Denmark on penalties after a 1-1 draw to lift the Artemio Franchi Cup, played between the champions of South America and Europe. Maradona even returned for that but the team was criticised for being too reliant on his slowly declining talents.

In the same year, Argentina retained the Copa América with a stubborn performance in Ecuador. In that tournament, many of their players seemed out of sorts. Fernando Redondo and Simeone were an exceptional pair in midfield, making them hard to beat, but with Batistuta underperforming until his two strikes in the final, Argentina lacked creativity and goals.

Ortega looked like the answer to that but he was in line behind Maradona. Like Borghi before him, Ortega went to a World Cup as Maradona's understudy – the troubling 1994 tournament in the US. They were room-mates and Ortega learned at the little master's feet. He came on as a substitute for Maradona in the opening 4-0 win against Greece, a passing of the torch to some extent.

Following Maradona's failed drugs test and expulsion from the tournament, Argentina became chiefly reliant on Redondo for creativity. While he could pull strings and create openings from deep, he needed a creative partner further up the pitch. Recognising that, coach Basile brought Ortega on as a substitute early on against Bulgaria and made him a starter in Maradona's role in the round-of-16 game against Romania, where the overawed 20-year-old was thoroughly outshone by a splendid Hagi. Ortega certainly tried – there were moments of characteristic invention and quality – but it was a huge ask for a young, still-developing player, and Argentina were eliminated after a thrilling 3-2 defeat.

By the 1998 tournament, Ortega was the starting number ten for Argentina and a megastar in his homeland. There was still time for him to live up to the Maradona comparisons, or at least to define his own career and achievements. After all, Maradona had flopped at his first World Cup in 1982. His old mentor Passarella was coach of a team that contained a clutch of quality players approaching their prime. Ortega's old River Plate colleagues Almeyda, Gallardo and Crespo were surrounded by players of proven class: Batistuta and Simeone; Juan Sebastián Verón, Roberto Ayala, Javier Zanetti and Claudio López. As is ever the case, Argentina looked genuine contenders for the trophy.

They appeared to be going through the gears in a deceptively strong group stage – shading Japan 1-0 in the opening game, then hammering Jamaica 5-0 with two goals from Ortega and a Batistuta hat-trick. Even a weathered, skilful Croatia team – who would eventually make the semi-finals – were beaten 1-0 to make Argentina group winners.

That put them into a tie with old enemy England in Saint-Étienne. If that game is chiefly remembered in England for Michael Owen's magnificent solo goal and David Beckham's red card for a reaction to Simeone's provocation, what is less celebrated was how brilliant Ortega was that night. Probing, teasing, he ran the Argentinian attack. England could barely get near him, and he looked on a different level to anyone else on the pitch.

That was until extra time, when fatigue was an unmistakable factor. As in the group games, Ortega looked short of match fitness after his months on the bench at Valencia. That may have guaranteed he arrived at the tournament uninjured but also ensured he arrived lacking match fitness. Nevertheless, Argentina won on penalties after a gruelling 2-2 draw, an emotional victory that seemed to drain them before their next game.

In the quarter-finals, they faced a gifted Netherlands in Marseille. After a frenetic start, and with both teams having scored, the game became a tight and physical battle. Argentina seemed to gain the edge when Arthur Numan was sent off in the 76th minute for a foul on Simeone. But Ortega, with the timing that played a big part in his persistent failure at the highest levels, self-destructed to cancel that out.

Ortega's stature and influence had been evident from the way the Netherlands played him – like Maradona in most Argentina games from 1982 on, he was suffocated and double-marked at every opportunity. The Dutch players were supremely athletic and experienced in the hard grind and professionalism of high-level European football. They knew how to deal with talented opponents so they fouled him when they had to but their focus and application was enough to stymie him without illegal play.

After the season he had endured at Valencia, Ortega was easily frustrated. In the 87th minute he squirmed into the penalty area and dived under an imaginary tackle from Jaap Stam, trying to earn a penalty. Beanpole goalkeeper Edwin van der Sar raced out to berate him for his play-acting and Ortega met him with a head-butt. Van der Sar went down and Ortega was shown the red card. A couple of minutes later, Dennis Bergkamp scored one of the great World Cup goals to seal the game for the Netherlands.

Argentina were out and Ortega was disgraced. The burden of trying to win a World Cup for Argentina as the number ten had proved far too much for a player with so much emotional baggage. Whereas even the combustible Maradona had kept his head against Germany in a World Cup Final, Ortega had lost his. Ortega's actions against the Netherlands seemed typically self-destructive and that sort of behaviour became more common over the next few years, even if generally they happened away from the football pitch.

* * *

Ortega's transfer from Valencia took him to Sampdoria in 1998 and, although his record on the pitch was similar to the one at Valencia, his talent was obvious. Most notably he scored a sublime and distinctively Ortega chip against Inter Milan, but his lifestyle was a distraction. There had been rumours about his drinking in Argentina but his success on the field kept them at bay. Italy, less enamoured with a foreign star and his ego, was a different story.

It might have been different had Sampdoria been winning but, under young coach Luciano Spalletti, they were struggling badly and the golden era of the early 1990s felt a very long time ago. When Spalletti was sacked, he was replaced by former Samp hero David Platt. He in turn was dismissed for not having the correct coaching badges but not before he dropped Ortega in favour of former Manchester United winger Lee Sharpe, whose star was in rapid decline. The club slid slowly and painfully towards inevitable relegation.

Ortega made it easy for coaches to drop him with antics in his personal life, where he still appeared to be attempting to live up to Maradona's legend. In December 1998, he was arrested and breathalysed in Rome after brawling with fans outside a nightclub. When Sampdoria were relegated, he was ready to move.

Paris Saint-Germain and newly crowned European champions Manchester United were circling but Ortega opted to remain in Serie A, joining Parma as a partial replacement for his 'Albiceleste' team-mate Juan Sebastián Verón, who had moved to Lazio where he would be instrumental in their success. At Parma he was reunited with Crespo in an obvious attempt to recreate their River Plate success. It didn't pay off. Although Crespo kept scoring goals, Ortega shone only sporadically and, while Parma won the Supercoppa Italiana, Ortega was never happy – and his football reflected that.

Meanwhile, the club was in financial turmoil and players needed to be sold to bring in money. Crespo was their most valuable asset and, when he was sold to Lazio for a world-record £35m, Parma also cut their losses on Ortega, transferring him back to River Plate in lieu of transfer money they still owed. His first stint in Europe had been an abject failure and he would henceforth always be known as a 'former new Maradona'. For all that, Ortega still had some memorable football to play, particularly in Argentina. The timing of his River return was perfect. Under coach Américo Gallego, a trio of exciting youngsters had burst into the first team, two of them already saddled with the 'new Maradona' tag so familiar to Ortega.

Pablo Aimar was a dreamy, elegant enganche, who generally played on the left and cut infield to create and score goals. Javier Saviola was a bustling speed merchant of a second striker, lithe and deadly in the box. Juan Pablo Ángel, meanwhile, was a Colombian poacher with the movement, instincts and finishing precision reminiscent of a young Crespo.

When Ortega joined them, they were labelled the 'Cuatro Fantásticos' (fantastic four) and their football thrilled Argentine fans. Ortega was back home, wearing a trademark headband and back to being adored by the River faithful. He claimed to be happy once more. However, the fantastic four rarely played together – Aimar and Ortega were both injured in the title run-in – and that beautiful side never won a trophy despite scoring 40 goals in 20 games.

Soon, Aimar and Saviola had both gone to Spain in lucrative deals; Aimar to Valencia, Saviola to Barcelona. Angel followed them out in 2001, moving to Aston Villa in the Premier League.

In their absence, Ortega embraced his increased responsibility and combined well with the new young star brought in to take Ángel's goalscoring burden – Fernando Cavenaghi.

Coached by Ramón Díaz, River had a balanced side mixing the youthful verve of yet another new Maradona contender in Andrés D'Alessandro, the maturity and energy of the similarly young Esteban Cambiasso, Cavenaghi's prolific pilfering of goals, and veterans such as striker Martín Cardetti and club legend Leonardo Astrada. That was enough to help them win another title, the 2002 Clausura, but Díaz, his seventh River title achieved, had a disagreement with president José María Aguilar and left.

* * *

European clubs were again sniffing around Ortega. Sir Alex Ferguson loved Argentinian football and was a long-time admirer of El Burrito. Instead, Fenerbahçe paid £5.85m to take him to Turkey, a sum that appeared to be a huge bargain given his form for River. Ortega was miserable in Istanbul, however. Despite solid performances, Turkish football was more comparable to the Argentinian league than the strength in depth he had faced in Spain and Italy. While he scored five goals in his 14 games, including one in a 6-0 rout of arch-rivals Galatasaray and contributed many YouTube-friendly clips of his skills and tricks, he was terribly homesick. He disliked the food, couldn't speak the language and found the culture too alien. Once more, the 'little donkey' showed his self-destructive stubbornness. Instead of knuckling down and making an effort to adapt, Ortega basically ran away. He showed up for an Argentina squad for a friendly against the Netherlands in February 2003 and never returned to Turkey.

His agent claimed Fener had promised to recruit more Argentine players and had broken that promise along with many others. Ortega had signed a four-year contract with Fenerbahçe, however, and they owned his image rights. The club complained to FIFA, which banned Ortega until December and fined him $11m. Embracing his self-destructive tendencies once more, Ortega sulked. He could not buy his way out of the situation with such a massive fine and no club rich enough to remedy the matter would consider him after the way he had acted towards Fenerbahçe. Despite being 29, an age when most players are at their peak, Ortega pulled another trick he may have learned from Maradona in their hotel room at USA 94 – he announced his retirement.

At that point, Ortega had been around Argentinian football for long enough that it felt as though everybody had either been a team-mate, a rival or coach of his at some point. His web of relationships and resentments was large and complex. At that low ebb, one old coach, Américo Gallego, saved him. He persuaded Rosario giants Newell's Old Boys to use some of the profit from the sale of Mauro Rosales to Ajax to pay off the rest of Ortega's contract.

After months of training alone to keep in shape and wondering whether he would ever play again, 'Orteguita' was back in Argentinian football. His decline was evident, however. Many speculated it was due to his drinking, which was reportedly much more serious than anyone knew – but he could still decide a game with a moment of genius, destroy a defence with the ball at his feet, and earn the adoration of a stadium.

Newell's had the right mix of youthful talent and experienced know-how, which had become essential if a side was to win the Argentinian title. Dominant centre-back Ezequiel Garay, cultured number eight Fernando Belluschi and creative second striker Ignacio Scocco were all set for bright futures. Ortega was the catalyst, however; a player who had been there and done it and knew what it took to win the title. In 2004, Newell's won the Apertura, a brilliant homecoming achievement for the now 30-year-old player.

He returned to River Plate in 2006 with Passarella again his doting coach but soon official confirmation of Ortega's alcoholism was a media story for the first time. He missed games and was escorted from the team hotel and training much the worse for wear. He went to rehab and came straight back into the team on his return but football and alcohol were the two addictions battling for his soul, and football was not winning.

When Passarella was sacked, his replacement was Diego Simeone, fresh from a triumphant title win as coach of Estudiantes and another notable figure from Ortega's past. If Simeone had been an uncompromising footballer, he was even more so as a coach. He had no time for Ortega's issues and would not indulge him as Passarella had. The Argentine media ensured Simeone was always aware of what El Burrito was up to as lurid photos and stories of his binges were regular front-page news. In that way, Ortega more than matched Maradona. Exasperated, Simeone dropped Ortega and put him on the transfer list just as River Plate were winning the 2008 Clausura.

The last few years of his career were a sad, repetitive round of loans to smaller clubs, an occasional moment of transcendent magic, a shocking incident or failure to appear, another round of rehab, then the news he was leaving the club. River loaned him to Independiente Rivadavia in the Nacional B, where he managed a year of mixed performances before expulsion and another loan to All Boys before a final few months at Defensores de Belgrano. Throughout, he was adored by the River Plate faithful and deemed one of the club's greatest legends. His essentially flawed nature made him relatable, another quality he shared with Maradona. When he retired in 2012, Ortega was generally seen as one of the biggest disappointments in Argentinian football for the way he had failed to fulfil his immense potential. But River Plate saw him differently. With 75 goals and a few thousand gambetas in 272 appearances, they loved him still, and he was given a farewell game in July 2013 at the Monumental. Not the new Maradona, then, but somebody singular and fascinating in Argentinian football all the same.

* * *

In his first spell at River Plate, Ortega had played alongside Marcelo Gallardo, another who was briefly anointed the 'new Maradona'. Gallardo was a very different player to El Burrito. Nicknamed 'El Muneco' (the doll) because of his round face and diminutive stature, at 5ft 7in Gallardo was much more slight than Maradona or Ortega.

He was also more cerebral; he played more like a classical enganche. Lacking pace and not quite as obviously a gifted dribbler, his game was founded on his reading of play and superb passing. He could shake off a defender or beat a man but did this generally to create space for himself so the passing sequence he envisioned opened up. To anyone who regularly watched Gallardo as a player, his later massive success as River Plate coach makes perfect sense. He always played as if he knew what would happen next, and watched the way teams played and looked to use his finely calibrated passing to exploit their weaknesses.

Born in the outskirts of Buenos Aires, Gallardo came through the River Plate academy, made his debut at 17 and was a first-team regular by his early 20s. He had already made his international debut under Passarella in 1994 and would go on to make 44 appearances for Argentina, scoring 13 goals. He was unlucky to play during the period when Argentina won nothing, with only an Olympic silver medal to show for his international career. He never even got to play at a World Cup, spending the entirety of the 2006 tournament on the bench.

Gallardo was not as spectacular to watch as most of the other players who had been compared to Maradona, which is perhaps why the comparison did not follow him around as it did many others. He was too different, too much his own man.

He won five titles during that first spell with River as well as one Copa Libertadores. After that he went to France, signing for AS Monaco in 1999 and quickly establishing himself as the creative cog of the team. Playing Gallardo's way with intelligence and perception, passing teams to death, Monaco won Ligue 1, Gallardo won player of the year, and the Maradona comparisons were rendered meaningless. Here was a player who defined his career on his own terms. He went to Europe and enjoyed great success but did it his own way, without controversy or media scrutiny. He just played good football.

Gallardo would return to River Plate twice more, winning another title in between more trophies with Monaco, PSG and DC United. Injuries hugely affected his performances towards the end of his playing career and he retired at Nacional in Uruguay, quickly segueing into the role of coach. Gallardo would win a title in Uruguay before he arrived at River, where he would win every possible trophy and cement himself as River Plate's greatest manager. Not a bad effort for another new Maradona.

Gallardo typically wore the number 10 shirt during his career, most of the new Maradonas did, although some were revealed to be suited to other shirt numbers and roles at some stage in their career, leading to the comparisons fizzling out. In Argentina, wearing the number 10 on your back is accepting a challenge – that shirt means something.

* * *

Perhaps the most baffling new Maradona was Fernando Redondo. 'El Principe' (the prince) earned his nickname as there was something truly regal about him in full flow. The Maradona comparisons basically came because Redondo was a hugely talented player. He had fantasy in his feet. He made great players look bad. He was special.

The comparisons did not hang around him long – he was too obviously different in his look, style and position – but the one way he lived up to Diego Maradona was in a sense of frustration. Although Redondo had a fantastic career, given the extent of his talent there is a lingering suspicion he could have been even better and done even more.

Unlike most of the players discussed in these pages, Redondo came from a middle-class background. Born in 1969 in Adrogué, an affluent Buenos Aires suburb hymned by Argentine writer Jorge Luis Borges, Redondo was raised by his ex-footballer father, a fanatical Independiente fan. However, like Maradona and Borghi before him, it was the football nursery at Argentinos Juniors that noticed Redondo's talent and he signed with the club at the age of 11. He would be in the first team by 16, although he was not a regular starter until he replaced World Cup-winner Sergio Batista in 1988.

Redondo played in defensive midfield, although he was far from a traditional Argentinian cinco. The number five is a special number in Argentina's football culture and, before Redondo, generally meant a player who relied on anticipation, aggression and pace to cover ground and cut out attacks. Tackles, fouls and controlling space were the tools of a cinco. When they gained possession, generally they laid it off simply and rapidly.

That was not Fernando Redondo. He played like a number ten, only a pass or two further back towards his own goal. His feet were quick, his touch deft, and he could pirouette and flick the ball around opponents with a dainty elegance that was stunning for a man with a 6ft 1in frame. Redondo was elegant and, with an upright posture, seemed to glide effortlessly around midfield, playing one, two and three-touch passing exchanges, shifting direction, pinging backheels to team-mates, dribbling when required to create space to get out of trouble. This was a defensive midfielder who played like an enganche.

Unsurprisingly, he revolutionised the position in Argentina. Since his pomp, a series of players have been called the 'new Redondo', which is a huge tribute to his gifts and impact. Fernando Gago and Éver Banega, for example, were both superb footballers with decorated careers – but neither was as effective as Fernando Redondo. The emergence of Enzo Fernández at River and progression to Benfica and the national team during the 2022 World Cup brought up those Redondo comparisons once more.

A legendary Argentinian number five such as Javier Mascherano was more classical in his approach but even he had to absorb something of Redondo's style into his game. That style was beautiful to watch, elaborate and composed. Redondo was a 'regista', a link between defence and attack, but he did not play many of the quarterback-style long passes beloved of Andrea Pirlo or obsess over endless passing like Xavi. He was more energetic, aggressive and more involved in launching attacks than he was in merely dictating pace – although he did that too. He was also Argentine and did the dirty work when he needed to. Powerful and rapid over space, his position generally set him against celebrated 'trequaristas' and playmakers. Redondo's battles with Rivaldo in classic clashes were epic and typically won by the Real Madrid player. He memorably wrested control of the 1998 Champions League Final from Juventus by asserting his dominance over Zinedine Zidane in the second half.

Redondo had left Argentinos Juniors for Tenerife in 1990, where he became the key player in a series of sides that overachieved. When coach Carlos Valdano left the club for Real Madrid in 1994, he took Redondo with him. By then, 'El Principe' had become a regular in the national squad. He was given his nickname by his Argentina midfield partner Diego Simeone, based on his calm elegance and good looks – with long hair flowing, he had something of the movie star about him. He had been called up by Bilardo for the 1990 World Cup but, in a sign of the wilful nature that would damage his legacy, Redondo refused, claiming he wanted to focus on his law studies. In later years he admitted he had not fancied being stuck on the bench in a Bilardo squad but, by the 1993 Copa América, he was a fixture in the squad and was part of the team that won the tournament.

By this stage the new Maradona stuff had faded away but the Argentinian public was excited by the prospect of seeing this dominant young midfielder playing alongside the real Maradona at the 1994 World Cup. Maradona's expulsion after two promising games destroyed that, and the huge burden of creating attacks from deep now weighed heavily on Redondo, who impressed even as Argentina struggled.

* * *

The national team is where many of the frustrations in his career lie. By the 1998 World Cup, Passarella was coach and, in an effort to reassert his legendary toughness, he banned long hair and earrings. Redondo, who had just won his first Champions League with Madrid, refused to cut his hair and missed the tournament. Here was a gesture worthy of Maradona in its mixture of arrogance and defiance. Little wonder Redondo became something of a legend when that personality was allied to his achievements.

He would add a second Champions League in 2000, making himself the standout player of a run to the trophy that included the destruction of England's champions Manchester United. That game was marked by the moment most football fans will remember Redondo for – what Madrid fans call 'el taconazo' – when Redondo nutmegged United defender Henning Berg with a perfect backheel, collected the ball on the byline and played a simple assist for Raúl to put Madrid 3-0 ahead. The moment was a microcosm of Redondo at the time. Audacious, ballsy and beautifully performed, it captured a player who was one of the only midfielders to truly dominate United's legendary midfield warrior and captain Roy Keane during that era.

Madrid fans adored Redondo, although he had started to miss games because of increasing injuries. After a 1999 call-up by Marcelo Bielsa, he would retire from the national team to focus on club football.

His 2000 transfer to Milan was agonising and controversial. Redondo claimed he wanted to remain in

Madrid – fans even picketed the ground in an attempt to retain him – but he was eventually sold to the Italians for £11m. The move was a failure. Redondo picked up a knee injury in training soon after and only managed 16 appearances in his four years at the San Siro, retiring after a second injury kept him out in 2004. He had refused to accept his salary during some of his lengthy absence, however, endearing himself to Milan supporters.

Only 34 when he retired, the frustration lay in the suspicion that, but for injury and his own principles, this genius could still have contributed for Argentina and Milan throughout the 2000s. His absence for Argentina in two World Cups and a series of Copa América tournaments was a huge loss and an obvious part of the reason the long trophy drought they were enduring began to elongate.

Still, he retired having changed the way his country thought his position could be played, with two La Liga titles and one Serie A alongside two Champions Leagues and one Copa América in a trophy cabinet few players could match. Only a talent as immense as Fernando Redondo's could win so many trophies and still be regarded as a 'what if'.

FOUR

Juan Román Riquelme, 'El Último 10'

THERE ARE great goals and then there are immortal goals. When Esteban Cambiasso connected with a Hernán Crespo backheel to drive the ball hard into the roof of the net in a World Cup group game in Gelsenkirchen between Argentina, and Serbia and Montenegro on 16 June 2006 to put the Argentines 2-0 up, an instant classic was recognisable.

It came at the end of a sequence of 24 passes involving eight players in a classic move redolent of the purest aesthetic of Argentinean football and la nuestra – moving the ball on the ground quickly in a sweeping sequence of short passes, back and forth, dragging the opposition all over the pitch until their defence leaves a gap that is ruthlessly exploited. It was the method Spain and Barcelona would be so acclaimed for a few years later – but Argentina played tiki-taka first.

The goal was a breathtaking thing of beauty and a pleasure to behold. What was so beautiful? There are few instances of mesmerising skill, nothing really spectacular beyond a couple of truly superb touches, but the beauty lies in the communal effort of a team, the combination of solid technique and hard work to create and exploit an opportunity. Pure football. Juan Román Riquelme football.

Riquelme did not score the goal or even provide the assist but this was his first World Cup with Argentina and he was at the peak of his powers. In the qualifying campaign for the tournament, after an indifferent spell, José Pékerman had come in as coach. He had nurtured Riquelme – and a couple of generations of Argentine talent – through the youth-team system at the AFA. Pékerman knew that, for all his placid appearance, Riquelme was the very definition of a 'mercurial' player and he understood how to get the best out of him.

Beyond that, Pékerman was the first coach of the Albiceleste to realise Riquelme was key to the success of the national team in that era. He was the greatest talent in Argentinian football and Pékerman saw if he could be made to feel comfortable and indulged to some extent on the pitch and in the football that was played, he would deliver. And deliver he did.

By that point in the 2006 tournament, Argentina were running smoothly. Drawn in the 'group of death' with old enemies the Netherlands, star-packed Ivory Coast and a rugged Serbia and Montenegro, they were still among the tournament favourites thanks to one of the most talented squads in Argentina's World Cup history and an excellent qualifying campaign.

Riquelme was in supreme form. Against Ivory Coast he strolled about as though playing in a pre-season friendly, regal in his air of existing above the fray, effortlessly finding and using pockets of space, setting the rhythm and dictating the shape and attacking angles of his team. Big-name Ivorian midfielders Yaya Touré and Didier Zokora looked at a loss on how to handle him.

After some early chances for the African side, a Riquelme free kick caused mayhem in the Ivory Coast defence, which Crespo exploited to stab in a loose ball. Then, in the 38th minute, Riquelme found himself in acres of space outside the box. Any club side in Argentina or Spain would have known not to allow that, but the Ivory Coast players had not yet organised themselves enough to pick him up. Riquelme looked up and played a trademark, perfectly paced and weighted through ball into the path of Javier Saviola, who had begun his run as soon as the number ten received the ball. He finished neatly and Argentina won 2-1 after a late Didier Drogba goal made things interesting.

Argentina's confidence going into the game with Serbia and Montenegro was buoyant. The Serbian defence was legendary – they had conceded fewer goals in qualifying than any other team – but Manchester United warrior Nemanja Vidić was injured and, when Maxi Rodríguez scored for Argentina after six minutes, any nerves they may have had were settled as the Argentines relaxed into the game. That meant they passed the Serbs and Montenegrins to death.

Riquelme was central to that. He jogged around in midfield, perpetually looking exhausted, playing one-touch balls, spinning away, slowing, standing still, receiving, giving, receiving, giving. What was fascinating was the eagerness of the Argentines to play the simple ball. Riquelme, the most technically gifted player on the pitch, was never afraid to play the ball first time back the way it came. He knew maintaining possession was more important than always seeking the killer ball, that even such a simple ball meant an adjustment had been made by an opposition defender. And for Riquelme, such adjustments were opportunities.

He was patient and waited for an opportunity, confident he would spot it when it came.

It came here, in the middle of that long passing move. It wasn't one of those through balls or a dribble – it was a change of pace. Cambiasso laid the ball off into the path of Riquelme who, with his back to goal and two defenders approaching, played it first time sharply back to number five Javier Mascherano, another easy ball. But the pace had been injected with Riquelme's instant touch and it would only gather momentum over the next five passes.

Riquelme's greatest gift was perhaps his ability to dictate the pace of a game, and here he had done just that. A great team moves as one to some extent, changing gears together, instantly, and in the next 15 seconds or so this team moved up a gear and could have scored before their opponents had even noticed.

The ball fizzed around between Mascherano, Sorín and Saviola before finding its way back to Riquelme. It came to him square, with a defender rushing towards him. Again, Riquelme upped the pace, perfectly flicking the ball first time off his outstep over the raised leg of the onrushing defender and into Saviola's path. And there it was; two Serbian players eliminated from the game, their defence suddenly teetering with one single flick of the boot. From there, the technical ability and understanding of Saviola, Crespo and Cambiasso took over, and the goal got the sublime finish it deserved.

As the team and fans went crazy, aware of how great a goal they had just witnessed, Riquelme turned to the bench and raised his arms to Pékerman as if to say: 'See? That's how Argentina plays football.' They would add four goals, including one apiece for young substitutes Carlos Tevez and Lionel Messi – just to emphasise their strength in depth – for a 6-0 win. This looked like being Juan Román Riquelme's tournament.

* * *

Riquelme was born in Buenos Aires on the eve of the June 1978 World Cup Final, the eldest of 11 children raised in San Fernando, a suburb with a high degree of crime and poverty. If his upbringing wasn't quite as deprived as Diego Maradona's, it was possibly more dangerous and complex. Journalists Nick Elliott and Ed Bearryman, writing for Dream Team in March 2016, alleged Riquelme's father was involved with gangs and youth-team match-fixing. A beginning in such a world only seemed to rob Riquelme of fear. He was never afraid to play football his way, to give his opinion or demand what he was worth. In that way, he was every inch the new Maradona.

There were other, superficial similarities. Like Maradona, Borghi and Redondo, Riquelme was spotted and nurtured by the Argentinos Juniors youth system. Platense had spotted him first but in his youth Riquelme was rangy and thin, and his physique apparently dissuaded the club from taking a chance on him. Unlike the celebrated trio, however, Riquelme didn't break through into the first team at Argentinos.

He was spotted playing as a more conventional central midfielder in the fifth tier for the U20s side by scouts for Boca Juniors and River Plate. A childhood fan of the Xeneize, Riquelme chose Boca and they paid $800,000 for his signature as part of a bundle of players, hinting at his huge potential.

His signing for Boca Juniors and destiny to wear the number 10 shirt meant the 'new Maradona' talk was inevitable – but it took him a while to make an impact. Riquelme needed to fill out, to some degree, and while his skills and vision were already celebrated, the strength that would later allow him to hold off opponents was not quite there in his skinny adolescent frame. Although he made his debut for Boca as an 18-year-old in November 2006 under Carlos Bilardo, he was in and out of the team for the next few seasons. Maradona's return seemed to usher Riquelme out of the first-team picture but it soon became clear from his cameos off the bench that Riquelme was the stronger player of the two, although not every coach would realise that.

More than many players, Riquelme's career was highly dependent on the influence of his coaches. Some of them loved Riquelme, admired his distinctive talent and trusted him. Those men would build and deploy a team with the intention of releasing him, putting him in a position to run the game for them safe in the knowledge that, if he was allowed to do that, his side would win the match. In his career, José Pékerman was one such fan, as was Manuel Pellegrini at Villarreal and the first real managerial admirer of his career, Carlos Bianchi.

Bianchi arrived at Boca in July 1998 having taken Vélez Sarsfield to three Argentinian titles and their first Copa Libertadores. He basically entrusted attacking responsibility for the team to Riquelme, perhaps seeing that with Guillermo Barros Schelotto slipping into the box from the wing and a rampaging number nine in the form of Martín Palermo, Riquelme would have numerous chances to play through balls and create goalscoring opportunities.

Riquelme was now fully developed and revelling as a daringly classical Argentinian playmaker, recalling the likes of Bochini and the Colombian Valderrama. He was a deceptive player. His laid-back posture, deadpan expression and air of tiredness seemed to blind some to his manifold qualities. He had little pace to speak of and his dribbling was not at the level of an Ortega or a Borghi, but Riquelme's vision and excellence of passing seemed almost supernatural. He seemed to sense gaps before they appeared and would angle balls on lines only he could see between defenders to the feet of his team-mates. He was devilishly impossible to dispossess, too, using his big frame to shield the ball and maintain space and time as the play shifted around him. When the right hole appeared in a line, he would see it, and send the ball on its way.

Riquelme's touch was sumptuous and he used his studs and sole more than most players. He would roll the ball under his foot, stroking it around on the grass, his torso bent over it, arms outstretched to hold off an opponent. That allowed him to receive the ball under immense pressure – sometimes surrounded by three or more players. Riquelme would hold it up, spin, shield, then unleash a trick or a flick – some of his caños are justifiably celebrated in Argentina – giving him that instant he needed to pick a killer pass. And although he wasn't a dribbler of the highest calibre, he could run the ball upfield well, his loping stride covering ground as he weighed his options, and he could always use trickery to dribble past one or two players.

His finishing was superb, too. During his time at Boca, Riquelme was often the best finisher at the club and scored plenty of goals – from long-range howitzers to angled clips past the goalkeeper – but he was a divisive player, even among supporters. Not everyone appreciated the old-fashioned beauty of his football.

His nickname, 'El Último 10' (the last 10), suggests that even in his early years at Boca, supporters were aware he was a throwback to another time and that nostalgia played a part in his cult appeal. Detractors criticised his lack of pace, which is often seen as a huge factor separating very good players from great ones. His tendency to fatigue late on in games was another stick used to beat him. But the main criticism of Riquelme revolved around his role – an old-school playmaker was seen as a luxury in the modern game. When all the attacking play went through one player, if that one player had a bad day the team had a bad day too. Teams knew that and set out to stop Riquelme influencing games.

The fundamental issue with this approach was Riquelme was so good – good enough and clever enough to perform even under that kind of pressure, especially in the context of club football in South America. Bianchi and Boca never asked him to do defensive work, which some saw as another flaw in his game. But his job was to get on the ball and make things happen. And he did that job with thrilling consistency in his first spell at Boca.

Boca won the 1999 Clausura and went 40 games without defeat. The following year, they won the Copa Libertadores, with Riquelme incredible in the quarter-final Superclásico elimination of River Plate. In 2000, Riquelme showed he belonged in elite company with his performance against Real Madrid in the Intercontinental Cup Final in Tokyo. That was early in the galácticos era with the likes of Luis Figo, Roberto Carlos and Raúl wearing the all-white of the Madrid giants.

Boca took an early two-goal lead, both by Palermo – one from a typically incisive long Riquelme pass – before Madrid began to ratchet up the pressure. That was when Riquelme turned on the style. He endlessly took hold of the ball in midfield and kept possession, tormenting legendary French defensive midfielder Claude Makélélé, wing-back Geremi and Madrid's own playmaker, Guti, to the extent all of them were guilty of multiple frustrated fouls on him. Riquelme nutmegged, dummied and bamboozled each of them, and was the best player on the pitch by a distance.

Boca won 2-1 and the talk linking Riquelme with moves across the Atlantic grew louder. He was no longer being compared to Maradona, except in expectation of a similar impact. Riquelme was obviously the greatest talent Argentinian football had seen since his old predecessor as Boca number ten, so the big question was whether his career could measure up.

He had already surpassed Diego at Boca in terms of trophies and impact. Riquelme won another Copa Libertadores there in 2001 and was voted South American footballer of the year, a title with a remarkably storied list of winners. When Bianchi left Boca, however, Riquelme was deprived of a key ally and mentor at the club. He lasted another season, marred by injuries and spells out of the team as well as arguments with the chairman and board about his contract. The fearless child of San Fernando once again showed his refusal to be cowed, by protesting in iconic style at the Bombonera, hands cupped to his ears in front of the directors' box as he celebrated a goal.

His family situation remained complex. During that season, one of his brothers was kidnapped, with the criminals demanding a ransom from the famous footballer for his safe return. With life in Buenos Aires and Boca Juniors losing some of its attraction, once his brother was released, Riquelme left for Barcelona in 2002, following the path established by Maradona, for a fee of £6.8m.

* * *

His career in Spain was again defined by his relationships with coaches. Riquelme arrived at a Barcelona coached by Dutch tactician Louis van Gaal, who had been hugely successful, if controversial, during an earlier spell at the club. Van Gaal had clashed repeatedly with star players over his tactical intransigence and the local media over just about everything else.

Riquelme was a replacement for Rivaldo at number ten. They were hugely different players; the Brazilian was very much in the Argentinian pibe mould of playmakers, with his agile dribbling and set-piece skills. Forebodingly, Van Gaal had insisted he play as a winger, despite Rivaldo arguing he was best utilised in the centre, behind the strikers.

On his return to Catalonia, Van Gaal allowed Rivaldo to leave with a year remaining on his contract rather than spend further months battling in the press and on the training pitch. But Riquelme was not a typical Van Gaal player either. Too slow, too unpredictable, he had been indulged and made central to everything at Boca, but the same could never happen at Barcelona where megastars came and went, many without making much of an impression.

Early on during his time there, Van Gaal told Riquelme he was a 'political signing' and indicated he was surplus to requirements. In truth, the Argentinian was the type of player Barcelona fans loved to see – a budding megastar, stylish and creative – but, as with Rivaldo, Van Gaal wanted him to play on the wing.

From being the main man at Boca, where everybody used him as a frame of reference on the pitch, to being shunted out to the flanks must have offended Riquelme's ego. As the season wore on, he played more games in European ties and the Copa del Rey than in La Liga, where Barcelona's form stuttered, a hint at his reduced status. Riquelme was also accustomed to having a huge network of friends, siblings and hangers-on around him. Deprived of that in Europe, his form suffered – he was miserable on and off the pitch.

Even when Van Gaal left in the middle of a bad season, replaced by Raddy Antić, Riquelme's poor form continued as he was misused and squandered, appearing mainly as a substitute. The frustration was that if he had been trusted and allowed to adapt in his natural position, he could have thrived at Camp Nou and been adored by fans who have always appreciated good football. Instead, Riquelme demanded a move.

When new coach Frank Rijkaard signed another Brazilian number ten in the form of talented showman Ronaldinho, they needed to lose a non-European player from their bloated squad. Villarreal, the little club from Castellón, near Valencia, were eager to add Riquelme to their South American contingent and he headed there in summer 2003 on a two-year loan deal. He was only 25 but appeared defeated in European football, signing for Spanish minnows to spend a season or two earning his wages without the uncomfortable spotlight.

Instead, Riquelme's defiance at Villarreal showed his mettle and the fighting spirit of a young man who had come from deprivation and was used to struggle. Villarreal was an unlikely but perfect setting for him to showcase his talent. 'The yellow submarine' were the only club in a town with a population of just 50,000, and had only been promoted to La Liga in 1998 after decades in the lower divisions. The rise was facilitated by billionaire chairman Fernando Roig, who identified South American football as a model for the kind of game he wanted his team to play. When Riquelme arrived, he brought with him an extended entourage of friends and family from Argentina and, although Villarreal already had celebrity players and a handful of other Argentines who would have helped the new boy settle in, Riquelme was the first true star to join the club.

A couple of key arrivals slotted into place at the start of the 2004 season. Chilean coach Manuel Pellegrini knew Riquelme from his time at River Plate and San Lorenzo, and understood how best to deploy this maverick genius. Pellegrini brought in another South American who had thrived in Argentina as a youngster but struggled at a European superclub. Uruguayan striker Diego Forlán had been sensational for Independiente in Buenos Aires, and Manchester United added him to their star-studded squad in 2002. He had been a cult hero at Old Trafford, scoring key goals in big games, but had been unable to find consistency, perhaps due to beginning many games on the bench as he failed to dislodge Dutch striker Ruud van Nistelrooy from his starting role.

Villarreal was a new start for Forlán, and he and Riquelme struck an immediate understanding. Forlán has since spoken about how Riquelme welcomed him to the club by inviting him for dinner on his first night – Riquelme made milanesa, the classic Argentine breaded beef dish – and brought Forlán into his inner circle, composed mainly of his huge family. Over the next few years, the Uruguayan would rejuvenate his career in great part thanks to the ammunition supplied by the Argentinian – nobody could read Forlán's rampaging runs quite like Riquelme could, and he would ensure the ball arrived where, and when, it needed to be.

Pellegrini was an intellectual coach – nicknamed 'The Engineer' because of his university education and the cerebral approach he brought to arranging a team – and he set up Villarreal in a 4-2-2-2 formation to maximise the talents he had. Riquelme was nominally placed on the left of midfield but mostly played in a free role, wandering inside and dictating play. To allow for that, Pellegrini used tireless runners such as the energetic and aggressive Spanish defensive midfielder Marcos Senna, the twin-engine runs of Argentina team-mate Juan Pablo Sorín, and Forlán's clever movement and hard work to buzz around him. Riquelme could drift, pick passes, set the pace, and make himself the heartbeat of every game.

For the first time, Spain and Europe saw the best of Riquelme. That Villarreal team was capable of beating anyone on its day and Riquelme was the main reason why. He scored a hat-trick against local rivals Valencia as Pellegrini's side put together a long unbeaten run in

La Liga in early 2005 to put themselves in European contention. Riquelme's understanding with Forlán kept the goals coming – the Uruguayan won the Trofeo Pichichi, awarded to La Liga's highest scorer, with 25 goals. It meant he also shared the European Golden Boot with Arsenal superstar Thierry Henry. As well as creating goals for others, Riquelme chipped in with a few of his own – 15 in that season. His quality was also recognised when Spanish sports newspaper *Marca* voted him the most artistic player of the season.

That was a typical response to Riquelme's football. Ronaldinho had unarguably been the best player in Spain that year, combining a thrilling series of flicks, tricks and outlandish dribbling feats with unbelievable goals, assists and dominant performances. But Riquelme was a close second, and the luscious, slow-motion beauty of the football he created was the sort of thing that appealed to football writers. His cult appeal was enshrined.

That was a huge point of difference between Riquelme's former 'new Maradona' tag and the real thing. He was destined to be remembered as underrated but loved by a growing band of football hipsters who swooned at his sumptuous passing and appreciated his control of tempo above Ronaldinho's more effective performing-seal antics – to borrow Sir Alex Ferguson's barb about Zinedine Zidane.

Villarreal claimed the highest finish in their history, third in La Liga, and qualified for the Champions League. Riquelme's importance to that effort was recognised by the club; buying out 75 per cent of his contract from Barcelona for €8m and tying him to a four-year contract.

He would be the key player, too, in a glorious Champions League campaign. Villarreal won their difficult group, knocking out Manchester United, who could only manage two draws against them, and Lille before eliminating Rangers on away goals in the round of 16.

That meant they faced Internazionale and several of Riquelme's international team-mates, including Walter Zanetti, Verón, Cambiasso and Julio Cruz. Riquelme rose to the occasion, running Inter ragged. He played extended sessions of keep-ball, constantly drew fouls, tried shots from unimaginable angles, and evaded tackles. Surrounded by international class such as Adriano and Álvaro Recoba, Riquelme looked as though he was on another level – a genius surrounded by the merely great. Villarreal narrowly lost the first leg 2-1 but triumphed 1-0 at home to eliminate the Italian side on away goals. That set up a tie in the heady heights of the semi-final against Arsène Wenger's Arsenal.

Everything was set up at Villarreal to allow Riquelme to succeed. He was indulged in his personal life and indulged on the pitch. He was given the central role he craved and made to feel he was the star of the show – and it worked. For a while, the criticism of his slowness, poor stamina and lack of defensive discipline faded away. He was acclaimed as a poetic footballer and the validation of the way he had always seen himself and seen football only made him better. But football is not so simple. Sometimes a single kick can decide a destiny and settle a career.

In the semi-final, Pellegrini's side lost a tight game 1-0 to a late Kolo Touré goal in north London. However, they were battering Arsenal in the return leg at the Madrigal, Riquelme central and pulling the strings. At his peak, central defenders could not deal with his touch or movement. He used the ball with almost unerringly acute judgement and, although Arsenal were obdurate and committed in defence, Villarreal should have scored three or four. In the final minutes, the Spanish side won a penalty. Riquelme was the team's penalty taker and his calm and clinical shooting meant he was efficient in the role. He hit the ball well but keeper Jens Lehmann guessed right and saved it. Arsenal had won the tie. Riquelme appeared devastated. A player who always accepted and expected the scrutiny when he failed to deliver, his miss had huge, immediate consequences.

And yet, for Villarreal to even gain a semi-final spot was an immense accomplishment and Riquelme was central to that. He headed for Argentina duty at the World Cup with his global profile at a new high, generally regarded as the greatest Argentina player of the era. That was new. Despite globalisation of the game, fans in Asia and Europe remain generally ignorant of the South American leagues. Players only really 'arrive' when they play in Europe, when they show they can compete in a 'proper' league. Despite his artistry and heroics with Boca Juniors, Riquelme's successes at Villarreal had proven his quality to a European football public.

* * *

His role in the national team had been similarly dependent on the identity and philosophy of each coach. Given his debut by Passarella in November 1997, Riquelme had been in many squads but few starting line-ups over the years. Marcelo 'El Loco' Bielsa was a coach with an extremely specific view of how football should be played – pedal to the floor, rapid in transition, hard-pressing football. Riquelme was never going to fit into Bielsa's system. He couldn't press, he liked to slow the pace or at least control it, and he chose when to flick the switch for a team into transition.

Nevertheless, Riquelme was considered for the 2002 World Cup – even Bielsa could see the playmaker could be a useful weapon to have in reserve. But he was returning from injury and Bielsa's team already had a very successful style – he used Verón as a deep-lying playmaker to start quick attacks and had the pacier Aimar to call on if he needed to introduce a number ten to change the game.

Bielsa again ignored Riquelme for the 2004 Copa América, preferring to turn to the energy and pace of River Plate wunderkind Andrés D'Alessandro, who had recently completed a high-profile move to Wolfsburg in the Bundesliga. So Riquelme, while not quite languishing in international wilderness, played a lot less than his talent demanded. That was until the arrival of Pékerman. In the aftermath of a heartbreaking loss to Brazil in the final of the 2004 Copa América and a mixed start to qualifying for the 2006 World Cup, Bielsa resigned, frustrated with the AFA, the Argentine media and the demands of coaching a team while being unable to drill them the way he could a club side.

Riquelme had starred for Pékerman in a succession of Argentina youth teams and the new coach turned to him immediately. He started his first-ever World Cup qualifier at the Monumental against Uruguay in October 2004. Wearing number eight, Riquelme did his thing the way he always did, without fuss but with spellbinding success. With his Boca team-mate Sebastián Battaglia protecting the defence and River Plate all-rounder Lucho González shuttling and creative in possession, Riquelme cut Uruguay apart, playing a key role in three of Argentina's goals in a 4-2 win. The Monumental roared its approval.

If Riquelme had been loved by Boca and Argentinos fans exclusively before that game – while being criticised by others for his old-fashioned style of play, placid on-pitch demeanour, apparent lack of passion and effort, and occasional quiet games – now even River Plate fans approved of him.

Galvanised, Riquelme inspired the Argentina side to become the first to qualify from South America for that World Cup, the peak coming with a classic Riquelme goal and performance at home to a strong Brazil side during a memorable 2-1 win. Not only was Riquelme playing well, he seemed to be loving it.

In 2005, Argentina played in the Confederations Cup, which was held in Germany as preparation for the bigger tournament taking place the summer after. They reached the final but were taken apart by a rampant, counter-attacking Brazil side with the fearsome forward line of Adriano, Kaká, Ronaldinho and Robinho. Riquelme started the tournament bossing games with apparent ease but seemed fatigued as the games ticked by; less dominant and active. Accordingly, Argentina drew their last group game, against Germany, and the semi-final against Mexico, advancing on penalties. Two old criticisms of the enganche returned: the notion he tired too easily despite his lack of defensive work, and the idea that if he didn't play well, the team struggled.

In Argentina, the slang 'pécho frio' (cold-chested) was applied derisively to Riquelme, suggesting he never tried hard enough. Pékerman, however, was determined in his defence of his talismanic playmaker. He made him captain of the World Cup squad and gave him the number 10 shirt, fully aware of the significance it had in a country firmly in thrall to the myth of Maradona.

The coach said: 'Some say Riquelme is slow – but he's not slow when he's in possession. It's the ball that should do the running, not the player.'

Pékerman also explicitly compared his number ten to Brazil's, who had just won the 2005 Ballon d'Or. He said: 'If Román played in Brazil he'd be Riquelminho and would be the world number one. I think the decision to choose Ronaldinho as the best in the world was unfair.'

That was clever coaching from Pékerman – he knew it was what Riquelme needed to hear. He needed to be loved and trusted and appreciated in order to play his best. Finally this heir to Maradona was going to lead his country into a World Cup, wearing the number 10 shirt just as Diego had done. He was at his peak and in a team designed to maximise his abilities. Argentina went to Germany among the favourites. The 6-0 annihilation of Serbia and Montenegro only added to the belief that, 20 years after Mexico 1986 and 13 years after they had last won a trophy, this could be their year.

Pékerman was canny. He ensured there was cover should Román suffer injury or fatigue. Pablo Aimar was in the squad, as were Carlos Tevez and Lionel Messi, all capable of impressing in the hole behind the strikers in their different ways. As it was, Pékerman's strange reluctance to use any of them when it really counted was to be his undoing. Just as in the Confederations Cup, Riquelme tired as the tournament wore on. His performance level dipped perceptibly, although he remained the dominant player in the team. He still kept the ball, created chances and occupied an inordinate amount of opposition attention.

Having won their group, Argentina were pushed hard by Mexico in their round-of-16 game. Riquelme was more effective than inspired, although he did create Crespo's opener. The game was won by a magnificent Maxi Rodríguez goal in extra time.

In the quarter-final, they faced old enemy Germany. As hosts, a vibrant young German side had performed better than expected in the tournament, scoring freely and playing some free-flowing, attacking football. Argentina and Riquelme toyed with them in the first half, monopolising possession and appearing threatening without making too many chances. When Roberto Ayala scored in the 49th minute, from another Riquelme assist, it felt as though Argentina would maintain the control created by Riquelme and Mascherano in midfield and hold out for a tight victory. But, with the stakes at their highest, Pékerman seemed to lose his nerve and withdrew Riquelme.

Rather than replacing him with Aimar or Messi, who would have been deft at keeping the ball and drawing fouls, Pékerman opted for the extra security of Cambiasso in midfield – and suddenly Argentina had lost control. This was all too familiar to fans.

In a November 2005 friendly against England in Geneva, Argentina had been leading 2-1 going into the last ten minutes of the game. Riquelme had been superb all night. England's Swedish coach, Sven-Göran Eriksson, was playing Tottenham's classy centre-back Ledley King as a holding midfielder but in that game Riquelme showed the folly of his selection. King later said Riquelme seemed to play the game at his own pace, yet had still run rings around him. Pékerman took off Riquelme in the 84th minute with Argentina still in charge, despite a thrilling performance from a young Wayne Rooney. But with Lucho González replacing Riquelme, some element of Argentina's poise had slipped and England scored two goals in the last few minutes, both by Michael Owen, to steal the game 3-2.

A similar scenario was just about to unfold against Germany in the World Cup. The Germans equalised in the 80th minute, were the more aggressive, energetic team throughout a goalless extra time, and then won 4-2 on penalties after misses by Ayala and Cambiasso. Argentina responded with fistfights and tantrums. It was now time for recriminations and regrets. Argentina were out, and Riquelme had played in his last World Cup.

Riquelme seemed to suffer in the aftermath. Aping Maradona, he quit the national team, publicly blaming Pékerman for taking him off at the worst time, when he was most needed. His form at Villarreal dipped and, again in the style of Maradona, he quarrelled with the club.

It became clear just how indulged he had been over previous seasons – he started games if he wanted to, no matter what shape he was in. Sometimes he didn't play because he claimed injury but the suspicion was that he just didn't fancy it. That was certainly true of the many training sessions he had missed, preferring the company of his entourage of Argentines. Villarreal even allowed him to return to Argentina for the birth of his son but, when he returned to Spain, he refused to train. That was the final straw. Chairman Roig admonished him in the media, which was never going to go down well.

Various clubs were interested. Everton had been linked with him in every transfer window, and Riquelme spoke after his retirement of his regret at not joining Manchester United at that point. But the fact he needed to be surrounded by his family and countrymen suggested there was only one solution. Román was homesick and, with his mother seriously ill, he returned to Boca Juniors on loan. By February 2007 he was back at the Bombonera and, although Boca were enduring a middling season in the Clausura, their attention was focused almost entirely on the Copa Libertadores – and that is where Riquelme belonged.

He was given the number 10 shirt, which he believed was his by right and tradition, and slotted into a Boca side that was already crammed with talent. Up front, Martín Palermo had returned from Europe to create a devastating pace-and-power partnership with the rapid running of Rodrigo Palacio and, with Riquelme behind them, they were an attack no side in South American football could contain for long. Román was given security in midfield by the experience of Neri Cardozo and the football intelligence and finesse of young Éver Banega, who might have been playing at number ten but for Riquelme's return. Instead, he proved a brilliant number five in Boca's system.

Riquelme thrived, scoring in every knockout round of the Libertadores as Boca eliminated Vélez Sarsfield, Paraguayan side Club Libertad and Colombia's Cúcuta Deportivo. He had returned from Europe with a better understanding of his own gifts and of the game itself, and he controlled games now with his positioning and consistently sublime use of the ball. Often, watching him at his peak felt like a masterclass – and it felt like he knew it, too.

In the final against Porto Alegre side Grêmio, Riquelme turned in vintage performances in each leg. He assisted Palermo for one goal and scored another in the 3-0 win in Buenos Aires before scoring a brace in Brazil to assure Boca won the trophy. To Boca fans, Riquelme had returned and delivered the Copa Libertadores. In the eyes of many, he was a greater icon of the club than Maradona had ever been.

* * *

At international level, Coco Basile had returned as boss after Pékerman's resignation following the World Cup. Basile's hardest task for the 2007 Copa América was choosing a squad from a huge production line of attacking talent, while his defensive options were more limited. He also had to convince Riquelme to return. He achieved that through flattery. Argentina should always be 'Riquelme plus ten others,' Pékerman said. Riquelme, always loving to be loved, returned to the fold. Basile's eventual starting XI for their opening 4-1 battering of the USA featured Riquelme and Verón in tandem, with Cambiasso and Mascherano behind, and Messi and Crespo up front. Tevez, Aimar and the lethal Diego Milito all began on the bench.

Argentina were devastating early on in that competition, like an improved version of the 2006 side. While Brazil counter-attacked their way past opponents, Nike still selling their style as 'Joga Bonito' (play beautifully), Basile's team played a joyous symphony of attacking football. Verón to Riquelme to Messi and back again was a terrifying sight for an opposing midfield and Argentina followed that game against the USA by beating Colombia 4-2. Having already won their group, Basile put out a reserve side for the last game against Paraguay, although that reserve side still featured the likes of Aimar, Fernando Gago, Palacio and Tevez. Paraguay were summarily defeated 1-0.

Aside from an injured Crespo, the starting XI were reunited for the quarter-final against Peru, and Argentina thumped them with four sumptuous goals in an unbelievable second half. Riquelme was sublime, scoring two and creating one for Messi with a trademark perfect pass.

Mexico were next, beaten 3-0, setting up a final against Brazil, who were playing without their biggest stars in the tournament, sporting a second-string squad that was still better than anyone else in the tournament except Basile's men.

The Brazilian strategy was clear from the first minute: they were going to kick Riquelme and Messi out of the game and counter-attack at a wicked pace. It worked. Júlio Baptista scored to give Brazil the lead in the fourth minute with a beautiful shot from distance after a long ball out of defence. Then Riquelme hit the post a few minutes later and Argentina looked to be awakening. It fleetingly looked as though Brazil would find themselves on the end of the same kind of hammering everyone else had. But Argentina were an attacking side, with a defence that was a mixture of ageing and fragile.

Brazil had plenty of pace up front and, after Baptista scored, Argentina had to chase the game. That left them wide open and Brazil scored twice more to see the game out 3-0.

Riquelme had again come so close and lost with the national side. If he had surpassed Maradona with Boca, he would never do the same with Argentina. He did lift a trophy, though. Chosen alongside Mascherano and Nicolás Pareja as overage players, he captained Argentina to the gold medal at the 2008 Olympic Games.

Olympic football is much more respected in South America than in most of Europe and seen as a useful proving ground for young players. That Argentina squad was a beguiling line-up of future stars including Sergio

Agüero, Angel Di María and Ezequiel Lavezzi, alongside Gago, Banega and Messi. Riquelme was the leader and stylistic influence on a team coached by Sergio Batista as they won every game and beat a strong Brazil side featuring Ronaldinho and Diego in the semi-finals before a 1-0 win over Nigeria gave them the gold medal.

Riquelme would play for Basile in the senior side again, captaining the team in the opening qualifiers for the 2010 World Cup, where he scored twice in the defeat of Bielsa's young and improving Chile side. But when his form dipped for both club and country and Argentina began to struggle, Basile was dismissed.

Even before that there was talk the youngsters in the squad were frustrated by the influence Riquelme enjoyed. Some were offended by his quietness and what was perceived by some as arrogance. There was also the Messi factor; did Argentina really need two high-quality number tens? Surely the immense, more flexible talent of Messi was enough now? With Basile gone, Román lost his chief protector.

Basile's replacement was Riquelme's old team-mate and idol, Diego Maradona, and some of the respect Riquelme has in Argentina came from the way he stood up to Maradona when so many others were cowed by the myth. Soon after he was given charge of the national side, Maradona attempted to motivate Riquelme on national television. It was a move that spoke of Maradona's volatility – as a player, he would have been enraged to be criticised in such a way by a coach on television. He would have responded in kind and felt passionately sure he was the victim but now, as coach, he was the one at fault, even if there was some truth in what he said about Román at that point.

Maradona said if Riquelme was not playing close to the opposition goal, beating defenders and feeding the strikers, he was 'no good to me'. He also claimed that, for him, the team had to be 'Mascherano plus ten others', in itself a direct repudiation of Basile's defence of Riquelme. Aside from the criticism masked in analysis, Riquelme was offended by the public nature of the event. He gave his own address to the press in which he never mentioned Maradona by name but said he would 'not play again while he is there'. He was true to his word and his international career, sporadically glorious as it was, ended with a whimper.

Riquelme won two more Argentinian titles with Boca Juniors but his powers were waning. In his early 30s now, he was not as mobile as he had been. The vision and ability to bend the flight of the ball to his will was undiminished, but he now decorated games rather than dominating them. And Maradona was not the only fight he found himself involved in – he had a long-running feud with fellow Boca legend Martín Palermo. They played together and Riquelme created goals for the target man, but they would celebrate separately before aiming barbs at each other in the media. The board at Boca was also a target of Riquelme's ire, but he still turned in some immense performances.

He seemed to reserve his best performances against Brazilian teams in the Copa Libertadores, resulting in a famous glut of Brazilian children born during the 2000s and early 2010s with variations of Riquelme as their first name. Brazilians know a player when they see one.

After much speculation, and the usual links with European, Brazilian and MLS clubs, Riquelme finally left Boca in July 2014 and returned to his boyhood club, signing for Argentinos Juniors in a pleasingly symmetrical move.

They were languishing in the Argentine second tier at the time and Román stayed there long enough to ensure their promotion back to the Primera, where they belonged. It was a sentimental gesture of such class that it was appreciated by football fans of all Argentinian clubs.

He scored five goals in 18 games and played those games his way: forcing his pace, passing, receiving, passing. He would be Juan Román Riquelme no matter where or when he played. When it was done and Argentinos were guaranteed promotion, he retired, and something of the soul of Argentinian football went with him.

When Zinedine Zidane – perhaps the greatest player of his generation – retired, his last game was for Real Madrid against Villarreal. Yet he waited on the pitch to make sure he got to swap shirts with Riquelme. Zidane knew what the Argentinian was, and what he represented. He had played against him and witnessed Riquelme's unique, pure football up close.

Riquelme's nickname, 'El Último 10', has been proven accurate since he stopped playing and football has continued to evolve. And while tens of players have been compared to Maradona since his retirement, only one or two have been compared to Juan Román Riquelme. He was just too singular, too refined. He was a one-off. No new Maradona, just Riquelme.

FIVE

Pablo Aimar, 'El Payaso' Javier Saviola, 'El Conejo'

RIQUELME'S DIRECT opposite at River Plate as he ascended through the youth teams was a skinny, lithe little artist by the name of Pablo Aimar. Their careers would intersect and overlap recurrently over the years, and although Aimar's talent would be overshadowed by his friend, his achievements were equally impressive.

Aimar's playing style was more Maradona-esque than Riquelme's. He was a dribbler, for one thing, capable of shifting through the gears with the ball at his feet and changing direction on the head of a pin. It was his dribbling style that first gained the attention of a scout in his hometown of Río Cuartoin in the Córdoba province. Aimar was elegant, his balance seemingly effortless and natural, something he never lost even as age and injuries took their toll. As he developed, he learned how to use the ball after he had beaten a man or two, and his vision and range of passing became just as dangerous as his gambeta.

Born in November 1979, Aimar first attracted attention playing as an attacking midfielder in the youth teams at his local club, Estudiantes de Rio Cuarto. He was there from the age of six until River Plate came calling in 1993. There was some sense he had been born to be a footballer. His father Ricardo was a player, turning out for Belgrano and Newell's Old Boys. His father also chose a middle name for his son with strong connotations in Argentinian football – he is named César after César Luis Menotti.

Once River had approached him, young Aimar had a big decision to make and he chose to move to Buenos Aires as part of the River academy. Aimar was academic, clever – he had a back-up plan to study medicine – but it was already evident, even at River surrounded by all the young talent in their ranks, that he was an unusually talented footballer.

He was right-footed but equally comfortable taking the ball on his left side. That allowed the elegant dance he performed whenever he had the ball at his feet to be so unpredictable and difficult to stop, and he rose through River's underage system with phenomenal speed.

Aimar made his debut for the senior side against Colón in August 1996 aged just 16, and from then on he began to gain minutes, mainly from the bench. In 1997, the wider world took notice of Aimar for the first time. Alongside Riquelme and other young talent such as Cambiasso, Wálter Samuel and Lionel Scaloni, he represented Argentina at the FIFA World Youth Championship in Malaysia. Aimar wore the number 10 shirt, like his childhood idol Diego Maradona, and he and Riquelme both shone as Argentina won the tournament with a 2-1 victory over Uruguay in the final.

Aimar was quicker and more direct than Riquelme, interspersing dribbles and passes. He was never afraid to throw in a bit of spectacular skill, earning him the nickname 'El Payaso' (the clown) for his showmanship. Later in his career, fans at Valencia would call him 'El Mago' (the magician), which tells you just how skilful he appeared in full flow.

On his return to Buenos Aires, Aimar became more important to River Plate under coach Ramón Díaz, who loved his side to live up to the attacking traditions that were so important at the club. River Plate under Díaz were in the middle of an immensely successful period. They won the Apertura and Copa Libertadores in 1996, and the Apertura and Clausura the following year. They had prolific, skilled Chilean striker Marcelo Salas up front, with Uruguayan River legend Enzo Francescoli in the hole behind, wearing the number 10 shirt.

Díaz then began to integrate a couple of talented youngsters into his team. Alongside Aimar there were strikers Javier Saviola and Juan Pablo Ángel. When Francescoli retired in 1997, Aimar was given his number ten, a signifier of the expectations already heaped on him.

The 'new Maradona' talk had begun years before, with the dribbling wonders he executed at youth level. Wearing a number 10 shirt was never a help where that was concerned. There were a few vague similarities. At 5ft 7in, Aimar was short, but whereas Maradona was squat and stocky, Aimar was slight. He looked weedy but could ride tackles on that graceful, deceptively fast stride of his. When he was running at pace, like Maradona he was extremely hard to stop. Minute adjustments dragged him beyond players and he could go either way, using either foot.

There was also the issue of fouls. Even in those early days at River, opponents did whatever they could to stop him. That mostly meant a series of violent tackles; –

desperate trips, barges, knee-high studs. Aimar took more than his fair share of knocks and, even in those first years in Argentinian football, was already starting to pick up injuries related to the physical play he was experiencing. But Aimar loved challenges. He spent 1998 teasing defenders – slipping caños through legs; facing up to opponents with the ball between his feet only to beat them with a feint and a slip as though just to show them he could; hitting shots from distance; and feeding Salas with through balls and sly assists. Like Maradona, he seemed to love playing football and bounced around the pitch full of energy.

He was a star in Argentina now and by 2000 was also River's starting number ten and probably the most important member of 'Los Cuatros Fantásticos', a group consisting of all three youthful attackers and the recently returned Ariel Ortega. Aimar was the most composed of the quartet, although they only all played together on a few occasions.

While Ortega dribbled, Aimar went on surging runs and sought to bisect a defensive line with a simple pass. At River Plate he was consistently excellent. In 82 games he scored 21 goals and provided 28 assists, maturing and improving all the while.

Maradona himself called Aimar his 'heir' and claimed he preferred him over Riquelme or Saviola, the other candidates at the time for the 'new Maradona' tag, although in that era Maradona was willing to give such juicy quotes about many players across the world, from Wayne Rooney and Cristiano Ronaldo to pretty much any young Argentine player who grabbed the media's attention.

But Aimar was different – the chosen one at that time – performing at a high level over a few years, with exciting talent and a great attitude. He suffered none of the complexities of Maradona and his struggles with authority, lacked Ortega's wild self-destructive streak, and was not as difficult to warm to as the unsmiling sphinx that was Riquelme. Aimar was likeable, approachable and open – he just happened to be a great playmaker.

* * *

When he was ready to leave River, a huge number of European clubs were after his signature. The usual wealthy Premier League giants were linked as well as the Serie A clubs that seemed to pursue every Argentinian star but Aimar, counselled by international team-mates Roberto Ayala, Mauricio Pellegrino and Kily González, joined Valencia. That Argentine trio had all been successful there and Aimar also looked to the historical examples of Mario Kempes and the more recent glory of Claudio López.

All those players set a precedent for Argentine players to thrive in the south of Spain. Aimar must have looked at what had happened to Ortega at the club and realised it was more due to personality issues and less to do with anything cultural inside Valencia itself. In January 2001, he joined Valencia from River Plate for £19.13m. That kind of fee, and the weight of past Argentinian heroics at the Mestalla, put him under pressure from the start. At that point, Valencia were coached by Argentinian Héctor Cúper, who was familiar with Aimar's strengths. Cúper's teams were compact and pressed the opposition before launching rapid counter-attacks.

Valencia fans are famously difficult to please, though, and Cúper was never all that popular despite taking them to the Champions League Final in 2000, where they lost to a Real Madrid side inspired by Fernando Redondo. Valencia's success was largely founded on a solid defence, with Argentines Ayala and Pellegrino as centre-backs, and some Spanish quality in central midfield, where captain Gaizka Mendieta was a rampaging force in any given direction, while Rubén Baraja kept things solid in front of the back four.

Cúper used Aimar on the wing and he was impressive early on, scoring on his league debut and playing a major role as Valencia reached a second successive Champions League Final. In that game, Aimar was withdrawn at half-time and Valencia went on to lose to Bayern Munich on penalties.

Cúper – his perennial nearly man status underlined with each passing season – left for Internazionale and for a while Valencia struggled to recruit a coach. Valencia occupy an odd position in Spanish football; a huge club in Spain's third city, they sit about fifth in terms of honours won in Spain. They have a huge and devoted fanbase who are unbelievably, almost comically, expectant and critical, while the Mestalla is a famously ferocious ground for an away team to visit. At that point, however, it had been three decades since Valencia had won the Spanish league and they were barely clinging on in the battle to compete with Barcelona and Real Madrid who, for all their drama and political issues, were as predictably successful as any clubs in Europe.

Valencia eventually chose Rafa Benítez, who had learned his trade in the Madrid youth teams before coaching with varying degrees of success at Valladolid, Osasuna and Tenerife, as Cúper's successor. Mendieta and Kily González had left for Lazio in the summer, so Benítez played David Albelda alongside Baraja at the base of the midfield and moved Aimar to his natural position – in the hole, behind a striker.

Aimar responded, regularly feeding giant Norwegian centre-forward John Carew and improvising most of the team's elegant, incisive attacking play as they mounted an unexpected title challenge, driven by the continued strength of their defence.

Aimar has spoken of his initial difficulty in adapting to football in Spain. Not to the pace or the quality but to coming from a River side that would regularly enjoy 70 per cent possession to a Valencia team that played in a reactive, defensive style. He had to learn how to be ready to make things happen each time he received the ball. He also had to put a shift in – Benítez would accept no passengers in his team.

Aimar had never been a Riquelme – he did drop back, he made tackles and tried to nick possession, despite his small frame. And his role at the heart of the attack changed the nature of the team's play; it was more progressive, more attractive than anything Cúper's side had served up. Valencia fans approved and results followed – Valencia won the 2002 La Liga title by seven points from Deportivo de La Coruña and Aimar was their best player. The new Maradona tag had melted away as his personality was so different and his success in Spain had shown his diffident desire to knuckle down and work hard.

* * *

In the next season the demands of the Champions League campaign took its toll on Valencia's league form. Although Aimar excelled in Europe, with five assists during the group stages and quarter-final, Valencia came a disappointing fourth in La Liga, missing out on Champions League qualification. Aimar was beginning to miss more games, too; the knocks and tackles he was regularly on the end of were plainly affecting him.

Although Valencia had another great season in 2003/04, achieving a double by winning the Spanish league and UEFA Cup, Aimar played fewer times than he had in the previous three seasons. He started the UEFA Cup Final on the bench, only introduced by Benítez in the 64th minute with Valencia already 2-0 up against Olympique Marseille.

Benítez fell out with the board at the end of the season, and Valencia went on to have three coaches over the next two years. Aimar struggled with his fitness and tactical changes, and seemed to be a player in rapid decline. In 2006 he left Valencia after five and a half seasons, four major trophies, 162 games and 27 goals. He was a club legend and a rare 'new Maradona' – he had come to Europe and unequivocally succeeded; playing well, winning trophies, avoiding scandals.

He joined Real Zaragoza, another of Spain's traditional 'big' clubs, who had been in slow decline for decades. Yet again he joined an Argentinian enclave. The Milito brothers, who were direct opponents and took part in an on-pitch, mid-game fight at Independiente versus Racing Club in Buenos Aires, were both in that exciting Zaragoza team.

Gabriel Milito was joined in defence by a young Gerard Piqué, on loan from Manchester United where he had failed to shift Nemanja Vidić or Rio Ferdinand from the first team, but he was easily capable enough for La Liga. Argentine creativity came from two players –

Aimar and another former River player, maverick Andrés D'Alessandro, on loan from Wolfsburg. Diego Milito was just hitting peak form in 2006, with 23 goals.

Zaragoza were one of the most exciting teams in Spain that season, with Aimar and D'Alessandro combining beautifully to set up Diego Milito, who was lethal inside and outside the box. Both playmakers scored a few too – Aimar scored five – and helped Zaragoza achieve a sixth-place finish. However, the next season was disastrous. Piqué and Gabriel Milito both left and the recruitment of an ageing Roberto Ayala wasn't enough to mitigate the loss. Aimar was again sporadically injured and, as the team's results indicated they would be involved in a relegation battle, media observers caught him and D'Alessandro squaring up to one another at training. D'Alessandro fell out with coach Victor Fernández soon after and was sent to train with the reserves. He left for San Lorenzo on loan. When Zaragoza were relegated at the end of the season, Aimar was off too, moving to Lisbon giants Benfica for £7.2m.

* * *

Benfica is a club that appreciates a fine playmaker. Club legend Rui Costa was one of the best attacking midfielders in the world of his generation and, in his new role as sporting director at the club, made Aimar one of his first signings, recognising the number ten could become a big player in the Portuguese Primeira. After taking a year to settle in under coach Jorge Jesus, Aimar was part of an attacking line-up of high-quality South Americans who would go on to terrorise Portuguese football.

He played in his natural role, as a classic number ten. He drifted, found pockets of space, dropped off to pick up the ball where he fancied, and crafted chances. Benfica drafted in his old River Plate partner in crime Javier Saviola to play as second striker. Their connection and understanding remained intact, and both played brilliantly off old-fashioned Paraguayan centre-forward Óscar Cardozo, who hugely benefited to the tune of 26 goals in the 2009/10 season. Many of those goals were created by another Argentine, the pacy, direct winger Angel Di María. With Brazilian Ramires joining in from midfield, Benfica were a joy to watch, with Aimar the conductor of every move. They romped to the Primeira title, scoring 78 goals in the process and adding the Taça de Liga (the Portuguese league cup) for a rare double.

Aimar stayed at Benfica for five years, confirming he was a serial football club monogamist. When he was happy and felt loved, he stayed. However, injuries continued to affect his appearances and performance, especially in 2012/13. He left Benfica at the end of the season having won the Taça de Liga three times alongside his league title and beloved by Benfiquistas. Jesus called him the greatest player he had ever coached.

At the age of 34 and increasingly injury-prone, Aimar's best realistic options lay away from Europe. Players of his generation were starting to choose the MLS for a good payday, a different lifestyle away from the pressure of football stardom in Europe and Latin America, and a league that was kind to ageing quality. Robbie Keane and Thierry Henry were there, alongside a host of Argentinians a rung or two below Aimar in terms of talent such as Federico Higuaín and his old River team-mate Mauro Rosales. Others were choosing the new football frontier of Australia for similar reasons and Italian legend Alessandro

Del Piero proved a number ten growing into his 30s could thrive there.

Aimar chose differently. Perhaps warmly recalling his success in Malaysia in the 1997 Youth Cup, in August 2013 he signed for Johor Darul Ta'zim of the Malaysian Super League. He was the biggest star and highest earner in the league but his habitual injury problems meant it was six months before he made his debut, and injuries would mar his spell there. He only played eight times, scoring two goals, before he was released in April 2014 in the middle of yet another long spell in the medical room.

* * *

His story with the national team was more complex than his club career; he always seemed to be playing second fiddle to others. Aimar made his international debut in 1999 and was part of Bielsa's squad for the 1999 Copa América, where both he and his friend Riquelme were below Ariel Ortega in the pecking order. Bielsa's team – that had not quite been indoctrinated in the Bielsa way yet – were outclassed in the quarter-finals by a sparkling Brazil team, however, and Ortega's star began to dim.

Aimar appeared to be a perfect Bielsa player – hard-working and energetic, accurate with his use of the ball, creative in tight spaces – and Bielsa regularly selected him, although he never became the talismanic figure for Bielsa's Argentina team as many had hoped. Early on, Ortega was in the way, but when Aimar was a bigger star Bielsa changed the focus of his side. Juan Sebastián Verón became the focal point of a team playing aggressive, European-style football, with Aimar often brought on in the second half to alter the rhythm of a match. In the disappointing 2002 World Cup campaign, Aimar was only introduced when an unfit Verón struggled and Bielsa needed to test other options, although when he was brought on for Verón against England in the 1-0 group-stage loss he created some bright moments.

Bielsa started him alongside Ortega against Sweden in the next game, a make-or-break tie to decide who qualified for the knockout rounds. But a nervy Argentina never quite hit their stride, Aimar included, and a 1-1 draw eliminated them from the tournament.

A few years later, when Bielsa was replaced by Pékerman, Riquelme became the team's creative leader. If Aimar played after that, it was as a second striker alongside Riquelme or starting because he was injured or unavailable. Their careers had overlapped and interlinked when they were kids at the World Youth Cup, young rivals for Boca and River, and in Spain at Valencia and Villarreal. Now they were rivals for the same position, although Riquelme generally had the edge over Aimar.

After Riquelme had fallen out with Diego Maradona around the qualifiers for the 2010 World Cup, Maradona needed an old-fashioned number ten to play alongside Lionel Messi, who was busy redefining exactly what a playmaker could and should do. After considering the likes of Daniel 'Rolfi' Montenegro, he turned to the old reliable figure of Aimar, who created a goal for Gonzalo Higuaín early on in a key game against Peru. That assist was a classic enganche moment. Aimar prodded a perfectly judged through ball into a gap, eliminating four defenders from the play, for Higuaín to run on to and finish. It was to be his final big moment in an Argentina shirt.

* * *

Aimar's career was ebbing away but, when he left Argentina, he promised he would return to River Plate. After surgeries on a recurrent problem with his heel, he rejoined the club in January 2015 and made his second debut when he came on as substitute against Rosario Central in May of the same year. The reception was phenomenal. River is a club with a very self-conscious sense of its heritage and history, and the romantic gesture by a returned conquering hero did not go unnoticed. That was his first game and, it would turn out, his last game too, and he announced his retirement in July 2015.

In another romantic gesture, he appeared alongside his brother in one competitive game for his boyhood club, Estudiantes de Río Cuarto, after his retirement and then he was gone, until he reappeared among the coaching staff for his nation in 2017 and 2018, passing on his lessons in magic and flamboyance to the U17 team before becoming part of Lionel Scaloni's staff for the triumphs at the 2021 Copa América and the 2022 World Cup.

Aimar helping to nurture young Argentinian footballers seemed right. First, because he had broken through at such a young age himself, and second, because another young player had long declared his love of Aimar. Lionel Messi admitted in an interview that Aimar had been his idol growing up and, after a break from the national team, Aimar's role with the coaching set-up was reportedly key to encouraging Messi to return to lead his country in the 2020s.

There were many similarities in their games. Aimar's influence might not have been as extensive or as important as Maradona's but in Messi, as well as in his own heroics for his clubs and country, he left a powerful legacy.

Aimar's former team-mate at River and Benfica, Javier Saviola, bore more resemblance to Romário than Maradona as a player but, when he first emerged in his teens at River Plate, there were enough similarities. Saviola's talent was undeniable and he seemed set for the sort of career that sends records tumbling. The new Maradona tag was unavoidable.

Saviola was brought up in Belgrano, a leafy district on the banks of the Río de la Plata in northern Buenos Aires. River Plate's Monumental stadium is located there, so it was no surprise that Saviola grew up idolising Ariel Ortega instead of Diego Maradona. But as a player, he was unlike either of those other porteños. At just 5ft 6in, Saviola was short and explosive, with a phenomenal burst of pace over a short distance. In addition, he was Argentine so he could deploy an arsenal of tricks and skills when he needed to. If his team-mates could feed him the ball in the box, Saviola was speedy and skilful enough to create a chance. If he created a chance – in his early days at least – Saviola could score.

The Romário comparisons came from that combination of technical ability and pace, and also the knack he had of coming alive as soon as he sniffed a goal. His movement was superb – he could drift and dart, and his pace meant that if he got even an instant on a defender, he was gone.

As a teenager, Saviola's finishing suggested the calm and precision of a born goalscorer. He placed shots into the bottom corners of the goal with amazing consistency. His nickname, 'El Conejo' (the rabbit), was prompted by his buck-toothed appearance but the fact he was also called 'El Pibito' (the little kid) – in reference to Maradona's 'El Pibe de Oro' name – suggests just how much potential Saviola had in his youth.

Indeed, despite a successful career, that huge potential means he is generally regarded as a talent unfulfilled. There is an entire generation of computer game fans that whisper the name Javier Saviola to one another. In the late 1990s and early 2000s, he was as close as the game *Football Manager* came to a sure thing – if you bought him as a teenager, he grew up to be the best player on Earth. Unfortunately, real life was to be a lot more complicated for Saviola.

As a player too, there was something of a rabbit about him – he scurried, he twisted and turned, defenders could not kick or pull him down. He had that magic only young players possess; a fearlessness and optimism that football would always work out for them. And when he burst into the River Plate senior team, a frenetic, pacy 16-year-old kid who had grown up only blocks from the stadium, he made anything seem possible.

He made his debut in 1998, meaning Saviola came into a team featuring the once-in-a-lifetime creative glut of Aimar, Ortega and Angel in and around him. For a player who had the skillset to play as an out-and-out centre-forward, a second striker or a playmaker between the lines, the sense of thrilling possibility, of interplay and positional fluidity was ideal. Saviola was an instant star and, alongside Aimar, was seen as the latest great talent from River Plate's incredibly consistent player factory.

During the next few years, as a teenager he would score 45 goals in 86 games. With River, he won the 1999 Apertura and 2000 Clausura titles, while his individual achievements were recognised when he was awarded the prestigious 1999 South American footballer of the year title by *El País*, still the youngest-ever winner.

Although he had made his international debut against Paraguay in August 2000, he was called up by José Pékerman to play for the U20 team at the 2001 World Youth Championship, which was to be played in Argentina. In retrospect, Saviola seems like that squad in microcosm – undeniably precocious and talented, it largely failed to live up to a sense of immense potential suggested by those exploits.

Players such as Julio Arca, Andrés D'Alessandro, Leandro Romagnoli, Alejandro Domínguez and Esteban Herrera looked like huge stars in waiting back then, and arguably only D'Alessandro came anywhere near fulfilling any of his promise. Instead, it was the defenders who would enjoy more consistent careers – Nicolás Burdisso and Fabricio Coloccini becoming intermittent fixtures in the national team. Saviola and Maxi Rodríguez would be the two attacking players with the clearest success in Europe, and both enjoyed good tournaments. Saviola was better than good and, with his nation's eyes upon him, he was sensational. He scored 11 goals in seven games, including a hat-trick against France, to win the Golden Boot while becoming the highest goalscorer in the tournament's history. If expectations were already high, he had just raised them.

* * *

By that point, anyone who understood football could see Saviola was not and never would be the new Maradona but, by now, Argentina was addicted to the search for an heir to its fallen idol. Maradona, constantly asked for his opinion on young players who displayed any skill, self-destructiveness, or any of his looks, stature or personality, did not help.

Maradona had been praising Saviola all year. When the maestro was hospitalised in 2001 with heart problems, the Argentinian media set up camp outside. Saviola, fresh from a triumphant season with River and his Argentina heroics, visited Diego and presented him with one of his shirts. When Maradona, Pope-like, waved to the media from the window of his hospital room, he did it wearing that Saviola shirt. The Argentinian football media, loving such symbolic moments, duly seized on this one.

Saviola seemed to play up to the Maradona talk when he chose the European club he would move to. Having been linked with the giants of Spain, Italy and England during the past few years, he signed for Barcelona in 2001 for £15m. Like Maradona, the Barcelona he joined was experiencing one of its regular, difficult transitional spells. Great rivals Real Madrid were launching the galácticos era having just signed Zinedine Zidane to pair with Luis Figo, who had been poached from Barça, a bitter indication of the relative confidence at each club.

Saviola was paired with another bright young thing in the form of Dutch striker Patrick Kluivert in a classic, almost old-fashioned strike partnership. Kluivert, tall, great in the air, powerful and deceptively skilful, led the line for Saviola to scamper into space and around defenders.

Saviola's finishing was still of the highest quality and he scored 17 goals in La Liga, a decent return for a 20-year-old in his first season in European football. He scored another four in other competitions as Barcelona made it to the semi-finals of the Champions League – but it was not enough;

in that tie they were eliminated by Madrid. And if Barça fans had been told they were getting the new Maradona, they soon saw Saviola, for all his quality, was not that. He and Kluivert were good, but they were not good enough to propel the team any higher than another fourth-place finish in Spain.

Saviola would spend three seasons at Barcelona, the aura of his potential gradually dimming. The reality of European competition has that effect on some young South Americans it seems. In Argentina he was special. A crack, a superstar. In Europe he was just another good player surrounded by good players from Nigeria, Brazil, Serbia and Sweden. Being good was not enough in Europe. He scored goals and consistently combined with an ever-evolving line-up of team-mates – his understanding with Kluivert and Ronaldinho was exciting – but by the end of the 2003/04 season, both he and Kluivert were unwanted.

For two years in a row, Saviola was sent out on loan. First, he spent a season at AS Monaco in France, managing seven goals in 29 games. In a supposed lesser league, these were not the figures of a prospective superstar or a new Maradona who had scored for fun at River Plate. A move back to La Liga saw him win the UEFA Cup with Sevilla in 2006, but his performances were similarly underwhelming, with nine goals in 29 games.

After playing well in the 2006 World Cup, he returned to Barcelona for another middling season, with ten goals in 24 games. Most of those appearances came because of injuries to the starters and, at the end of the season, Saviola left Nou Camp to join Real Madrid.

In the recent past, players who had swapped the Catalan capital for the Spanish capital had been vilified and endured horrendous stick when they made their return. Michael Laudrup was terrified into anonymity by the hostility the Nou Camp generated when he returned with Madrid. Figo was only slightly more effective during his legendary 'pig's head' game a few years later. And Saviola? When he moved in 2007, it seemed like nobody really cared.

He had become so unimportant to Barcelona – both the club and the fans – that allowing him to leave for their greatest rival was not seen as that big a deal. Especially as he arrived at a squad containing a bewilderingly glittering stable of attacking talent: Ruud van Nistelrooy, Raúl, Arjen Robben, Robinho and Gonzalo Higuaín all competed for places. Saviola had left a club where he was well down the pecking order for a club where he was still well down the pecking order.

During his two years at Madrid, he scored just four goals in 17 appearances. In 2008, he did win the league title that had eluded him at Barcelona but all his spell there really did was confirm his decline. He was enshrined as a player who had peaked in his teens, and every conversation about him was as somebody who had once been seen as the next Maradona.

* * *

From 2009 to 2012, perhaps finally free from all the pressure in Spain his big-money transfer and all the media talk had guaranteed, he had his best period in Europe, playing for Benfica. With old team-mate Aimar behind and target man Óscar Cardozo alongside, he won one league title and three Taça de Liga cups, scoring 24 goals in 69 games and embracing his role as a second striker. He was no longer considered for the national team at this point, usurped by younger, better players, but still he plugged away in Europe, becoming a journeyman striker for three years.

First, he played for Málaga in 2012 and 2013. The club was still coping with the consequences of an injection of cash from new Qatari owners, and under Manuel Pellegrini the squad was stuffed with talent, including plenty of attackers from across South America.

There was Brazilian Júlio Baptista; Uruguayan Sebastián Fernández, who enthusiastically engaged in a direct battle for the role of second striker with Saviola; Paraguayan Roque Santa Cruz; Chilean Pedro Morales; and another young River Plate starlet in the form of Diego Buonanotte. Saviola did fine, scoring eight goals in 26 games, many from the bench, but at the end of the season he was off again, moving to Athens giants Olympiacos.

The Greek league has hosted several ageing Argentine players over the years and Saviola did well enough for a 31-year-old whose primary gift – his pace – had ebbed away. He still had his movement and skill, and that was enough in Greece. He scored 12 goals in 26 games and then left for Verona in Serie A for the 2014/15 season. The step back up to Italian league football was too much for him, though, and he struggled for form and fitness, scoring just one goal in 15 appearances.

After that, Saviola did what so many Argentinian players did in their 30s – he went home. Back to Argentina, back to River Plate. On 30 June 2015, his return was announced. He played 15 games that season, remained on the bench while Marcelo Gallardo's side won the Copa Libertadores by beating Tigres UANL in the final in August, and failed to score any goals. In January, he announced his retirement. He was just 34.

His international career followed similar themes. After the initial burst of raw talent, his later, more ordinary achievements could not be seen as anything other than a disappointment. After his heroics in the 2001 World Youth Championship, he was in and around the Argentina side under Marcelo Bielsa for the next few seasons. Bielsa claimed Saviola was not ready for the 2002 World Cup but, in reality, he already had a selection dilemma with a declining Gabriel Batistuta and a prime Hernán Crespo in his squad. Saviola would have been just another problem.

Instead, Bielsa took Saviola to the 2004 Olympic Games, where he played, scored and won a gold medal while being utterly outshone by Boca Juniors' young tyro, Carlos Tevez. When Pékerman took over, his knowledge of Saviola's qualities from Argentina youth teams meant he was a firm favourite, and he played in the 2005 Confederations Cup and 2006 World Cup, where he struck a nice partnership with Riquelme and scored in Argentina's opening victory against Ivory Coast. But the coming of Messi, Higuaín, Agüero and Tevez meant the end of Saviola's time with Argentina and, after two years without a call-up, he announced his international retirement in 2009.

Of all the new Maradonas since the 1980s, Javier Saviola's tale is the most classic example of a young South American star, hyped by his domestic media, who never really lived up to it all once he was in Europe. Robinho and Pato, Matías Fernandez and Nicolás Lodeiro, James Rodríguez and Enner Valencia all had similar experiences to some extent. But none of them, for all the expectation each created, had been compared to Diego Maradona as a 16-year-old. That created its own pressure and, for Saviola as he aged, it was a pressure he struggled to cope with.

SIX

Carlos Marinelli, 'Dieguito' Cristian Colusso, 'El Chiri'

FOR DECADES, Argentinian players were a common sight in Italian, Spanish and increasingly French, Portuguese and German football. Maradona's career was indicative of the trend throughout the 1990s and 2000s – quality South American footballers came to Europe. But England had always had a more complex relationship with Argentinian football.

The rivalry between the countries and their troublesome ties in World Cups in 1966 and 1986 is a symptom of that, displaying Argentina's customary insecurity before their former quasi-colonial overlords and Britain's superior dismissal of the South Americans.

But in the late 1970s, with transfers growing increasingly expensive within the British game, little history of players from other parts of Europe moving to England, and attracted by the talented players showcased by the 1978 World Cup, English teams looked to Argentina to find strong players at reasonable prices. Cosmopolitan north London club Tottenham Hotspur, with an image for stylish football and a certain sophistication, were at the vanguard of that movement. In 1978 they pulled off the surprise double signing of midfielders Osvaldo Ardiles from Huracán and Ricardo Villa from Racing Club. Both players were seen as successes and their stays and achievements in Britain did a lot to encourage other clubs to take a chance on fancy foreign players.

'Ossie' Ardiles and 'Ricky' Villa won the 1981 FA Cup for Spurs, with Villa scoring a ludicrously good goal in the final. It remains one of the most famous in English football history. He stayed at Tottenham for five years, while Ardiles made himself a beloved treasure in London, spending a decade at the club before spells at Blackburn Rovers, Queens Park Rangers and Swindon Town, plus an unsuccessful stint as Tottenham coach.

In the same era, Sheffield United were in advanced negotiations to buy a young Diego Maradona from Argentinos Juniors. They eventually baulked at the price – there must have been some massive regrets about that parsimony only a couple of years later – and turned their attentions to his contemporary, River Plate's reserve playmaker Alejandro Sabella.

Sabella lacked pace but was elegant and intelligent, and he played most of his River career as understudy to Norberto Alonso, only getting a regular starting place in his favoured position during Alonso's year-long adventure at Marseille in 1976. During the junta era, the Argentinian economy struggled, with even footballers feeling the pinch. Added to that, Sabella was educated and liberal – he had worked in the Buenos Aires slums with Perónist groups, helping the poor – and the moral accommodations he had to make to stay in Argentina must have been exhausting.

So, when an English club wanted to pay him good money to spend a season or two away from a turbulent Argentina, running their midfield at the age of 24, he said yes and spent two good seasons at the Blades, then another at Leeds United after Sheffield United were relegated to the old Third Division. Leeds at least offered him top-flight football and were one of the giant clubs of England. He struggled in that season, though, and returned to Argentina to win two titles at Estudiantes de La Plata.

All those players had been signed for their flair – they were all creative midfielders – but they showed Argentines were workers too, soldiers when they needed to be, and could adapt to the rigours and sometime brutality of the British game. The same era saw 1978 World Cup winner Alberto Tarantini flee a contract dispute at Boca Juniors for a difficult season at Birmingham City. He was something of a bad boy, signed for his defensive combativeness and roving, driving energy from full-back. He attracted attention after some excellent performances in the World Cup and, for Birmingham, his £297,000 transfer was a huge coup.

Tarantini has since claimed he had to leave Argentina after he soaped his genitals before shaking hands with General Videla in the dressing room during the World Cup. He also claimed he had asked too many questions about his friends, who were among the thousands who had been 'disappeared' by the military dictatorship. Life in Argentina was difficult, and even the protection offered by being a national hero for his role in a World Cup win offered only so much insulation for a visible, charismatic figure such as Tarantini.

But he had a bad season. Birmingham were already in the relegation places when Tarantini arrived and his marauding style did not really fit with a Birmingham side too dependent on the injured Trevor Francis. He also struggled to adapt to a Midlands winter and met the aggression of the English game with his own. He knocked out Manchester United's Jimmy Greenhoff in an off-the-ball incident, which was unseen by the referee in a 5-1 win but breathlessly reported by the English football press, who loved Tarantini's curly-haired hatchet-man image. Then he waded into the crowd at the end of another loss in a season full of them and exchanged punches with a Birmingham fan.

Despite his huge wages, revealed a few years ago after his contract was leaked online, when Talleres de Córdoba came in for him in 1979, he returned to Argentina after only 23 games for Birmingham.

During the subsequent two decades, only a few Argentines took the gamble of moving to England. Most of the high-profile foreign imports in the 1980s came from Scandinavia and the Netherlands, both areas where English football was closely followed. Footballers from Rotterdam or Oslo would not be put off by a rainy midweek cup tie in Carlisle, and most already spoke English.

England's success in the 1990 World Cup and the coming of the commercial behemoth that was the Premier League changed all that. The English game became more middle class, more marketable internationally, more financially attractive. Players came from all over the world – suddenly England's top division had Nigerians, Italians, Peruvians and Russians alongside the Irishmen and Danes who had been a feature for decades. Some of those foreigners were huge successes, and even the failures held a certain cult appeal.

English clubs that had never been successful were suddenly wealthy. The TV money generated by a league sporting superclubs such as Manchester United, Liverpool and Arsenal, all of them with squads of international stars, trickled down to clubs that might have traditionally been regarded as second or third-tier sides. Some of those sides spent big or had good seasons, made it to the Premier League, spent only a season or two competing with the big clubs, and then sank back down. Some of them bought foreign players to make themselves more instantly competitive, which rarely worked.

Those clubs and the glamour they brought to the Premier League made other clubs more attractive investments. Ultimately this would lead to Russian oligarch Roman Abramovich buying Chelsea and Manchester City's acquisition by oil-rich owners, which would warp the very nature of football in Europe, but in the 1990s it meant local businessmen might be able to buy the club they had supported as a child. So it was with Jack Walker, who bought Blackburn Rovers in 1989 and invested enough for them to win the Premier League in 1995. They would later buy another young Argentine attacking midfielder in the form of Mauro Formica, but he was never quite a 'new Maradona', for all his evident promise.

Steve Gibson would have hoped to emulate the success of Walker and Blackburn when he became chairman and majority shareholder of his boyhood club, Middlesbrough, in 1994. Gibson installed Manchester United and England legend Bryan Robson as manager and gave him enough money to start filling his squad with internationals from other leagues. During the next decade, Middlesbrough, a town of about 160,000 people on the northeastern edge of Yorkshire, played host to Brazilians Juninho, Emerson and Branco; Juventus and Italy forward Fabrizio Ravanelli; gifted Croat Alen Bokšić; George Boateng; Hámilton Ricard; Christian Ziege; Yakubu; Gaizka Mendieta and Abel Xavier, to name just a few.

Before that, 'Boro' had been a club of little distinction, generally moving between the second and third tiers and overshadowed by the two traditional giants of football in the northeast of England – Newcastle United and Sunderland. But Boro's new approach suddenly gave them unimaginable glamour and a profile, and other foreigners would come to a club where Ravanelli and Juninho had played.

They had some success too, and a mixed era of relegations, promotions, a European run and cup finals all followed. They also changed football in England. If Boro could do it, anyone could. Anyone could buy a foreign artist to play in an obscure English town for a club founded in the 1800s, anybody could challenge the big clubs of London and the northwest of England with stylish sophistication. Middlesbrough never abandoned their policy, even as the results fluctuated. They even looked to expand their policy of buying foreign talent. Instead of just buying proven performers, they started to look at young prospects. One such prospect was Carlos Ariel Marinelli.

* * *

Marinelli was born in March 1982 and raised in Villa de Mayo in the Buenos Aires suburbs. Like Maradona, Borghi, Riquelme and Redondo before him, he came to everyone's attention in the youth system at Argentinos Juniors. He had played at their feeder side, Club Parque, but his vision and touch saw him brought into the Argentinos sides.

From there, he attracted admiring glances and went to Boca Juniors as part of a package of several players, including Riquelme and Coloccini. Under the microscope at Boca, Marinelli progressed rapidly, and that might have been where his issues began. Everything came easy and so early to Marinelli, until it didn't.

He arrived at Boca in 1997 at the tender age of 15. Quickly, his coaches at Boca were rhapsodising about his ability to see two or three moves ahead, and his evolving quality in the youth teams there meant he made his debut for the reserves in August 1999.

He had already made something of a stir for the Argentina youth teams, too. In 1998 he had been called up to play in the U17 World Cup (the 'Mundialito') in Salerno by coach Hugo Tocalli, and he was in terrific form as Argentina reeled off a string of impressive victories to win the tournament. That was when the first mentions of the dreaded 'new Maradona' were attached to his name.

Tocalli and then-youth-system supremo José Pékerman were suitably wowed and selected Marinelli for the Argentina squad for the South American U17 Championship in Uruguay in 1999. After a good start with Marinelli in the team – although quiet against strong opposition – Pékerman dropped the playmaker for the games that looked as though they might be dogfights. In particular, the grit and toughness always asked of an Argentina side in any game against Uruguay was something Marinelli might be lacking, and he was left out of that clash.

Goalkeeper Germán Lux and Coloccini were the stand-outs in that close draw, and in the semi-finals Pékerman again left out Marinelli for the big clash with Brazil. He was brought on in the second half with Brazil two goals up, and soon after created a goal with a cross to give Argentina hope of a comeback. It was hope Brazil swiftly squashed with a third goal.

The third-place play-off at the tournament had more meaning than most. Not just because it was against old foes Uruguay but because the winner would qualify for the World Youth Cup in New Zealand a year later. Again, Marinelli started on the bench. When he came on, Argentina were losing, and they went down 4-2 to a rampant, free-scoring Uruguay side.

This tournament was a telling experience for Marinelli. His talent was undeniable but as players around him began to develop physically, he seemed to struggle. He was not strong enough yet, and although coaches and fans believed he had plenty of time, that would be a problem throughout those crucial formative years of his career.

In July 1999, a few weeks before his actual debut for the reserves, Marinelli toured the UK with a Boca Juniors U19 team. Watching as Boca played a mixed team of Middlesbrough youth players was manager of the senior side, Bryan Robson. He was stunned by the dazzling performance of the youngster, who seemed to perfectly fit the profile of players his club were pivoting to target. He was young, developing, technically exceptional, relatively cheap and had great resale potential.

Boro opened negotiations during that tour and, after a series of complications involving Marinelli's father and his rights to his son's gains as a minor, the Teesside club paid Boca £1.5m for the number ten in October 1999. Marinelli arrived to great fanfare, the Maradona comparisons acknowledged and ludicrously emphasised in the British press, the expectations of any South American arriving in the country now stellar. Initial impressions were positive. Marinelli scored the winner with a free kick in his debut reserve game on a midweek night against Barnsley, watched by 10,000 people when the crowd was usually in the hundreds. He followed that with another goal in his second appearance.

For the reserves, he was playing as a second striker, given liberty to drop off and dictate attacks from the hole. He scored nine goals in ten games and crafted a series of assists and it looked as though all the praise was justified. Robson gave Marinelli his full debut on Boxing Day at Hillsborough, the home of Sheffield Wednesday. He was training with a team full of class and experience. As well as talented foreigners such as local legends Juninho and Ziege, there were former Manchester United and England stars Paul Ince and Gary Pallister alongside the sporadic genius of Paul Gascoigne.

For his part, Marinelli was 17 years of age and had never played for the Boca Juniors first team. All his competitive football prior to arriving in England had been in the youth teams or reserves. Boro were comfortable in mid-table, Wednesday rooted to the bottom, but English football is unpredictable and the Owls won the game 1-0. Marinelli came on in the second half and made little impression.

* * *

From there, the story of this new Maradona in England is assembled from bits and pieces of every story of every skilful foreign player who came to play in the UK in that era only for it to not quite work out. He was too young, too far away from his family and friends, too culture-shocked, too delicate for the physical power of the football, too injury-prone, too unsuited to all but one position.

After a start that was mixed and with clear evidence of his potential, he played games mostly for the reserves for the rest of that season. Marinelli plainly needed time to bulk up and adjust to English football. In summer 2000, Boro sold Juninho and Ziege but recruited high-class players in Bokšić and Christian Karembeu. Marinelli was given a semi-promotion to the senior squad, with the intention of playing him more as the team struggled. He was generally positioned on the wing, where Robson believed his dribbling and passing ability could frighten teams, but he saw himself as a second striker.

A recurring ankle problem that began in his first season together with a battle to find consistent form and the expected homesickness of a teenager living a continent away from his home affected his mood and chances of putting together a run of performances. The suspicion remained that he was too lightweight for England, and his toughness and work rate were questioned. He had a Riquelme-esque reluctance to track back and do the hard work demanded by English crowds and coaches, without the Riquelme genius. That persistent ankle injury also suggested his durability was a genuine issue but its chief repercussion was to rule him out for long periods of the season when he could have been adjusting to the pace and ruggedness of Premier League football.

In a pivotal game, he was given a starting role against fellow relegation candidates Bradford. In the second half, with Boro 2-1 down and threatening only from set pieces, Marinelli, who had been playing well and been creative and positive in a dour, physical game, had a moment that encapsulated his time in England. He received the ball, jinked his way past one player, pulled off a slick drag-back to escape another, and then an errant touch left him having to commit himself to a 50:50 to keep hold of the ball. He went over the ball, took some of the man – perhaps in an effort to prove he was, after all, tough enough for this league – and got a straight red card for his troubles. Although the game ended as a 2-2 draw, Marinelli's fragile spirit sank and Robson – together with new coach Terry Venables – gave him another spell in the reserves to rebuild his confidence. It all damaged his standing in the Argentina youth teams.

Marinelli had been playing regularly alongside the likes of D'Alessandro, but his injury and long spells on the treatment table meant he missed out on the squad for the 2001 U20 South American Championship, where he would have been expected to flourish. A season in which many expected this new Maradona to live up to his billing had turned out to be a disaster – he had played 13 games, been sent off in one, and lost his place in the Argentina youth squad. The injury he had picked up was dominating his career, too.

* * *

In the next season, Marinelli showed the best form of his Boro career – when he was fit. Again, he spent stretches injured, but under Steve McClaren he was far more consistent and assertive in his football. He played 27 times that season and scored a couple of goals.

It was obvious by now that the Maradona comparisons were ridiculous, but Marinelli still looked as though he might develop into a fine attacking midfielder. He might have been expected to kick on in the next year, with two and a half years in England under his belt, and more first-team experience. Instead, he wilted.

In and out of the team and squad during the first few weeks of the season, Marinelli started to complain to the media about his lack of opportunities. He was quoted as criticising the youth policies in English football to the Argentine media and, after he wasn't selected in the months leading up to Christmas, Boro began negotiating with Boca Juniors to take him back on loan.

Boca coach Óscar Tabárez, with his Pékerman-like devotion to youth, was keen on the move but, when the veteran manager returned to the role of Uruguay head coach, he was replaced by Carlos Bianchi, who wasn't interested in Marinelli.

As an alternative, the youngster followed the old Maradona pattern – when seeking to leave one European league, head to Serie A. He arrived at Torino, who were fighting relegation, with a similar fanfare to the one that had greeted his Boro entrance. Any set of fans, no matter how cynical, would be excited by the prospect of a new number ten once billed as the new Maradona and Marinelli won cult status with a debut assist and a goal against Modena in his second appearance. The Italian press hyped him up and his performances were creative and enterprising. He had some dynamism from his time in England to add to his Argentinian gambetas. He seemed more street-smart and experienced, and he looked perfect for Serie A. Until the Turin derby. Then, his immaturity revealed itself again as he shoved a referee and received a red card and lengthy ban. Torino were relegated, but their fans sang his name during their long slow run of defeats as they slid out of the league.

As many Argentines have, Marinelli liked the culture, the city and the language. He was willing to stay to get Torino promoted but his father entered negotiations – as he had done during his move to Middlesbrough – and the deal fell through. Marinelli was forced to return to Boro having spent weeks doing his best to leave. Nonetheless, he was embraced by the team. Juninho had come back and he helped Marinelli refocus on committing himself and starting again.

Marinelli did his best during a brief return. He impressed McClaren enough to earn a start in the first game of the 2003/04 season, where he scored in a 3-2 defeat to Fulham. But when he was substituted, Marinelli reacted with petulance, that immaturity again evident. It must be hard to be the new Maradona only to find yourself constantly substituted by a club involved in endless relegation battles. His contract, up at the end of the year, was terminated by mutual consent in November 2003. Marinelli was now free to go to whoever would have him.

After that, he became a journeyman. Any hope of ever playing for Argentina or an elite club disappeared when his return to Boca Juniors turned into a non-event, with just three appearances of little note. Marinelli was still not to Carlos Bianchi's taste and his role in a goal scored by Vélez Sarsfield in his debut seemed to cement that. He lost possession and failed to track back. Vélez scored. Bianchi was seemingly assured that his instincts were faultless.

In the reserves, Marinelli got himself sent off, something that was becoming a habit at this point. From there he went to Racing Club, where he played more – mostly coming off the bench – without really impressing or scoring. Racing lost almost every game he played and, when Torino showed interest in his return to Italy, he paid €30,000 of his own money to buy himself out of his contract to return to Turin. Still in Serie B, he made his debut in January 2005 against Hellas Verona and, in typical Marinelli fashion, got himself sent off for slapping an opponent. After his suspension he did relatively well, playing 15 more games and scoring once, to help Torino into the play-offs and ultimately promotion.

However, the club was in huge financial trouble and, once the Italian FA scrutinised the accounts, their unsustainable debt – alluded to by Marinelli in subsequent interviews when he talked about the awful facilities – meant they were condemned to remain in Serie B. Their finances were in such a state they could not afford to keep an underperforming luxury like Marinelli.

He moved again, this time to Sporting Braga in Portugal in January 2006. There he made a handful of appearances, playing his usual game of fancy tricks on the ball and absolutely no defensive work, before an injury forced him to return to Argentina for treatment and rehabilitation. His contract at Braga ended so his next stop was the MLS, an increasingly attractive option for Argentinian number tens of a certain level. But those players would move as 'franchise players', enabling the clubs to attract quality veterans and pay them more than the average American professional would expect.

Marinelli had lost so much lustre he was not even a franchise player. Instead, he had two seasons with the Kansas City Wizards after they saw videos of him on a pre-season tour of Argentina. This was probably his most consistent spell after Middlesbrough, and it shows how he had declined. In Kansas, he was a solid player, making 41 appearances over two seasons, scoring one goal and providing six assists as the Wizards made it to the 2006 play-offs. After a less impressive second year in the US, the club declined to renew his contract and he was on his way again, the words the 'new Maradona' destined to ever hang heavy around his neck.

First, he went to Millonarios of Bogotá. In classic Marinelli fashion, he only played 11 games but was sent off three times. When the club terminated his contract, he sued them for non-payment of wages– a legal battle he won in 2015 leaving Millonarios having to pay him $550,000. He had already had a trial at Huracán and been in negotiations for a stint with Argentinos Juniors but, in December 2009, he signed for Primera B side Aldosivi, who would spend the season fighting relegation. Now 27, Marinelli helped save Aldosivi from dropping down a division and, at the end of that season, he returned to Europe, joining ETO FC Győr of Hungary in September 2010. Aldosivi team-mate Agustín Briones made the same move but Marinelli and his family failed to settle and he cancelled his own contract after two games.

In January 2011, he returned to South American football when he joined Universidad de San Martín de Porres in Peru, lined up as a replacement for another Argentinian ex-golden boy, Pablo Vitti, who had thrived in the Peruvian league. Marinelli, with his pace and some of his litheness faded and an increasing tendency to need rest to see off injuries, spent the last three years of his career in Lima, with an impressive (for him) 77 appearances, seven goals and two red cards, although he was injured more and performing less in that last year.

In 2014, at the age of 32, he retired and became a football agent. For all that his career looks like squandered potential, Marinelli played and lived in eight countries alongside some greats of the game, made himself a good living, and became a cult hero to different sets of fans. If he is a cautionary tale to anybody billed as the 'new Maradona', he is still a comfortable, successful one.

* * *

Perhaps only Cristian Colusso rivals Marinelli in terms of players compared to Maradona who became baffling wanderers. Like Marinelli, he found himself playing at an unfashionable English club before a string of clubs in different countries.

Born in Rosario in February 1977, Colusso emerged as a talented youngster at Rosario Central, where he made his debut in 1994 at the age of 17. As was the case with so many of the players given the burden of expectation, Colusso's gambeta was the thing that made him stand out. His dribbling was distinctive, brave and thrilling enough to earn him the 'new Maradona' tag and, when he turned it on for 'El Canalla' against Maradona's Boca Juniors at the Bombonera with a scalding attacking performance, Diego, always eager to associate himself with young Argentinian talent, encouraged him during a short chat.

Colusso was also dazzling when Central won the CONMEBOL Cup against Atlético Mineiro, losing the away leg 4-0 before winning the home leg by the same score and prompting a penalty shoot-out. Colusso missed his kick but Central still won the cup.

His form in the Primera and for Argentina's youth teams was enough to draw the attention of scouts and the media, and there were already rumblings of him moving to Europe. Colusso's subsequent career suggests he suffered from terrible luck – some decisions went as badly as they could have done and he missed the crucial windows of opportunity in his career.

First, in 1995, he was called up to the U20 Argentina squad by Pékerman for the 1995 World Youth Championship in Qatar, where he would have contested the number 10 shirt with Lanús' Ariel Ibagaza. But Rosario Central refused to release him and he was denied some crucial experience and exposure, an awareness that must have seemed crushing once Argentina won the tournament in his absence.

Worse was to follow. In 1996 he moved to Seville in a big-money, big-publicity transfer. His agent was Roberto Rodríguez and, in one of the quirks of football in Argentina, he owned the rights to Colusso as a player. This is not uncommon with youngsters in Argentina, and Rodríguez appeared to do everything right. He sold Colusso to Sevilla for more than £1m, a huge profit, while the player was already in Andalucía as Sevilla were keen to blood him in their youth teams as early and quickly as possible.

Colusso would end up playing only six games for Sevilla in two years – not because of injury, form, managerial change, homesickness or any of the other problems South American players endured playing in Europe – but because of a problem with his contract.

Rodríguez sold Colusso to Sevilla for almost three times the amount he paid for his rights but, once Sevilla looked into the deal, they wanted to know where the rest of the money had gone. During the investigation, Colusso found himself isolated and under fire from the Spanish media. Colusso – still only a teenager – ended up training alone in a situation that lasted for more than two years. The player's development was understandably badly affected. He was eventually allowed to train and play a few games with Sevilla B but the experience had affected his mental health and he saw a psychiatrist to help him cope.

In 1997, Sevilla granted permission for him to move to Club León in Mexico on loan, mostly to protect an investment in danger of withering from a lack of competitive football. But Mexican football is a different beast, and he took time to adapt.

Just as he was beginning to find his feet, Colusso suffered an injury to his knee, cracking the patella, ruling him out for an extended period. León's doctor removed fluid and Colusso returned to Argentina for treatment but the Mexican club were furious, accusing him of trying to leave by stealth. He was sent back to Sevilla, still only 21, to train with the youth teams and Sevilla B.

Unlike so many other players in these pages, it feels as though Colusso was never really given the chance his talents deserved, as if he was strangled at birth as a footballer. Those wasted years at Sevilla damaged him, and he never recovered. Nobody ever spoke of him as the new Maradona any more. In 1999, he and Sevilla terminated his contract by mutual agreement.

As Argentinian players are wont to do, Colusso fled back home. He rejoined Rosario Central while his former agent Rodríguez began working at Real Madrid, a neat encapsulation of the balance of power in European football. But the magic was gone. Colusso spent that season in Rosario mostly on the bench, acclimatising to being a player again, recovering his fitness, trying to leave his trauma behind. The days of him as the young star of the team seemed long ago.

He moved to Atlético Tucumán in the Argentinian interior in 2000 and played 19 games over two years, without ever appearing special. Then began the nomadic period in his career. A loan spell at Oldham Athletic on the outskirts of Manchester saw him billed as a 'former U20 and U23 Argentina star', and his touch and undoubted skill on the ball looked impressive set against the football commonly played in the English third tier, where Oldham were trapped.

Colusso saw this as a chance to lure a club from the wealthier Championship or even the Premier League but, in spite of some good performances, it didn't happen. The club wanted to keep him, and he wanted to stay, but after weeks of negotiations he returned to Buenos Aires, later blaming rules on the number of foreigners allowed. He had played 13 games and scored two goals at Boundary Park.

After that it was to be a club or even two clubs a year. In 2002, he was at lower-league Carrarese in Tuscany, Italy. In 2003, he returned to Buenos Aires to spend some time at Almirante Brown. In 2004, he took a big but well-paid risk and joined Union Sportive Madinat Blida in Algeria. There he alleged he was left imprisoned in a cockroach-infested apartment until the Argentinian consulate intervened.

South America was a more familiar option and in 2005 he returned from his north African trauma to join Universidad Católica del Ecuador. In 2006, he moved to Deportivo Anzoátegui in Venezuela but in 2007 he came back to Argentina once more to play for tiny San Martín de Mendoza in the third tier. He was only 30, and perhaps no other player once compared to Maradona had seen his stock fall so rapidly or so far.

In 2008 Colusso retired, dedicating himself to coaching young players. He said his dream had always been to play for Rosario Central and, once he had achieved that, at the age of 17 no less, everything else was an unexpected bonus. But he is still perhaps the greatest cautionary tale of any player mentioned here. The new Maradona tag was an unwanted burden for Colusso; it brought attention that only magnified his struggles and ultimately became a joke applied to him to give any story a sense of irony.

SEVEN

Andrés D'Alessandro, 'El Cabezón'
Darío Conca, 'El Mago'
Walter Montillo

ANDRÉS D'ALESSANDRO is perhaps the most famous example of what had become a new trend in South American football in the late 2000s. He returned from the relative failure of spells with European clubs to enjoy huge success, not in Argentina but in another South American country. He was also the first 'new Maradona' to do so, and perhaps the last, as the rise to prominence of Lionel Messi in this era tilted the axis of Argentinian football. But other number tens followed his example, and the ubiquity of Argentine playmakers throughout football in the Americas – in more or less every major league, from Canada through Mexico to Chile – is yet another legacy of Maradona's career.

Another sparkling talent off the River Plate production line, D'Alessandro was born in April 1981 and raised in La Paternal, the Buenos Aires district that is home to Argentinos Juniors. He inherited his father's love of Racing

Club and his idol was the Uruguayan playmaker Rubén Paz, a gifted, burly contemporary of Maradona. But instead of the Racing academy or the football nursery at Argentinos Juniors, D'Alessandro was part of the River Plate system from the age of nine.

He was a scrawny child. His nickname, 'El Cabezón', means 'big head' and comes from his appearance as much as his ego. That big head atop a twisting, turning skinny body is an image that would excite supporters from England to Brazil over the next few decades but, as a little boy, it meant he was perceived by many coaches as being too frail for the battles required in football.

D'Alessandro often started games on the bench but was devoted to his career. His family were working class and, with a mother who worked in administration at a school and a taxi-driver father, young Andrés had to take a 40-minute bus ride across Buenos Aires to train at River in Belgrano.

He needed to go to bed early to make sure he got enough sleep to help him grow and, because he had to set off so early for games and often arrived home late, when he was old enough he took on jobs to help out financially – working as an apprentice plumber and delivering pizzas.

At 18, he had filled out and his talent meant he was impossible to leave on the bench in youth teams. He signed his first professional contract with River Plate and could suddenly afford to move his family to a better house.

D'Alessandro began to dazzle in the reserves. He was dynamic, imaginative and flamboyant, with an eye for a spectacular goal. He was also ostentatiously left-footed, with tremendous balance that allowed him to ride tackles and change direction in a flash. The new Maradona talk had already started as people paid attention to River's youth teams, where he stood out as the type of player who excited supporters.

His trademark move was a 'la boba' – a half drag-back, followed by a nutmeg – that he discovered while playing futsal as a child. Watching him execute it regularly over the years was to appreciate his explosive elasticity and the speed of his feet. He would play the ball beyond an opponent and they would often freeze in shock as he charged past them. He was also as liable to try an outrageous flick or backheel as he was to play the ball simply. But he had a fine range of passing – arrowing curling through balls into the box from either flank (he obviously preferred the left) and excelling at high-speed, one-touch interplay. In short, he seemed to have it all. The next big Argentinian star.

His temperament, however, may have been the thing that most resembled Maradona. D'Alessandro always had an edge of furious intensity about him. His goal celebrations were passionate, eyes-rolled-back-in-his-head stampedes towards the fans. He loved an overreaction to a tackle, could lash out in the heat of a game and picked up a lot of cards for silly fouls and petulance. Whereas contemporaries like Riquelme seemed cool and dispassionate and Aimar just loved playing, D'Alessandro really cared.

He made his River Plate debut in May 2000 against Unión of Santa Fe, on the day River were crowned champions. In the next few seasons, he began to feature more often under first Ramón Díaz and then Manuel Pellegrini. With stars such as Aimar and Saviola leaving in 2001, he became more important to the team and eventually assumed the number 10 shirt in recognition. D'Alessandro scored his first goal in September 2001 against Estudiantes and began to bag trophies – Clausura wins in 2002 and 2003.

He was crucial to those triumphs as the team's creative outlet and eventually he became River Plate's youngest-ever captain. In that spell he made 70 appearances and scored 20 goals. He was a consistent performer – with assists and passing masterclasses accompanying the exhibitions of skill and golazos he contributed.

Maradona, of course, weighed in, comparing him favourably to Rivaldo when asked who the best player in the world was and admitting he felt D'Alessandro resembled him as a player. European giants were circling – there were links to the usual suspects in England and Spain – but it was Wolfsburg who finally brought D'Alessandro to the Old World, with an £8.55m deal in July 2003.

* * *

Wolfsburg was a relatively young club in the traditional world of German football. The city was only founded in 1938 – known initially as the less catchy Stadt des KdF-Wagens – for workers at the nearby Volkswagen facility. The club itself was founded in 1945 at the end of the Second World War. After years of moving between divisions, Wolfsburg only established itself as a solid Bundesliga club in the late 1990s. The signing of D'Alessandro, therefore, was a huge statement of intent. The club's record signing, a player wanted by the big guns of European football, he showed Wolfsburg were ambitious – but it never really came off.

D'Alessandro thrilled in flashes in Germany, with a few performances that convinced fans and the media he had adjusted, but after a few seasons it was clear something was missing. This was not the 'new Maradona' they had heard about or the player orchestrating the attacks for River Plate. At first, the traditional excuse was used – he was adjusting to the tempo and physicality of German football – but as his second season showed no real improvement, D'Alessandro began to look like one of the many failed transfers that had befallen Argentinian talent over the years.

Was European football beyond him? It didn't look like it when he ran games, creating strings of chances and scoring eight goals in his eventual 61-game spell in the Bundesliga. But he was also a liability in his self-control, earning yellow cards and a sending off in his first season as he struggled to deal with a new environment and huge expectations. Also, he was no more than good in many games, and more was expected of this young talisman of Argentinian football than 'good'.

The Argentina youth teams offered D'Alessandro an escape from his purgatory in Germany. He had already been one of the stars of the stunning Argentina side that won the 2001 U20 World Championship in Buenos Aires. Under Pékerman's coaching he began the tournament on the bench with the old-fashioned class of Leandro Romagnoli of San Lorenzo as the starting playmaker, but injuries saw him make the starting line-up as the tournament continued. Playing alongside his free-scoring club-mate Javier Saviola, he won the Silver Ball as the second-best player at the championship, and a bright international future beckoned.

After his struggles in his first season at Wolfsburg, senior coach Marcelo Bielsa selected him for the U23 side that competed in the 2004 Olympic Games, alongside a host of other young stars, including Carlos Tevez of Boca Juniors and Javier Mascherano, another River Plate product.

Again, D'Alessandro played well as Argentina dominated the tournament to win the gold medal. He was the perfect number ten for a Bielsa team – his ceaseless energy and inventiveness suited the high-tempo pressing game and rapid transitions of 'El Loco' and his football. Accordingly, Bielsa also selected him for the 2004 Copa América squad that same summer. In Peru for that tournament, he wore the number 10 shirt and scored one goal, in the side's thrilling 6-1 win over Ecuador. Argentina reached the final where they were beaten on penalties by Brazil, with D'Alessandro missing his spot kick.

After an exciting summer of representing the Albiceleste, D'Alessandro returned to another disappointing year at Wolfsburg. The 2005/06 season saw his attitude worsen and in January he was dropped by coach Klaus Augenthaler, who even joked about not needing him to be Maradona in a barb about his lack of defensive work, which had become a theme with D'Alessandro in Germany.

At that point his status in the Argentina team was also unclear. Juan Román Riquelme had been finally given the number 10 shirt, and there was little sign he would relinquish it. Even if he did, Pablo Aimar's success at Valencia made him a high-quality replacement. And a young Rosario boy who had been poached at a very young age by Barcelona looked as though he would inherit the playmaker role sooner rather than later and was already in the squad from 2005 onwards. For all D'Alessandro's undoubted quality – even his flashes of genius – he was made to look distinctly average when compared with young Lionel Messi.

D'Alessandro responded to criticism of his defensive work in the German press, basically claiming it wasn't his job. If this suggested anything apart from the fact 'El Cabezón' was still an appropriate nickname, it was that he was clearly aiming to get out of Wolfsburg as soon as possible. So it was that in January 2006 he moved to Portsmouth in the Premier League on loan. Coach Harry Redknapp – always a fan of skilful attacking players – rhapsodised about D'Alessandro as the kind of talent you could build a team around and put him straight into a side that was embroiled in a bitter relegation struggle.

He found his feet quickly, coping with the blood and thunder of English football well enough to suggest his struggles in Germany were about more than just the physical demands of the league. He scored a phenomenal goal against Charlton and began to do what he was supposed to do, what he was expected to do – dictating play, crafting attacks from the flank and the hole, giving Portsmouth the quality edge they had been lacking. In a league full of skilful players and megastars from different continents, D'Alessandro fitted right in. He was inescapably a short, Argentine playmaker, a brilliant dribbler, an excellent passer of the ball, tough and passionate, and exciting.

Portsmouth avoided relegation and the Pompey supporters adopted D'Alessandro as a cult hero and the kind of player they had not seen much of on the South Coast. Redknapp wanted to keep him but negotiations dragged on, with D'Alessandro's wage expectations too much even for big-spending Portsmouth. Instead, he followed his averred desire to play in La Liga and signed for Real Zaragoza on loan in June. He had a quietly influential season there, alongside Aimar and Milito, as Zaragoza finished sixth and qualified for Europe.

D'Alessandro finally seemed to have matured as a player and person. If his football was less flashy, he was more consistent and less temperamental. If the Spanish media had questioned whether he and Aimar could play in the same team, they proved more than capable of adapting. Aimar had a free role from the classic number ten position, whereas D'Alessandro could move infield from the left. They swapped and played off one another to often devastating effect. D'Alessandro played 36 games that season with two goals and nine assists, his strongest year in European football. Zaragoza rewarded him with a full contract, buying him for £3.15m from Wolfsburg.

In typical D'Alessandro fashion, he messed that up thanks to a training-ground row with Aimar. D'Alessandro needed to be restrained as he threatened his compatriot, all of it caught by TV cameras and coach Fernández, leading to him being criticised for his attitude. His wife was pregnant with their second child and D'Alessandro said they wanted to be back in Argentina for the birth, having suffered in isolation for the birth of their first child in England. That would ultimately lead to him leaving the club and Spanish football to return to Argentina.

* * *

Instead of the much-anticipated return to River Plate, D'Alessandro joined his old mentor Ramón Díaz at another Buenos Aires giant, San Lorenzo, for £3.15m in February 2008. Like many of the players who followed in Maradona's footsteps, D'Alessandro seemed to need to be loved to play to his potential. He needed the crowd's adoration, the coach's arm around his shoulder, his team-mates' trust. D'Alessandro knew Díaz admired him and so he performed, excelling as San Lorenzo mounted a challenge for the Copa Libertadores. Their status as the only one of the five 'grandes' of Argentinian football – the others are Boca, River and the Avellaneda duo of Independiente and Racing Club – not to have won the South American Championship was a sore point among the club's devoted fanbase. Even supposedly smaller, less heralded clubs such as Estudiantes, Vélez Sarsfield and Argentinos Juniors had won it, but San Lorenzo in that era felt very far from winning such a competition. Instead, they lurched from one crisis to another, with the 2007 Clausura under Díaz their first title in six years.

They had a good go at the resulting Libertadores under Díaz and the key tie came when they were drawn against D'Alessandro's beloved River Plate, managed at that time by Diego Simeone. Having won the first leg at the Nuevo Gasometro 2-1, D'Alessandro was relentlessly booed at the Monumental by fans who felt betrayed by his signing for another Argentine club. Every touch was met with a wave of hissing.

River roared into a 2-0 lead but San Lorenzo pulled a goal back before Gonzalo Bergessio equalised from a D'Alessandro corner to take the tie to 'El Ciclón'. They were eliminated in the quarter-finals by LDU Quito in a penalty shoot-out and, when Díaz left the club at the end of the season, D'Alessandro did the same. Not back to Europe, where the idea of him as the new Maradona had died a slow death, or even home to River, where, despite the boos, he was still adored. He chose to play in Brazil.

Argentina and Brazil have been locked in a duel for supremacy in South American football for almost a century. The national teams play probably the biggest international derby there is, with fortunes swinging either way. At the time of writing, they had played 109 games, with Brazil winning 43 and Argentina 40, with 26 draws. Brazil have won five World Cups to Argentina's three. Argentina, meanwhile, have 15 Copa América titles to Brazil's nine. Maradona's main rival for the title of the greatest player of the 20th century is Pelé, and FIFA memorably and controversially created a second award for the Brazilian in 2000 after Maradona had comprehensively won an internet poll to be proclaimed player of the century.

At club level, Argentine clubs have won 25 Copa Libertadores titles to the 22 achieved by Brazilian clubs. Historically, players from one nation rarely played their club football in the other; Argentines and Brazilians usually made their way across the Atlantic to Europe. In 2008, Argentinians were starting to be more commonly seen in North America – in the MLS and in Mexico – and there had always been a trickle of players to Peru and Colombia. But even though they shared a border and many cultural similarities, you found few Argentinians playing their football in Brazil.

The shifting economics of South America changed that. The fast-growing Brazilian economy meant an injection of cash into Brazilian football, while Argentina still felt the effects of the horrendous financial crisis from the early years of the century. Even the biggest Argentinian clubs are effectively selling clubs and, following the Maradona example, any top-class youngster is off to Europe almost as soon as he has made an impression. That all began to change in 2005, when Corinthians from São Paulo paid Boca Juniors £13.5m for Carlos Tevez. At the same time, they took Javier Mascherano from River Plate for £10.62m.

Corinthians are traditionally one of the two or three biggest and best-supported clubs in Brazil, but that kind of money had always been beyond them. Now we were witnessing a European transfer policy happening in South America.

It worked, too. Tevez and Mascherano inspired Corinthians to a Brazilian title and other big Brazilian clubs began to look south for players. Number tens were in particular demand, partly because Brazil did not produce them in the same quantities as Argentina. Brazil had responded to the failure of the divine 1982 side – where three or four playmakers co-existed – and the growth of power and conditioning in the European game by attempting to match it.

Although the favelas of Brazil's cities still threw up great attacking midfielders in that era, they were not as intrinsic to Brazilian football as they were to Argentina. Every club in Argentina had a number ten playing at a decent level and usually a number eight capable of playing as a variation on the role – maybe even an additional winger or second striker who liked to drift between the lines. Brazilian football hungrily eyes these players. D'Alessandro was probably the most famous example – as a new Maradona his capture by Internacional of Porto Alegre was a huge coup. And at Inter, D'Alessandro had finally found a home.

* * *

It may be relevant that Porto Alegre is the southernmost major city in Brazil, with some similarities with Argentina – churrasco instead of asado, chimarrão instead of yerba maté – but it seems more likely that the gratitude and love the supporters showed him straight away won D'Alessandro over. Their mutual love affair was sealed when he starred in his first 'Grenal' derby between Inter and Grêmio. He chipped in with a goal and two assists and, over his long years in Porto Alegre, he always did well against Grêmio, winning 13 of 27 games, only losing five, and scoring eight goals.

In truth, it may have been the maverick streak in D'Alessandro that allowed him to succeed in Brazil. It was that factor that had sunk his European era but, for an Argentine in Brazil, a big head and stubborn sense of self is a desirable quality. He not only survived Brazilian football, he smashed it, making 285 appearances for Internacional between 2008 and 2022 and scoring 46 goals. In that time he became a naturalised Brazilian citizen, club captain, earned himself a recall for Argentina – for a friendly against Spain in 2010 under Sergio Batista – and was awarded *El País*' prize for South America's footballer of the year in 2010.

He also collected the trophies that gave his career real shape and importance: six Campeonato Gaucho titles in addition to the really big ones – the Copa Sudamericana in 2008, the Recopa Sudamericana in 2011 and the Copa Libertadores in 2010.

He is as big an idol at Inter as any player ever has been, the fans identifying with a player who was working class, like them, who gave his all on the pitch, as they would have. In Brazil, Argentinian players are admired for their competitive spirit and fight, just as Maradona was, and D'Alessandro allied that unmistakable rage in battle with his explosiveness and quick football brain.

It was not all good, however. Transfer rumours swirled every window, linking him with moves to the MLS, back to Germany or to the newly rich Chinese Super League. In

2016, after a season when he had missed stretches through injury and seemed oddly out of sorts, he returned to River Plate on a year-long loan to spend a season playing under Marcelo Gallardo. Stationed on the left wing, he was obviously overjoyed to be back home – he burst into tears at his unveiling – and, now a veteran, combined well with some of River's latest generation of attacking talent. In that year he won a Copa Argentina and another Recopa Sudamericana to add to his impressive trophy cabinet, playing 17 games and scoring two goals.

His return to Inter was solid but the team was less successful and, with his powers waning, he left for a year at Nacional of Montevideo in 2019. Nacional had become adept at wringing the last year or so out of declining greats over the previous decade, with his River coach Gallardo and Uruguayan legend Álvaro Recoba both following that route, but D'Alessandro's spell at the club was undistinguished aside from a win in the Uruguayan Super Cup.

He returned to Inter for the last six months of his career, retiring in April 2022 in front of a packed Beira-Rio, where he scored against Fortaleza and was held aloft by his team-mates. In his odd, latterly glittering career, he had shown another route was possible for a new Maradona without becoming a wanderer or dropping down divisions.

* * *

In the same era, a few other Argentine number tens played in Brazil, with just as much success. Perhaps the most important was Darío Conca, who was briefly best known for his wages when he was the third-highest-paid player in world football behind Lionel Messi and Cristiano Ronaldo.

From General Pacheco in Tigre on the northern edge of Buenos Aires, he emerged at local club Tigre, making his debut at the age of 15 in the Nacional B. River Plate, always hungry for young talent, took notice, and he joined their academy in 2000. But Conca, while talented and short at 5ft 6in, was no 'new Maradona', while River had a surfeit of young attacking talent. He was competing with D'Alessandro and Ortega, then later with Cavenaghi and Falcao.

Conca made his River debut in November 2003 under Pellegrini and managed 14 appearances and two goals during the next year but his talent was not quite definitive enough to guarantee him a place in an ever-shifting River Plate team. He was a fine passer of the ball, he could dribble and gambeta beautifully, but a lack of pace meant he could rarely beat a man decisively. He took high-quality set pieces, worked hard and read the game expertly but he wasn't good enough for River Plate. Perhaps he simply wasn't ready for that era? River sent Conca on a series of loans, first to Chilean club Universidad Católica of Santiago, where he thrived in a slightly weaker league. He made 65 appearances and scored 13 goals over two seasons between 2004 and 2006. When he returned, he was off again in 2006 for an underwhelming 13-game stint at Rosario Central.

Conca got his first taste of Brazilian football in 2007 when he went on another loan, this time to Rio giants Vasco da Gama. Evidently Brazil suited him. He made 30 appearances that season and scored six goals, impressing the Brazilian media and Vasco fans. The rhythm of football in Brazil was different to Argentina and that may have suited a foot-on-the-ball playmaker, as Serbian legend Dejan Petković also learned to his benefit during a successful career as a playmaker at a series of Brazilian clubs, including Flamengo, Fluminense, Santos, Vasco, Goias and Atlético Mineiro. Similarly, Chilean maverick number ten Jorge Valdívia was making himself a legend at Palmeiras.

The pausa worked well in Brazil, and a cerebral number ten could use the space created by rampaging wing-backs and disciplined shuttlers to craft openings. Fussy Brazilian referees protected talented players in a way their Argentine counterparts did not, and Conca suddenly blossomed. Following that Vasco loan, he was loaned to Rio grandees Fluminense in 2008, and a legend was born. At Flu, he turned that loan into a three-year transfer and between 2008 and 2011 was perhaps the best player in the Brazilian league, scoring 21 goals in 111 games. He won a series of individual accolades in 2010 and 2011 as Flu won the 2010 Brasileiro championship.

Argentina was nonplussed. Conca was a virtual unknown there and, although he had appeared for the U20 team in 2002, had never been awarded a senior cap. There was talk of him declaring for Brazil but nothing came of it in an era when there were a couple of Brazilian number tens emerging.

* * *

While Conca and D'Alessandro were showing the legacy of Maradona and mystique of the Argentinian enganche could endure, even in Brazil, they were joined by Walter Montillo. He had emerged at San Lorenzo in 2002 and showed huge promise, appearing regularly during the next few seasons before going on loan to Morelia in Mexico in

2006. After returning to San Lorenzo and still finding himself unable to break into the first team, he moved to Universidad de Chile in 2008.

There, just as Conca had done at Santiago rivals Universidad Católica, he did well, winning a Chilean title, his brilliant performances against several Brazilian clubs in competitions drawing the attention of some big clubs. Montillo moved to Belo Horizonte club Cruzeiro in 2010 and was a consistently impressive performer – scoring 23 goals in 89 games over two seasons to become the club's all-time leading foreign goalscorer. He moved to Santos in 2013, replacing young but old-school Brazilian playmaker Paulo Henrique Ganso after he had left for more money at São Paulo. Montillo largely maintained his performance levels behind the young prince of Brazilian football, Neymar.

His sustained quality earned him a call-up for Argentina in 2011 and over the next two years he won six caps, including a couple in World Cup qualifiers. By that point he was being named alongside Conca and D'Alessandro as a definite trend in South American football.

Conca – perhaps the most impressive and surprising performer of the trio given his relatively unheralded arrival – was being linked with big-money transfers to other countries. When he did leave Flu, it was for Guangzhou Evergrande in China for £7.35m. His salary stunned observers worldwide. The Chinese club paid him £7.25m a year.

After South America, Conca found Chinese football easy. He played 65 games for Evergrande between 2011 and 2013 and scored 33 goals. He won the Asian Champions League and five other trophies as well as a plethora of individual honours.

His wages and performances drew attention to the Chinese game and encouraged other players to follow his lead. In 2015, for example, Montillo copied his compatriot with a move to Shandong Luneng, where he spent two seasons. Other South Americans – such as Hulk, Lucas Barrios, Colombian playmaker Gio Moreno and eventually Javier Mascherano – would follow their example, giving the Chinese Super League some much-needed glamour.

Conca and Montillo both returned to Brazil; Conca to Flu in 2014 and Montillo to Botafogo in 2017. Conca would be lured back to Asia by the promise of more riches, however, signing for Shanghai SIPG in January 2015. He was 34 and, although he remained a solid performer, his three years at Shanghai failed to match the success of his first spell in China and he was loaned to Flamengo in 2017, although he featured little. In 2019 he moved to the US and Austin Bold in the United Soccer League and managed three games before announcing his retirement.

Montillo, meanwhile, had returned home after a disappointing time at Botafogo to join Tigre in 2018, scoring six goals in his 34 games there. After that he returned to U de Chile and had a fine last season there before he, too, announced his retirement, in 2021.

Between them, these three players showed that the playmaker was now an Argentinian national product, recognised and respected across the world. Established on the genius of Diego Maradona, the validity of Argentine claims to owning the number ten position were being asserted daily by Lionel Messi until even Brazil had to accept them. D'Alessandro, Conca and Montillo were a big part of that acceptance.

EIGHT

Carlos Tevez, 'El Apache'

SETTING ASIDE any footballing similarity, Carlos Tevez is probably the closest thing we have had to a 'new Maradona' in spiritual and emotional terms. A short, dark, passionate product of the slums of Buenos Aires, all sweat, fight and hustle, 'Carlitos' was adored by the people of his country and city. They called him 'The People's Player' and, for a few years, opinion polls, internet forums and radio phone-ins were full of people arguing that he deserved a place in the Argentina side ahead of Messi.

Few players have been loved as much in their homeland as Tevez. As with many Argentine playmakers he was forced to adapt his game as he aged and moved to Europe. His qualities were perhaps more flexible than those of a Riquelme or an Aimar, and so when he arrived in Europe he became more of a pure second striker – his energy and invention meaning he was a success at each of his European clubs.

Tevez had an amazing career, winning accolades, trophies and adoration at a series of huge clubs but also falling out with coaches, fans and executives in almost every place he played. Had he been born in another time, he would probably be better appreciated as an Argentine number ten. However, at different points in his career he had to share a stage with Riquelme and Messi, and those comparisons place his talent and achievements into a context that is perhaps unfair.

Tevez's early life is so filled with tragedy it was turned into a TV drama, which also speaks to the popularity the player enjoys in Argentina. Like Maradona, Tevez hails from an infamous Buenos Aires barrio. Ejército de los Andes is a public housing project created in the 1960s and used to resettle the population of a shanty town that was moved from the Retiro district in the run-up to the 1978 World Cup. The area is densely populated, with drugs and criminal gangs a huge issue. When a journalist was writing a story about a murder in the area in the 1980s, he nicknamed it 'Fuerte Apache' after the American movie *Fort Apache the Bronx* starring Paul Newman as a cop in an area with a horrific crime rate. The tag stuck – and such a place would mark Carlos Tevez's life before he was even born.

Tevez's biological father was shot and killed when his mother was six months pregnant with him. She would leave when Carlos was only six months old, whereupon he was adopted by his mother's sister and her husband. When he was a toddler, Carlos pulled a kettle off a stovetop, scalding himself across the chest and neck; scars he would proudly bear as a badge of honour throughout his career. Tevez never cared how he looked as a player but as a child the injuries meant he spent two months in hospital.

Life in Fuerte Apache was hard and dangerous, but Tevez has said he would not change it for anything. Like Maradona, that struggle gave him his fire and grit, a determination most players could not compete with. He was a warrior, forged by the mean streets he lived in.

As a youth, he played for All Boys in Floresta, but his skill and drive quickly attracted bigger fish and his name was changed by his adopted parents from his birth father's 'Cabra' to his adopted father's 'Tevez' during a contractual dispute once Boca Juniors came calling. The legal loophole allowed Tevez to join Boca at the age of 13 and he immediately began impressing Argentinian football fans and coaches.

* * *

He already displayed all the qualities that would drive him to success across three continents. He was incredibly sturdy and powerful, with a barrel chest and broad shoulders, short powerful legs and a low centre of gravity, all recalling Maradona, as did his burst of pace over short distances. Tevez could use his build and power to hold off opponents with his back to goal but was also a fine dribbler and liked to shoot from distance if he spied an opportunity. That made him an excellent forward in the modern-day mould. He was able to play as a centre-forward, lacking only aerial prowess, but was perhaps better suited to the role of second striker, where his tactical awareness and eye for a pass made him as much a creator as a goalscorer. Those qualities meant he would also find himself in the hole as an attacking midfielder at different points in his career.

What set him apart from many of his talented peers in Argentine football, however, was his commitment. That made him a great fit for European football once the high press became a common tactic. Tevez would run, hustle and harry the opposition all game and, if he recovered the ball high up the pitch, he knew just what to do with it. His strength and surging acceleration were ideal components for the highest defensive player. He was rapid into the tackle and must have been a nightmare for a centre-half to play against, giving opponents no rest, always competing, sweating, battling, always willing to make defenders look stupid.

Tevez made his senior Boca Juniors debut in October 2001 at the age of 16, featuring sporadically. The 2002/03 season was when he established himself, playing 32 games and scoring ten goals as a precocious, fearsome 17-year-old.

Argentinian and Boca football fans love a young star, especially one who comes from a slum, as it reassures them that their image of themselves, their football and their club is not fiction or a marketing ploy. Tevez was seen as the future from an early age. He was so confident, so perfectly himself, and so good at football. A famous photo of Tevez was taken when he was still emerging in the youth teams. It shows him alongside Juan Román Riquelme, already in the senior squad and a bit of a talisman. They are on the pitch at La Bombonera, Riquelme in his Boca kit, Tevez in the tracksuit of a ball boy. Riquelme is tall, almost willowy; Tevez shorter, wide-eyed. Both look like boys, with a rawness to them.

For all the similarities in their rough beginnings and shared love for Boca, they could have been deliberately designed as opposites in terms of the way they approached the role of the number ten. Whereas Riquelme was elegant, artful, above the fray even as he orchestrated it – a regal quality to his facial expressions as much as his playing style – Tevez was a warrior. He was in the trenches, head down, battling; flashes of sublime skill carved out through work and ferocious will, a snarl on his face as he did his job. He celebrated goals joyously, ensuring his obvious bond with the fans on the terraces grew. Here was a player like them, who celebrated goals like they would celebrate them if they were on that pitch. They never played together for Boca; in fact Tevez more or less replaced Román as the idol of the fans when he began to mature into his role in the team in 2002/03. He was a modern forward, it seemed, playing across the attacking areas of the pitch, dropping deep, racing into the channels, loitering in the six-yard area.

Boca gave Tevez the number 9 shirt and in that first four-year spell at the club he scored 38 goals in 110 games. The next season he was awarded the number 10 shirt and seemed to relish all that the shirt meant and the responsibility he now bore. Tevez was a 'clutch' player, and every fanbase loves one of those; he scored vital goals in big games and showed up and played better when it meant something.

The 2003 Copa Libertadores Final against Santos? Tevez scored and was voted player of the tournament.

The 2004 Copa Sudamericana Final against Bolívar of Bolivia? Tevez scored.

The 2004 Copa Libertadores 'Superclásico' tie with River Plate? Tevez scored and did a chicken dance in direct reference to the River fans' 'las gallinas' nickname, getting himself sent off for provocation. Boca fans lapped it up, especially as Boca won the game on penalties.

Tevez was at one with the fans. In that era he won the Copa Libertadores, the Copa Sudamericana, the 2003 Apertura and the 2003 Intercontinental Cup. He was the young shining star of Argentine football – but he was also showing signs of wanting to leave.

The young boy from Fuerte Apache had an unavoidable edge to him; he could be blunt and truculent. His discipline wasn't always great. Like Maradona, he was often highly provocative during interviews; he could respond to the endless questioning of Argentine football journalists with dramatic statements that were then blown up by the press. With the usual links to European superclubs echoing, Tevez turned up to a press conference wearing a Manchester United jersey. He made ambiguous statements about his plans.

Although Tevez was famously in love with Boca, that love was far from evident in his behaviour in his last season at the club. The Argentine media reported his every utterance breathlessly. His personal life was messy, a fact reportedly dissuading European clubs from risking his transfer. Tevez claimed he was sick of the attention and intrusions. He said he needed 'tranquillity', even as he was a feature in Argentine tabloids for his friendships, nocturnal activities, and relationship status. Not that the Argentinian public cared. He was relatable. The people's player. He was already a national idol due to his exploits at the Olympics.

Tevez first gained attention beyond Boca for his performances for Argentina at the 2001 U17 Championship but it was when Marcelo Bielsa selected him for the squad for the 2004 Olympics that Tevez truly announced himself. He was in some ways a perfect Bielsa player. His energy and pace meant he could press for a whole game and was brilliant in rapid transitions. And, just as he had been doing for Boca, he performed in the biggest games.

Bielsa surrounded Tevez with a squad filled with class and talent; from a strong back line including Heinze, Ayala and Coloccini to a commanding midfield based around

Mascherano and Lucho González and a dynamic, fluid forward line with danger from every player – D'Alessandro, Saviola, Kily González, Mauro Rosales and César González all interchanged from game to game, each offering slightly different skillsets.

Tevez had the luxury of doing what he did for Boca, only here the supporting cast was better – he dropped off, dribbled, picked passes, made near-post runs – and his talented team-mates played off him and used his abilities to a frighteningly high level. Tevez was the player of that Olympic tournament, scoring eight goals in six games. All sorts of goals, too: a spectacular volley, an opportunistic flick, a placed finish from a one-on-one. That would become another characteristic of his – he was both a great goalscorer and a scorer of great goals.

Argentina won the gold medal – their first since 1952 – and Tevez scored the winner in the final against Paraguay. For all that the goldfish bowl of Argentinian and South American football sometimes overrated its own importance – especially in that era when it wasn't always possible to stream games online from anywhere on Earth – the world started to take notice of Tevez. Bielsa rewarded the majority of that squad with places at the Copa América only a few weeks later. Argentina again reached the final, with Tevez – again – scoring the goals that counted with the winner in the quarter-final against hosts Peru and the opener in the semi-final win over Colombia. Argentina were seconds from winning their first major tournament in a decade when, with devastating timing, the brilliant Adriano scored a 93rd-minute equaliser for Brazil. Tevez, exhausted from a summer of hard running, had already been subbed off by the time Brazil won the game and the trophy on penalties.

* * *

It turned out that Tevez's future was not as simple as who he wanted to play for; there was also the complicated and mysterious issue of his ownership. Alongside Argentina team-mate Javier Mascherano, Tevez signed for Corinthians of São Paulo in January 2005 for £13.5m and youth-team players worth £1.5m. Corinthians, very much in the mould of Boca Juniors, styled themselves as the 'people's club' of Brazilian football but were owned by London-based Media Sport Investment (MSI), fronted by Iranian-born, British-educated businessman Kia Joorabchian. In an article published in August 2011, *The Guardian* claimed Tevez was 'owned' by Joorabchian, Georgian billionaire Arkady Patarkatsishvili and Russian businessman Boris Berezovsky. Lawsuits around MSI, Corinthians and these three men rumbled on in Brazil and Europe for years but, what is not in doubt, was Tevez's signing by Corinthians was a statement of intent by a club set on winning trophies. A South American transfer record, Tevez was an almost immediate hit on the pitch.

With the intelligent, tactical Mascherano at the base of midfield, Tevez was given license to run the attack. He responded by driving the team to the 2005 Brazilian title, scoring 46 goals in 76 games across his two seasons there. Tevez made Brazilian football look easy. He won the CBF player of the year award, the first foreigner to do so since 1976, but at 21 years old he was plainly too good for South America – he was ready for Europe.

First, he was part of the Argentina squad at the 2006 World Cup in Germany. Tevez was not first choice; Riquelme owned the playmaker role and the number 10 shirt with Aimar in reserve. Behind them, Tevez's status as the next big thing in Argentinian football had been usurped by a little Rosario-born wonder boy who had been developing at Barcelona for years. A much-heralded 18-year-old Lionel Messi was in the squad with the world waiting to see whether he could perform at that level.

Argentina's attacking power at that tournament was frightening in terms of variety and talent. The classy Hernán Crespo was the seasoned, starting number nine, with Javier Saviola opening the tournament as the second striker. Julio Cruz was on the bench if the team needed his aerial power when playing more direct. Rodrigo Palacio, of Boca, provided raw pace and dribbling ability.

Tevez and Messi both came on and scored in the 6-0 group-stage slaughter of Serbia and Montenegro. Both started the final group game, a semi-meaningless 0-0 draw with the Netherlands, while both were again late substitutes in the round-of-16 victory over Mexico. But this was Riquelme's team and his domain, and Tevez was not quite the same player he had been at the Olympics. He appeared tired or overawed and, for all his hard work, his dynamism looked muted. Despite that, he remained creative and a great runner, he dribbled, he tried things; he was busy and industrious. Accordingly, Pékerman showed faith in Tevez and he started the quarter-final exit to Germany, playing the entire game, chasing and harrying but still curiously off-colour. Penalty misses by Ayala and Cambiasso meant Tevez never got to take a spot kick as Argentina tumbled out of the tournament.

* * *

Tevez and Mascherano had both polished their reputations in Germany so it was something of a shock when they ended up movving to West Ham United after the tournament. West Ham are one of the grand old English clubs, with successes – a trio of FA Cup wins and a Cup Winners' Cup stand out – and a history of producing some fine players across more than a century. Their fans like to half-jokingly claim they won the 1966 World Cup because of the huge contribution West Ham players made to the England side. The club has a classy sense of tradition and history, with a reputation for entertaining football. In the Premier League era, however, West Ham had become a mid-table side – when they were not suffering a series of relegations and promotions throughout the 1990s and 2000s that is.

They had also become a reliable producer of young talent. Four of England's vaunted 'golden generation' emerged at West Ham: Joe Cole (the 'cockney Maradona'), Frank Lampard, Rio Ferdinand and Michael Carrick. All four were sold after a season or two in the first team, however. West Ham had become a selling club, not the sort you expected to sign young Argentina internationals such as Tevez and Mascherano. Indeed, while Brazilian authorities were investigating the Tevez transfer to Corinthians in 2005, the Premier League would eventually launch its own investigation into Tevez and Mascherano's arrival at West Ham. Officially, Tevez cost West Ham £13.5m. Rumblings around the affair eventually led some of the clubs who suffered relegation in West Ham's stead to attempt to sue the Premier League for allowing the transfer to go ahead rather than imposing a points deduction, which would almost have certainly doomed them to relegation.

Tevez's time at Corinthians had ended in turmoil after he refused to play. Mascherano, meanwhile, was involved in a fight during training, captured by news cameras, and stormed dramatically off the field. The Argentinian duo's early months at West Ham were not exactly the glory supporters were expecting either. Tevez and Mascherano both struggled to settle under coach Alan Pardew and the club endured a nine-match winless streak, failing to score in seven of them. Mascherano was out of the team, with Hayden Mullins surprisingly preferred by Pardew, while Tevez reacted to being substituted in a November game against Sheffield United by throwing a tantrum. His team-mates decided Tevez should donate half his wages to a children's charity and wear a Brazil shirt in training as punishment. Tevez, with characteristic wilfulness, donated the money but refused to wear the shirt. Even after spending a couple of years in Brazil, there are some things a proud Argentine just cannot do.

The poor spell meant West Ham were dumped out of the UEFA Cup and League Cup and were deep in a relegation battle before December. Pardew was duly sacked, and Tevez, finally acclimatising to English football, began to show his true quality under experienced replacement Alan Curbishley.

Despite a disappointing season from their team so far, West Ham fans already loved Tevez; his warrior qualities are the kind of things all English fans love to see in their players. He ran and battled and chased lost causes. Used to the working-class crowds at Boca and Corinthians, he understood the East End support at the Boleyn Ground and knew how to play to it. In March 2007, he hit peak form. Tevez scored six goals in the final ten games, helping West Ham beat Arsenal, Everton and – on the final day of the season – champions Manchester United. West Ham were fined for irregularities in the Tevez transfer but no points were docked and Tevez was allowed to play. Frankly, he was the main reason West Ham stayed up. Hammers fans voted him player of the season, and they adore him to this day.

That final-day goal against Man Utd was a hint of what was to come as Tevez joined the champions' formidable squad in August 2007 after a protracted dispute between West Ham and Joorabchian that ended up in court. In Manchester, he became part of one of the best forward lines the Premier League had ever seen. Alongside Cristiano Ronaldo and Wayne Rooney, Tevez played in a free-flowing, creative, ferociously competitive attack. A year later, coach Alex Ferguson added the classy promptings of the Bulgarian Dimitar Berbatov to the mix. In the 2007/08 season, the original trio were peerless, scoring a combined 79 goals and contributing 29 assists. Of those, Tevez scored 14 and made ten, but he was perhaps the catalyst.

Rooney and Ronaldo already had a fine, blossoming relationship before Tevez's arrival and, alongside Messi, were arguably the two greatest young talents in European football. Ronaldo back then was a different player from the focused goal machine he evolved into at Real Madrid. For United, he was a winger who became a forward, a dribbler with silky skills, fast feet and a natural ability to entertain. His ego was already huge but he could be a great team-mate too, and he and Rooney complemented one another well. There were similarities between Tevez and Rooney, too. Both were street footballers, stocky and pugilistic, who played with a mix of rage and joy. Both evolved into strikers and, while Tevez was probably the better dribbler, Rooney was a more natural playmaker with his love of dropping into midfield, natural ability to see things before they happened, and need to dictate.

It is amazing the three forwards were able to play so well together but they interchanged, played no-look passes and backheels, and created goals for one another as if it were a game just between them. For the first time at club level, Tevez was not the biggest star in the team. In fact, he was probably third in the pecking order in that front line, and the talent around him often made him look ordinary. On those days when he was not quite at his best, Tevez contributed his usual hard running. He single-handedly tore across the box and terrorised defences. Especially in the Champions League, centre-halves looked panicked and uncertain when he was racing at them.

Rooney had comparable energy but less discipline; he would drift back and find himself in defensive positions. Tevez's example of how to defend from the front was good for him, too. With that front three plus Paul Scholes, Owen Hargreaves and Michael Carrick in midfield and a fabulous defensive pair of Nemanja Vidić and Rio Ferdinand, United won a league and Champions League double when they beat Chelsea in Moscow in May 2008. Tevez, unsurprisingly, scored a penalty in the shoot-out that won the game.

Tevez's time in Europe had seen him win the sport's biggest prize in only his second season but the move to a superclub had also put his talent into context; nobody compared him to Maradona any more – he was merely a very good player who had come from Boca. In December, Tevez added the Club World Cup to his list of titles when United beat LDU Quito of Ecuador. But as the 2008/09 campaign wore on, there were rumours Tevez would be leaving at the end of the season. It emerged that he was on loan from West Ham as United had baulked at his huge transfer fee. The expectation from Tevez and his people was that the deal would be made permanent after his heroics in that first year – but it wasn't so simple. He had always been a prickly character, and that was not something a coach as disciplinary and detail-focused as Alex Ferguson would accept.

Even though Tevez never learned English, on the pitch he still performed, scored and battled. He was still Carlos Tevez. Fans began to chant 'Fergie, sign him up' whenever he played and always responded to his effort and chasing of lost causes. United won another league title in May and Ferguson announced negotiations were under way to sign Tevez on a permanent basis. But the relationship between player and club had been damaged – as it had been at Boca and Corinthians – and Tevez moved to Manchester City, newly buoyant on a mattress of oil money after their purchase by Abu Dhabi United Group the previous summer.

* * *

His signing was a symbolically powerful one – a statement of intent from a club that had lived in its neighbour's shadow for so long. The famous 'Welcome to Manchester' billboard with a picture of Tevez in sky blue alluded to the fact that Old Trafford is located inside the City of Salford – part of Greater Manchester but historically with its own local government – while City's stadium is inside Manchester proper. More than that, it was 'noisy neighbours' City teasing United.

The odd thing about Tevez's time in England is that for all his goals and trophies in Manchester, only West Ham fans seem to recall him with true fondness and appreciation. His legacy and the ending of his spell at each Manchester club means he is regarded with some ambiguity by United and City fans. At City, Tevez was the main man in his first season, something he must have needed after being down the pecking order at United. Under a coach who was just as prickly as he was, Roberto Mancini, Tevez responded and scored 29 goals in 42 games. He led the line, he finished, he created but although there were rumours he had cost City a British record £47m – a sum denied by the club and MSI – and he won the 'Etihad player of the year' and players' player of the year awards, City ended the season without a trophy.

In the summer, Mancini made him club captain and City strengthened their squad considerably thanks to the club's new riches. It worked; they won the FA Cup in 2011, beating United in the semi-final and Stoke City in the final, but Tevez, despite scoring another 23 goals in 44 games, had shown his difficult side again. In December he had submitted a written transfer request, citing a breakdown in his relationship with several executives. City refused his request and he soon withdrew it but this attention-grabbing behaviour was reminiscent of Maradona in all the wrong ways and, for all his undoubted talent, Tevez was not Maradona. He was seemingly missing his family – another familiar tale from Argentine players in Europe. Tevez's wife and two young daughters were living in Argentina, having found it difficult to settle in the northwest of England.

Tevez was 25 and had always been a player who thrived on his own emotions, and now they were sabotaging him. Added to that, Manchester City had already grown beyond their reliance on him as a marquee player. They had other players who had become more important, who shaped the way they played football. Spaniard David Silva was an elegant, imaginative playmaker very much in the Argentinian mode, and he was the architect of their attacks, brilliant at finding space and picking passes, able to set and conduct a rhythm. Yaya Touré, meanwhile, combined marauding runs from midfield with goals and provided a huge presence across the pitch. Vincent Kompany was the real leader of the team and a brilliant centre-back. He would assume the captain's armband in summer 2011 after the FA Cup win.

Also that summer, while Tevez was back in Argentina bad-mouthing the club, City brought in another young Argentine striker who had been compared to Maradona – Sergio Agüero – and Bosnian target man Edin Džeko with the intent to forge a new strike partnership. With Tevez linked with a move to Italy and Agüero's transfer from Atlético Madrid prompting much excitement, Tevez lost his guaranteed starting place in the 2011/12 season. But he had shown professionalism; he claimed he wanted to stay. He got his head down and trained hard. He did what he could when called upon.

Tevez's versatility favoured him. He could play his own way, with all the usual pluck and verve. He could play off Džeko, looking for knock-downs from high balls, flicking crosses towards the striker in the six-yard box. He could also play alongside Agüero, creating the kind of intuitive interplay and trickery he had enjoyed with Rooney. He could link with the electric Mario Balotelli, too, reading his runs and finding him with flicks and clever passes.

But having left the red shirt of United for the sky blue of City, seemingly drawn by the promise he would be the most important man in the team, Tevez became frustrated as the season wore on. That came to a disastrous head during a Champions League game versus Bayern Munich in Germany, with millions watching on TV.

City were 2-0 down before half-time against an imperious, clearly superior Bayern side. Tevez would later claim that he was sent to warm up about 35 minutes into the game, and continued to do so for almost half an hour after that. When the first substitution was made, he was furious not to be involved. When Mancini called for him a few moments later, Tevez refused to enter the game. He and Mancini traded angry words, followed by shouts and hand gestures. The cameras caught it all, of course, as did the Allianz Arena, the entire City backroom staff and substitutes, the mass of English football, the players, fans and journalists. Tevez, a player almost defined by his commitment to the cause, had refused to play.

In his post-match interviews, Mancini made no attempt to conceal his fury and contempt for a striker he had always seemed to get along with very well. He said he wanted Tevez out of Manchester City and claimed he would never play for the club again. The British football media echoed those thoughts. Tevez was condemned by ex-pros, pundits, fans, bloggers and columnists. The extremely public nature of the spat in such a high-profile game, at a time when City were still struggling to make themselves a serious club at that level, was unfortunate and seemed to undermine the very project itself.

Tevez and his people went into damage-control mode. He claimed it was all a misunderstanding, although he and Mancini had argued in a mixture of English, Italian and Spanish so it was a spectacularly multi-lingual misunderstanding. He was suspended by the club for two weeks, then placed on gardening leave and warned to stay away from the club and training ground. Tevez did what any Argentine star would do in such circumstances – he fled back to Argentina where he knew he was still loved. Even that was more complicated than it might have seemed, though, as his international career had stalled by that point.

* * *

After his role in the disappointing exit from the 2006 World Cup, when he was still a young tyro establishing himself alongside Messi in a team beginning to transition to a more youthful line-up, Tevez became a reliable player for Argentina. He was part of the dazzlingly talented squad at the 2007 Copa América but, again, his international teammates had a way of putting his talent in an unflattering context. He did not quite match up to Crespo as an out-and-out goalscorer, Riquelme was supreme as playmaker, and Messi was too abundantly superhuman for any coach to leave out regularly. So Tevez began most of the tournament on the bench.

He came on and did his thing, scoring against the USA in the first game after replacing Messi. Crespo then injured himself scoring a penalty against Colombia but coach Alfio Basile replaced him with Diego Milito, a more superficially similar forward. Milito lacked some of Tevez's scurrying intensity but could lead the line in swashbuckling fashion, was great in the air and likely to score every kind of goal. But it didn't quite come off for Milito versus Peru – it never did in his international career, really – and Tevez started the semi-final win against Mexico and the final against

Brazil. He didn't score in either game and, while Riquelme remained imperious and Messi was tightly marked and could blame his lack of impact in the final on his youth, Tevez's relative anonymity resembled the way he had performed against Germany in 2006 – he tried and tried but it just wouldn't happen.

Tevez played regularly in the qualifiers for the 2010 World Cup. As usual, he courted controversy with two red cards in a three-game spell, but his Maradona-esque appeal to the Argentine public allowed those acts of stupidity and petulance to be seen as signifiers of his passion and spirit. Once Maradona took over as coach, Tevez's involvement was assured. The old master had spoken about his appreciation of Carlitos on many occasions and regularly turned to him when Argentina needed a result as qualification looked in doubt.

Tevez was always game but his final international record is telling; in his 76 appearances for his country he only scored 13 goals. Still, Maradona's Argentina squeezed into the World Cup and Tevez played at the tournament, scoring twice against Mexico in an otherwise frustrating series of performances.

By now, with Riquelme gone, the attacking complexion of the side was dictated by Messi, while Tevez competed with several high-quality rivals to play alongside him, including Angel Di María, Gonzalo Higuaín, Ezequiel Lavezzi, City club-mate Agüero, Martín Palermo and another rising star in Javier Pastore. Argentina went out with a limp, inept performance against old enemy Germany and Maradona was replaced as coach by his 1986 team-mate Sergio Batista, who had done well with some of the youth teams. He steered a young team into the 2011 Copa

América, held in Argentina. Tevez was in and out of the starting line-up, again because of a lack of goals and some mixed performances.

He was not alone in that – only Messi and Mascherano were untouchable under Argentina's coaches in that era – but Tevez never lost the faith of the Argentinian public. When an Argentina team was announced over the PA at home games, while Messi's name drew muted applause, Tevez's was the spur for celebration and chants. He was still the footballer of the people and his very public struggles, so human and tied to his emotional state, only made him seem more Argentinian to his compatriots. Meanwhile, Batista's midfield and attack were rejigged and tinkered with from game to game, and Tevez went from bench to starter and back.

Argentina struggled to a quarter-final tie against a formidable Uruguay in Santa Fe, where a turgid game eventually went to penalties. All ten penalty takers scored except Tevez, whose missed kick sent Uruguay to the final and an eventual Copa triumph. After that, Alejandro Sabella was appointed Argentina coach but Tevez was not part of his plans and he was not selected for the national team for three years. Conspiracy theorists in the Argentinian press put the blame on Messi but Tevez's inconsistent form and personal struggles were more likely reasons, as was Sabella's preference for a solid defensive base and searing pace in the forward roles. He already had Higuaín and Agüero as his strikers; Tevez was a luxury and Sabella was not prepared to sacrifice a more pragmatic selection for him. That meant, of course, that Tevez missed the 2014 World Cup, by which time he was playing in Serie A with Turin giants Juventus.

* * *

His crisis at Manchester City had been resolved in February 2012, when the club formally allowed him to rejoin the squad. For his part, Tevez pledged his gratitude to the club, made a formal apology for his behaviour, and withdrew the appeal he had lodged for the fine they had imposed on him. But – as well as being photographed by paparazzi playing golf during his suspension – he had spent weeks looking for a transfer away from England.

Tevez being Tevez, he gave his all when he returned to the team. He scored goals and provided assists as City won their first title of the modern era with an exciting victory over Queens Park Rangers at the death on the final day of the season. It tells its own story, however, that it was Agüero, in some ways Tevez's successor, who scored that famous winner and not 'El Apache' himself. He was just not as important at City as he had been.

As if in response, Tevez found another way to court controversy as, during City's victory parade through Manchester, he held aloft a sign reading 'RIP Fergie' in a final insult towards his former United boss. It seemed a sentiment from the barras bravas traditions of Argentine football but many members of the English football press were appalled.

Tevez would stay one more season at City, showing he remained a potent force with 17 goals in 47 games before a spell that had been on life support since the Munich incident ended with his June 2013 move to Juventus for £12m. His time at Juve was tremendously successful. He scored 50 goals in 95 games across two seasons and won two Serie A titles, a Coppa Italia and a Supercoppa Italia. He was named 2013/14 Juventus player of the season and

2014/15 Serie A player of the year. He scored seven goals in his side's run to the 2015 Champions League Final, where they suffered a 3-1 loss to an immense Barcelona side orchestrated by Messi.

The difference from his years in England was that, at Juventus, Tevez was treated like the galáctico he plainly believed he was. When he arrived he was awarded the sacred number 10 shirt that had once been worn not only by Omar Sívori but also by Michel Platini and most recently by golden boy Alessandro Del Piero. Tevez was a senior pro now, experienced and laden with honours – and he acted like it. He shouted and cajoled and demanded better. Playing as a second striker behind young Spaniard Alvaro Morata, his hard running and effort inspired the forward to up his own work rate. And in the slightly slower surrounds of Italian football, Tevez's dynamism, allied to his unquestionable technical quality, turned him into the game-winning star he had been in his youth. He was also fitter than he had been for years; he looked trim and motivated. Juventus fans loved him.

Tevez said he would only leave Juve for his first love and, in interviews during his second season, admitted how much he wanted to return to Boca before he retired. He got his wish with a June 2015 move back to Argentina, which involved Juventus taking five young players, including Rodrigo Bentancur, in exchange. And if Tevez had been loved at Juventus, nowhere was he as adored as he was at Boca Juniors. He joined a team with another recently returned star, Fernando Gago – once tagged the 'new Redondo' – but Tevez was instantly the biggest attraction in domestic Argentine football. He set about proving he deserved that tag in his usual all-action fashion, scoring nine goals in 18 appearances as Boca won a double of league and cup. Tevez was still a little too good for Argentinian football, it seemed, although he never made it look easy. That wasn't Carlitos's way.

He started the 2016/17 season in a similar vein, scoring five goals in 11 appearances early on and combining well with Darío Benedetto, a reliably voracious goalscorer in Argentina, but Tevez had his head turned. Chinese football was seemingly on the rise, swamped with cash by businesses hoping to ape the success of the Premier League across Asia and looking to lure more South American players following the success of Darío Conca and a couple of others. Chinese Super League side Shanghai Shenhua offered Tevez an obscene amount of money he just could not refuse. He later admitted it was a mistake, but a salary of £635,000 a week meant it was a very well-paid mistake.

* * *

Tevez signed a two-year contract but later claimed he realised as soon as he landed in China that he should have stayed at Boca. He joined a club with some pedigree and a tradition of signing 'marquee' players. Nicolas Anelka, Didier Drogba and Tim Cahill had all enjoyed well-renumerated spells in Shanghai, while Uruguayan Gus Poyet was the newly appointed coach when Tevez arrived. There were other fellow South Americans to ease him in – Colombians Fredy Guarín and Giovanni Moreno, an Argentine-style enganche who had risen to prominence at Racing Club – but Tevez never looked settled or all that interested. On the pitch he was his usual blend of industry and sparkle but in his nine months of appearing for the club on a semi-regular basis, he scored only four goals in 20 games. For a player of his calibre, in a league generally perceived as a low-wattage option for declining stars in search of a payday, that was a huge disappointment. Calculations estimated that each of those four goals cost the club $10m and Tevez's spell had dissolved into media criticism and spats with coaches long before he returned to Boca.

He had picked up a calf injury early on in his time in China and was pictured with his family enjoying Disneyland while his team-mates were involved in an away game. Fans were not impressed and questioned why he was not undergoing treatment to return to the fray. He had arrived in Shanghai accompanied by an entourage of 20 – with his immense wages he could certainly afford it – but he struggled with the culture, language and food. His persistent calf injury reduced his time on the pitch and his effectiveness when he did make it into games. Fans claimed Tevez was displaying a lack of interest and nicknamed him 'Homesick Boy' – perhaps it is catchier in Mandarin?

The club allowed him to seek treatment for his calf injury in Argentina but he returned weeks later, overweight and unfit, with new coach Wu Jingui dropping him from both legs of the Chinese FA Cup Final in which Shenhua defeated local rivals Shanghai SIPG, who had their own highly paid South Americans in the form of Brazilian stars Oscar and Hulk.

Tevez, never the most diplomatic, didn't help himself when he criticised the standard of the football in Asia, comparing it unflatteringly with what he had seen in Europe and South America and claiming it would still be unable to compete in 50 years' time. He was on his way back to Argentina while his team-mates were lifting the cup and in January 2018, little more than a year after he left, he was back at Boca Juniors. He labelled his Chinese spell a 'holiday', claiming he wanted to win the Copa Libertadores with Boca and was aiming to play for Argentina at the 2018 World Cup in Russia.

His final spell as a player at Boca was again a success. Tevez scored 31 goals in 113 games, won two league titles, and was again the talismanic presence Los Xeneizes showed such unqualified love for – but he was undeniably in decline. He affected games less, ran less, assisted less. That magic sparkle he had always had in addition to his ferocious joy in combat was only sporadically visible amid the injuries and bouts of arguing with the Argentine media. He was never really a serious option for the Argentina squad in 2018, having not played in the side for years, his spot taken by his successor at Juventus, Paulo Dybala.

The climax of his career should have been a Copa Libertadores triumph in the two-legged final in 2018, when a Superclásico of such magnitude broke Argentinian football. River Plate were coached by Marcelo Gallardo, playing exciting, stylish and successful football. Boca, under old legend Guillermo Barros Schelotto, were less attractive, but still a powerful unit.

The tie was chaos. The first leg at La Bombonera was postponed just two hours before kick-off due to torrential rain that made the pitch unplayable. When the game was rescheduled for the next day, it ended in a 2-2 draw. It was the kind of stage beautifully suited to Tevez in his prime but, only half-fit, he came on as a late substitute with little impact.

The second leg was also postponed following an attack on the coach carrying Boca's squad to the Monumental.

The coach had driven down the streets where River fans traditionally gather before games. Missiles thrown by mobs of River fans broke the windows and tear gas made it on to the bus, seriously affecting several Boca players. The game was abandoned and the clubs fought a running argument with the football authorities and Argentine media about what should happen next. A month later the game was finally rescheduled – on another continent. Real Madrid's Bernabéu was chosen as a neutral venue, in December 2018. Tevez was a largely anonymous late sub again, unable to prevent a 3-1 River win.

In June 2021 he announced he was leaving Boca, claiming he was physically but not mentally able to keep playing for the club. A year later Tevez officially retired. The loss of his father to Covid-19 in February 2021 had hugely affected him and, without his 'number one fan', he felt unable to keep on playing. Tevez had a great career by most standards. He thrived almost everywhere he went. He won trophies in every country except China, played alongside many of the great players of his generation, was adored by fans for his approach to the game, and always gave the media great stories about his life and career.

The comparisons to Diego Maradona started early and, for all his undoubted talent and skill, it was more of the similarities in background and attitude that gave them oxygen. He was a new Maradona in those respects and in the way he seemed to suffer for his brilliance, the way he took it out on the world around him, his rage and passion and love of football. Those are the characteristics that made him so compelling to watch and such a beloved figure in Argentina.

NINE

Lionel Messi, 'La Pulga'

STUDYING TEVEZ'S career, it is instructive to note how often his path was affected by the existence of Lionel Messi. Like Maradona before him, Messi's talent throws a shadow across his generation of players. His closest rival for the title of the world's greatest player for almost two decades, Cristiano Ronaldo, is constantly compared with him, their successes scrutinised and contrasted, their careers inextricably linked and discussed in the context of one another.

After a time, the Argentina squad – and arguably the Argentina coach – was selected to allow Messi to be as happy as possible with the national team. If you were an Argentine footballer, you needed to get along with Lionel Messi and even play in a way that allowed him to express himself – or you might not get many chances with the national side. That might sound extreme, but Messi is a genius. Messi is worth it.

With all the players I have already mentioned in this book, the key question applied to them all at some point was: is he the 'new Maradona'? Messi, however, is different. With Messi, that question eventually became is he better than Maradona?

The story of Messi's career in youth football is one of teams honoured for their greatness – and the common factor in those teams was little Leo Messi. Born in June 1987 to a middle-class Rosario family – his father managed a steel factory while his mother was employed in a workshop – Messi grew up surrounded by the game, playing with his two older brothers and his cousins the Biancucchis. These cousins would both go on to be professionals.

Messi's childhood in football is a story familiar to many Argentine boy geniuses. He played for his local club, Grandoli, from the age of four, with his father as coach, then joined the club his family supported, one of Rosario's historic giants in the form of Newell's Old Boys.

Of course, Maradona had spent time at Newell's, a detail that would be used extensively later to encourage comparison of the number tens. Messi had, it would emerge, been in the crowd on the day Maradona made his Newell's debut. He had been given his first Newell's shirt as a present on his first birthday. His brothers had played for Newell's youth teams. Newell's was already part of his identity and, over the next few years, it would become even more so.

Messi's team became known as 'La Máquina del 87' (the machine of 87), and they developed a reputation as an almost unbeatable side. Messi already had his own reputation. Éver Banega, who would become part of an impressive Rosarino contingent in the Argentina squad through the 2010s alongside Mascherano, Di María, Lavezzi and Garay, has reminisced about playing for his youth side Nuevo Horizonte against tiny Messi for Grandoli, claiming Messi's kit was too big but he would still make them all look stupid.

VHS footage of him from that era reveals a talent eerily similar to the one he showcased regularly for Barcelona and Argentina years later: dropping his shoulder; manipulating the ball under his dipping, hovering body; drifting effortlessly past players and riding despairing tackles, his mop of hair flicking and flowing as he runs, head up and scanning; finishing with style and nervelessness.

At Newell's he cemented his reputation as something special. He scored four goals on his debut, a sign of things to come. Eventually there would be 500 goals in his six years at the club and, even then, he was something intrinsically Argentinian, a gambeta phenomenon. His dribbling was supernatural, and he was competitive. He wanted to win. Quiet and shy, most of the time functioning as just one of the boys on the team, when the whistle blew, he was something else.

His maternal grandmother was the one who took him to games and training, forging a bond that is still evident with his characteristic goal celebration, pointing to the heavens and in effect dedicating every one of his many goals to her. Of Italian descent, Messi has spoken of her role in insisting he make his debut for the team playing in the league a year above his; of the coach's fear that this tiny kid would be hurt and of his grandma's confidence that he would be fine.

He was, obviously, more than fine. That team went three years in 'baby football' unbeaten, winning tournaments across Argentina and in other parts of South America. It was filled with good players and, when they passed into U11 football and were suddenly playing on full-size pitches, their success continued.

The coaches and players all knew how good Messi was, that he was special, but his physical development was a problem. When he was ten, Newell's sent the 4ft boy to a doctor and he was diagnosed with a rare hormone deficiency that was preventing him from growing at a normal pace. The Messi family was comfortable by Argentine standards. His father had medical insurance but the treatment for the hormone deficiency cost $1,000 a month, so Newell's agreed to partly fund the medication, wanting to protect the potential jewel they had on their hands.

Messi injected himself daily. Already his nickname 'La Pulga' (the flea) had taken hold and he did not like it. Thankfully the treatment was painless and quick. In later decades, when Messi and Cristiano Ronaldo fans argued their respective merits on web pages and social media, those treatments would be labelled by Ronaldo fans as 'performance enhancing drugs' in an effort to suggest Messi's achievements were due to chemical assistance. But his supporters rightly suggested that all the medicine did was allow him to be normal; what made Messi beyond normal was the talent he had been born with, the thing that made him seem extraterrestrial.

Messi went on scoring goals and winning tournaments but amid the flood of European scouts in Argentina looking for the next Maradona, Batistuta or Kempes, Messi somehow flew below the radar, overshadowed by the likes of Leandro Depetris, another Rosario boy whose team beat Messi's Newell's in a final in Córdoba during that era. Depetris joined AC Milan at the age of 12 in 2001 and, after five years there without breaking into the first team, he had an equally unsuccessful loan back at River Plate. He became a decent journeyman with a few solid years at Brescia but his career was marked by a slow drift down the divisions. At that age in the football town of Rosario, however, Depetris was far and away the more famous player.

* * *

One big European club had noticed Messi, however, and the growing crisis in the Argentinian economy soon enabled them to make their play. Beginning in 1998, Argentina lurched from one financial problem to the next, linked to the weakened state of several other economies and worsened by huge government debt and rampant corruption that led to a financial crisis in 2001. By then, Messi had already left the country. The start of the crisis in 1998 and 1999 affected football clubs, too. Newell's had financial problems and the money for Messi's medication could no longer be found. He had already been scouted by River Plate, where his idol, Pablo Aimar, had emerged, but they too were reluctant to pay for treatment for a youth-team player who might never live up to his obvious potential.

His family had links to Italy and Spain – more specifically Catalonia – and Barcelona, no stranger to picking up young Argentine creative players, had taken note of Messi. In September 2000, his family flew Lionel to Spain for a trial. Charly Rexach, team-mate of Johan Cruyff at Barça, a Spain international and La Liga-winning coach, realised how urgently the club needed to tie Messi down to a contract. The tale of Rexach hastily scrawling a contract on the back of a napkin in a restaurant has become legend but it does indicate that he knew there was something special in the boy he had watched dazzle on the pitch. Rexach was a director at the time and, after that napkin contract, there were months of issues with Newell's in Argentina over Messi's legal ties.

His team-mates in Rosario had been informed Messi was ill while he was in Spain and he returned only briefly before the entire family moved to Barcelona in February 2001 – and that is where the 'Messi as the new Maradona' narrative starts to break down. Maradona's relationship with Argentinian football culture was baked in. His relationship with Boca Juniors and their fanbase was something he was never shy about professing, and he responded to other clubs in his career more or less in terms of how similar they felt to Boca.

Messi, however, for all that his love of Newell's cannot be questioned, left Argentina at such a young age there would always be questions over how deep his connection with Argentinian football ran.

For at least the first decade of his career, he was associated more with Barcelona than he was with Argentina. While the club had dozens of other great players in his time there – Ronaldinho and Eto'o, Iniesta and Xavi, Puyol and Suárez, Neymar and Villa, Busquets and Fàbregas, Henry and Alba, Alves and Piqué – nobody was as symbolic of Barcelona in the late 2000s and throughout the 2010s as Lionel Messi.

He got off to a rocky start, though. Newell's were contesting his transfer and, in the early 2000s, European clubs were not as slick and well-practised at buying youngsters from beyond the continent. The arbitration dragged on, meaning Messi was only allowed to play in friendlies and Catalan league games, which meant he was struggling to integrate into the side.

He was also suffering from a niggling ankle injury and intense homesickness once his mother and siblings returned to Rosario, leaving him in Barcelona with his father. Most youngsters from beyond Catalonia at Barça's famous La Masia training facility live on the grounds, but Messi had an apartment with his father nearby. That meant Messi spoke so rarely to his new team-mates they believed he was mute. Until that is, as is so often the case with stories of the young Messi, they witnessed him on the pitch.

When his issues were finally sorted and a trip to the 2002 Maestrelli youth tournament in Italy allowed him to bond with his team-mates over a series of pranks and PlayStation FIFA tournaments, the wondrous team Messi was growing into began to develop its own legend.

In that team, Messi had another two greats of their generation as team-mates: the aristocratic Gerard Piqué as a graceful, ball-playing centre-back (later nicknamed Piquenbauer), and the cerebral promptings of Cesc Fàbregas in central midfield. Coached by Tito Vilanova and adopting the 3-4-3 formation of Cruyff's 'Dream Team', that youth side became all but unbeatable.

'Generación del 87' graduated to the Cadete A bracket as they aged and won matches by ridiculous scorelines. Players had contests to see who could score the most goals in a game. Amid all the talent and collective strength, however, Messi stood out as a phenomenal talent. He scored 40 goals that season – the only one in which he stayed with the same team from start to finish. The season was capped by a famous Copa Catalunya Final in which Messi started the game wearing a mask designed to protect a cheekbone he had injured in a game against the same opponents, local rivals Espanyol, the week before. Messi had been told he could not play unless he wore the mask but he ditched it after 15 minutes and swiftly scored two goals – the second with what would become a Maradona-esque gambeta past defenders – and was promptly substituted. Barça won 4-1, sealing a treble in what would be the final match featuring the trio of future stars.

By now, other European giants had noticed the talent in the side and Premier League clubs in particular were ready to flex their financial muscle. Fàbregas, aware that the route to the first team at Barça was blocked by Xavi, Iniesta, Busquets and a host of foreign imports, joined Arsenal, where the manager Arsène Wenger had guaranteed him a place in the first-team squad. Piqué left for Manchester United, where serving as understudy to the likes of Rio Ferdinand and Nemanja Vidić and suffering against the muscular forwards of English football transformed him into a complete centre-half. Both would eventually return to Camp Nou – but Messi never left.

Arsenal also came for Messi but Barcelona were well aware of what they had and rapidly funnelled him through their development system so he would not feel bored or question his future at the club. In the 2003/04 season he played for Juvenil B, Juvenil A, Barcelona C and Barcelona B – each a step up in quality and physical difficulty. Messi glided through it, showing his sense of competitiveness and toughness to be playing with grown men at the age of 16. By now, he had caught the eye of others outside the club. His talent was something rarely seen – and people were excited by it.

* * *

On 16 November 2003, Messi made his debut for the Barcelona first team in a friendly against José Mourinho's Porto to mark the opening of the Portuguese side's Estádio do Dragão. He missed two good chances through poor decisions – forgivable surely for a kid – and recalled coach Frank Rijkaard reminded him of that at the final whistle. But the coaching staff had been impressed and Messi began training regularly with the reserves. When senior players from that era are asked about him, their recollections inevitably involve stories of Messi's frightening raw ability embarrassing established internationals by dribbling past them.

At that point, Messi's close control was twinned with an explosiveness that made him a torment for anybody tasked with taking the ball from him. He could beat a man from a standing start. He would occasionally beat a player, turn back, then beat him again. He attracted fouls but had adjusted his stride so he could surf challenges.

Maradona comparisons were inevitable, and they only threw into relief the changes in the game since Maradona's era. Where Maradona had endured assaults in every game – watching the tackles on him in every single game at the 1986 World Cup is especially instructive and today he would draw a couple of red cards for opponents – Messi emerged in an era in which skilled players were protected by referees. Tackles from behind had almost been outlawed, with only the most clean and perfect permissible. Any studs-high challenges were met with a card, generally a red. Shoulder-barges had to be subtle. Holding, raised arms and elbows were all likely to bring instant sanctions.

Messi obviously benefited from this protection as it allowed him to play in a way Maradona was never allowed. It was also a time when sports science began to revolutionise the game. Players lived better, played faster, ran more, ate healthier, slept well, and worked out regularly. Once his hormone treatment was complete and Messi found himself taller than Maradona at 5ft 7in, he did not need the painkillers and anti-inflammatory injections Maradona required throughout his career. While Maradona found a love of cocaine and partying in Naples didn't seem to impede his football brilliance, Messi settled down to a quiet life devoted to football and his relatively young family. His freakish consistency is proof enough that this lifestyle choice helped to prolong his career.

It would be almost a year after his debut before Messi played a competitive game for Barcelona's first team. In that time, Argentina were busy ensuring he would be representing his country instead of declaring for Spain. Due to his roots in Europe and eventual nationalised status, Messi had dual Argentine–Spanish citizenship and could choose to represent either nation. Rexach had notified Spain's underage system of Messi's quality after his arrival in Catalonia and their pursuit of him was advanced and persistent. But Messi refused. He was a proud Argentinian, surrounding himself with his family, eating Argentine food and drink, listening to Argentine music, watching Argentine movies and TV, and never losing his Rosario accent. His girlfriend and eventual wife was his childhood sweetheart from Rosario, while his father and brother eventually ran most of his business interests.

He was never going to choose Spain over his homeland but the AFA took steps to make his decision easier. In June 2004 two friendlies were arranged with the sole purpose of confirming Messi's registration as an Argentina international. In the first, an U20 Argentina side loaded with talent, including Lavezzi and Garay, hammered Paraguay 8-0, with Messi scoring a trademark dribble and finish around the goalkeeper for the seventh. A second game against Uruguay showcased Messi's growing comfort as he scored twice.

His increased prominence and the nasty habit English clubs had developed of stealing young talent had alerted Barcelona that they needed to keep Messi happy. He had signed his first professional contract in February 2004. It had a €30m buyout clause that increased to €80m once he made his debut for Barcelona B in March that year. Barça knew what they had at this point. In Argentina, the Maradona comparisons had begun. The dribbling, the short stature and low centre of gravity, the Barcelona connection – all were played up.

Messi had an aura around him for Argentina fans before most of them had ever seen him play. Even players shared it. Agüero has spoken of a vague awareness of a young Argentine burning through the Barcelona youth system and not realising that the youngster he met at the underage camp at the training complex in Ezeiza, where his U16 squad and Messi's U17 mixed, was the wonder kid until he asked outright and other players laughed at him. Messi was already elite within the elite. He was also ready for his first real season as a professional.

At the start of the 2004/05 season, he was a fixture in the Barcelona B side in the Segunda Division, the third tier of Spanish league football, but the senior pros who trained with him and saw his quality behind the scenes were pressuring coach Rijkaard to promote the gifted youngster to the first team. Rijkaard eventually relented and Messi made his debut as a late substitute against Espanyol on 16 October. He featured nine times that season, playing a small part in Barcelona winning their first title in six years in a side where Ronaldinho was very much the leading man. It was Ronaldinho who assisted Messi's first Barça goal against Albacete in May, and Ronaldinho who greeted his Ballon d'Or win with the quip that he wasn't even the best player at Barcelona.

Messi also played in the Champions League that season and returned to the national team set-up to play in the South American Youth Championship. Held in Colombia in February, Messi scored five goals, including the winner against Brazil to guarantee Argentina third place and qualification for the FIFA World Youth Championship. However, he lacked the strength and stamina of many of his team-mates and opponents – something he would determinedly rectify when he returned to Spain, hiring a personal trainer – and had generally been used as an impact sub when his sinuous, tricky dribbles would prove horrific for opposing defences.

Europe's giants had taken notice of this scampering little genius and bids were being readied. More attention would be directed his way after the FIFA World Youth Championship, held in the Netherlands in June. Argentina had a strong squad including future stars such as Pablo Zabaleta, Lucas Biglia, Fernando Gago and Sergio Agüero, but they began with defeat to the USA. Messi started the tournament on the bench, the coaching staff still suspicious of his lack of size and strength, but after the other players appealed, he started the knockout games and showed sensational form. He drove Argentina to victory in the tournament, winning the Golden Shoe and Golden Boot for best player and highest scorer.

This was a player already too good for underage football and, on his 18th birthday, Messi signed a new contract, his first as a first-team player. His buyout clause was now €150m, a sign that Barcelona were well aware of the interest he was attracting. That interest was formalised after he earned rave reviews and a Camp Nou standing ovation for his performance in a pre-season Joan Gamper Trophy match against Juventus. Juve coach Fabio Capello asked to take Messi on loan but Inter Milan had already made a bid, seemingly prepared to pay his buyout clause in full.

* * *

It was when Messi became a first-team fixture at Barcelona that the comparisons with Maradona became a regular occurrence. By that point it was obvious to all that Messi was exceptional, a once-in-a-lifetime talent. He was left-footed, a magician, a brilliant dribbler. He was like Maradona. Paradoxically, his career and Maradona's were already hugely different. Messi's move to Barcelona was so much earlier, his development much more gradual and controlled by the club. He was quiet and modest. He was astoundingly consistent. He lacked Maradona's exhibitionism, arrogance and charisma – but he went out and performed wonders. Increasingly, he delivered when it mattered.

Over the next season or two, Messi did things the media in Spain and Argentina pounced on, such as his mesmeric, wondrous dribble from near halfway to score against Getafe, which was compared to Maradona's 'goal of the century' against England in 1986. He also scored a goal with a handball that was compared to the 'Hand of God'. Increasingly, however, Messi was showing at Barça that he was nothing like Maradona. He was a team player, more tactically disciplined and aware of systems. For all that, coaches rapidly realised he was best allowed to do what he wanted and find spaces wherever he wanted; early in his career he had the energy to drop deep and carry out the defensive work. There were no feuds, no scandals, no off-field exploits, just wonderful football. Soon Messi had replaced a Ronaldinho who had lost form as Barcelona's best and most important player. He was still growing and suffered injuries but over the next few years Messi's excellence became monotonous, his efficiency an almost supernatural fact of football.

Messi hitting new heights coincided with the arrival of Pep Guardiola as Barcelona coach and the dominance of tiki-taka in Europe via Barça and the Spanish national team. Messi played in front of the finest midfield in football at the time, with Xavi, Iniesta and Busquets all providing him with passes. He used those passes to destroy teams. The numbers are breathtaking: Messi won La Liga ten times with Barcelona between 2004 and 2019; won the Copa del Rey seven times in the same period; and the Supercopa eight times.

In Spain, for Barcelona to not win the league, another team needed to make a mighty effort or something had gone terribly wrong at Camp Nou. Real Madrid spent huge amounts of money in an attempt to foil the Catalan side, bringing in high-quality, expensive coaches in the shape of José Mourinho and Carlo Ancelotti, and a series of 'galácticos' such as Messi's eternal rival Cristiano Ronaldo, Gareth Bale and Luka Modrić. Even when Real were successful, often in the periods when Barça sides were in transition or riven by internal politics and poor transfer windows, Messi remained untouchable. In 2010/11, he scored 53 goals in 55 games. The season after, he scored 73 in 60. Then 60 in 50. Rarely had numbers like that been seen before and with such freakish consistency. The fact Ronaldo was just about matching him for Madrid made La Liga the must-watch league of that era.

Messi scored 672 goals for Barcelona in 778 appearances, a mind-boggling statistic. And it wasn't just goals. Ronaldo had arrived at Madrid and honed his game so all he really did was score. The Ronaldo from Sporting Lisbon and his first years in Manchester – all stepovers and showboating – was gone, replaced by an assassin who ruthlessly took his chances. Messi changed his game too, but the dribbles and assists remained. What always seemed evident when the two were compared was that once Ronaldo's physical gifts began to fade, he started to struggle. So much of his game was about power and pace and, from 2020 onwards, his achievements and performances dipped. With Messi, however, there was always the idea he would adapt; his game was richer and his arsenal more varied. He could drop and dictate play, he read the game so well, he could play every type of pass. His pace and trickery were key, but there was more. Alongside the goals, Messi incessantly created chances for his strike partners. He finished his time at Barcelona with 269 assists. He could prompt and strategise in-game then find a way to execute. His genius was multifaceted.

Alongside all the Spanish titles, he won the Champions League four times, a trophy that had always eluded Maradona and is seen by many as the greatest club prize in modern football. Indeed, his performance in the final against Manchester United in 2008/09 felt like the final confirmation of his status as the best in the world. Here was a player who could take a football match and bend it to his will; flitting in and out of space, scoring goals, joining in with the tiki-taka when he chose to, terrifying a defence seen as the best in Europe at the time.

Messi finished that tournament as the highest scorer, with nine goals, and third in the assist charts with five goals created. That was something he accomplished time and again in the Champions League during the next few years. Those wins were accompanied by three European Super Cup triumphs and three FIFA Club World Cup titles. The individual honours also began to pile up to a ridiculous extent: seven Ballon d'Ors, six European Golden Shoes for top scorer across the continent, six wins as La Liga's best player, 14 times voted Argentine player of the year.

Even all that success and acclaim misses what made Messi so sublime – he was consistently the best player on the pitch. In games filled with superstars and world-class players, he was better. It became a common theme on social media and from players to talk about him as an 'alien'. He played football on another level. Thierry Henry spoke with awe about how Messi could pick up the ball in training, beat half the team and score. Henry had played with Zidane and Bergkamp but had never seen anything like Messi. Zlatan Ibrahimović, never the humblest about his own gifts, was similarly awestruck by Messi, labelling him a 'genius'.

When Messi scored his 644th goal, one of his many corporate sponsors, Budweiser, sent an individually inscribed bottle to each of the goalkeepers he had scored against. The bottles were numbered with the goal, game and date. Rather than being annoyed, most of the keepers seemed to recognise the worth of being linked to Messi in that way. Social media was filled with 'victims' pictured with their bottles; in some cases, multiple bottles for the many goals he had put past them. Those keepers knew Messi was football history and, by conceding to him, they became part of his legend.

* * *

Game after game, week after week, season after season, Messi was amazing, yet all the while humble. He was still married to Antonella. They had three children, and Messi was a devoted father. Team-mates loved him. His interviews were fascinating because of who he was, even though he rarely said anything interesting. His fame was so immense a cult built around him that turned every utterance into a story. Fans became fascinated by his friendships with other players because they had so little to go on otherwise. His bromance with the much more voluble Uruguayan Luis Suárez seemed particularly interesting. The way he adapted his game to play alongside Suárez and would-be rival Neymar at Barcelona was telling. Messi had an ego, alright, but he let his game do the talking. Even an ego the size of Neymar's had to bow down before Messi's consistent delivery of quality football.

The media storm surrounding Messi's tax issues barely touched him personally. He just got on with his job and getting on with his job had come to define him publicly; he never made grandstanding speeches at press conferences like Maradona. Messi's fame had transcended the game to some extent. Alongside the more publicity-hungry and naturally photogenic Ronaldo, he was among the world's highest-paid sportsmen between 2009 and 2020.

At first his endorsements were all sporting – football video games, Adidas, etc. Ronaldo aped David Beckham, creating a brand around his own glamour, physical appeal and appearance. The fact Messi showed no interest in that only made him more likeable and relatable, and gave the Messi–Ronaldo rivalry another dimension. He was Adidas's biggest marquee player, with his own line of merchandise and, although he advertised various other brands, he seemed barely aware of the circus around him. Those brands shifted as his fame grew – he was now the face of airlines, soft drinks, skincare products, telecommunications, car manufacturers.

In an era when it was routine for people outside the football world to complain about the vast wages earned by footballers, Messi was often used as a defence of those wages – he was worth it. People paid for TV channels in order to watch him play. Any visit to Camp Nou during his peak years would highlight the effect of his fame; tourists came to see Messi, not to support Barcelona. He was bigger than the club for a time, a tourist attraction in his own right. Ronaldo regularly found himself heckled during matches by opposition fans just repeating Messi's name at him, as if to remind him that no matter how good he was, he was not the best. And Messi? He just got on with his job.

Messi was not the new Maradona it turned out – his career at Barcelona had lasted longer than Maradona's entire career in Europe at three clubs – but there was the distinct possibility he was a better player. Many were arguing that Messi was the greatest player the game had ever seen, even relatively early in his career. His consistent achievement and the amazing quality of his play gave their argument plenty to work with – but in Argentina, there were doubters.

Maradona played in a radically different era and it is fair to suggest that, had he played on modern surfaces, with modern footballs and modern fitness approaches and nutrition, he would have been even better. Most pertinently, Messi never had to face the violence that was routine for Maradona. Messi was protected by referees, by the very rules of the game. His entire generation were. Maradona performed his miracles against players shamelessly trying to hurt him. Messi often played against opponents frightened to even tackle him. But Maradona had achieved nothing like Messi's Barcelona success. Instead, what he had done was something far more important to the Argentinian public – he had won Argentina a World Cup. Could Messi do the same?

* * *

Messi's full Argentina debut came during the Pékerman era with a substitute appearance against Hungary in a Budapest friendly on 17 August 2005. The fixture was soaked in symbolism. Maradona's debut had come against the same opposition, when he was 16 years old, in February 1977. He had entered the game in the 62nd minute, while Messi was introduced in the 63rd. Messi's debut was a disaster, however. He was sent off after only two minutes when his vigorous attempts to shake off the clawing attention of Vilmos Vanczák were interpreted by the referee as a deliberate elbow and he was shown a straight red card. He went back to the dressing room and sobbed.

Pékerman was already convinced, however, and Messi was a regular member of the squad from then on, appearing in World Cup qualifiers against Paraguay and Peru before the year was out. Despite carrying an injury for the latter part of the season, Messi made the squad for the 2006 World Cup. His versatility in attack made him a useful option from the bench, although there were already calls for him to be a regular starter.

That team was dominated by Riquelme as the number ten, with Aimar as his understudy. Messi was there more to play on the wing or as a second striker, and he played – and scored – as a substitute in the 6-0 destruction of Serbia and Montenegro, then started the 0-0 against the Netherlands, with Argentina having already qualified for the knockout rounds. He was again a substitute against Mexico in the round of 16 but made a big contribution, his running and cunning stretching the Mexican defence in extra time, and he had a goal controversially ruled out for offside before Maxi Rodríguez's stunning winner.

The Argentinian press was on Pékerman's back about starting Messi against Germany in the quarter-finals, especially given the tiredness creeping into Riquelme's performances as the tournament wore on. In that match against Germany it seemed nicely poised for Messi to replace Riquelme as the orchestrator of the attacks. Riquelme had run the game for an hour, setting the rhythm, moving the ball and directing his team. Argentina were winning.

When Riquelme was withdrawn after 72 minutes, however, he was replaced by Esteban Cambiasso, a more defensively minded central midfielder. Pékerman's thinking was clear; he wanted to ensure continued control. He then withdrew Hernán Crespo, offering another opportunity to introduce Messi up front alongside Carlos Tevez, but instead he chose Julio Cruz for his aerial ability. Messi stayed on the bench and Argentina lost on penalties, having surrendered control and momentum. The Argentine press battered Pékerman for taking off Riquelme and ignoring Messi.

Nevertheless, Messi's international potential was overwhelmingly obvious. He had become the youngest-ever Argentinian player at a World Cup, the youngest scorer at the tournament and the sixth-youngest in history. He had scored one and assisted one in two substitute appearances and one starting role in a virtual dead rubber. If Maradona's first World Cup had ended with underperformance and the suggestion he had failed to live up to the hype, Messi's merely suggested there was much more to come.

Pékerman's resignation meant Alfio Basile returned to the role he had occupied in the early 1990s. Basile was a coach who loved beautiful, exciting, attacking football and his squad was bewilderingly talented in the forward positions; probably the best in my lifetime.

Riquelme remained the creative fulcrum, with Aimar as his lieutenant. Juan Sebastián Verón, enjoying an Indian summer at Estudiantes, vied with Lucho González for the role of the number eight alongside Riquelme, with Javier Mascherano and rising star Fernando Gago as the choices for the crucial number five role at the base of midfield, with Cambiasso able to play either position. The strikers were awesome – Crespo; the generally unsung but lethal Diego Milito; Tevez; Boca's rapid and prolific Rodrigo Palacio; and Messi.

Argentina were favourites for the 2007 Copa América title and destroyed every team they played on the way to the final. Riquelme's combinations with Messi and Verón were a joyful exhibition of passing football, touch, movement and awareness. The team were obviously loving it – but everything went wrong in the final. A Frankenstein of a Brazilian side consisting of squad players, youngsters and veterans under the tactical eye of the defensively inclined

Dunga set out to stifle Argentina. More specifically, their physical treatment and tactical fouling of Messi and Riquelme were reminders of the way the beautiful Brazil side from the 1982 World Cup had treated Maradona. On both occasions, it worked.

An early thunderbolt golazo from Júlio Baptista meant Argentina were chasing the game, which perfectly suited Brazil who could only really play on the counter. After Riquelme hit the post in the eighth minute, Argentina's heads dropped and Ayala's own goal made the task even more difficult. Messi kept playing and trying, while Brazil kept fouling, and at that age he could not force the issue the way he would in later years.

The 3-0 Brazil win meant it had been 14 years since Argentina had won the Copa América, an eternity for a country that had grown accustomed to footballing success. Basile and the team were roundly criticised, although there was great appreciation for the performances of Messi, who won the award for young player of the tournament. But there was hope despite the despair at losing a final to the old enemy. Argentina had Messi, and he was young. Surely plenty of Copa América wins would follow?

That hope seemed to be borne out by his crucial role in the Olympic gold Argentina won in 2008 in Beijing, where Messi joined the squad against the wishes of Barcelona, the first piece of outright proof that Messi loved playing for his country. Under the eye of Sergio Batista and again linking up with Riquelme with support from many youngsters he knew well from youth teams such as Agüero, Di María, Banega, Gago and Zabaleta, Messi was in supreme form. He was elusive and deadly in each appearance, scoring and assisting as Argentina imperiously swept to the gold medal, including a memorable 3-0 semi-final win over Brazil. It seemed like the beginning of a long era of international success.

Argentina had the best player in the world – again – and he would guide them to trophies.

Looking back at Messi's international career, that 2006/07 team was the best he played in and he was not even near his peak at the time. In subsequent squads, however, fundamental flaws would undermine progress through various competitions. While Argentina consistently produced elite attacking players – players who would not even make the squad would have been stars in many national teams – there would be a long-term struggle to develop defenders who were at a similar level. Once the likes of Roberto Ayala, Wálter Samuel and Javier Zanetti retired, that weakness was exposed.

Players who were good enough for the Argentinian league often struggled when they arrived in Europe, where the football was harder, faster and more tactically sophisticated. Some Argentine defenders made the grade at big European clubs but often their coaches recruited and organised to complement them. Nicolás Otamendi, for example, had Manchester City's financial muscle ensuring his deficiencies were covered by the recruitment of Vincent Kompany and John Stones. Ezequiel Garay had so many injury problems it was hard to read how good he was on a consistent basis.

Argentinian centre-backs tended to be good footballers and canny in their gamesmanship but looked vulnerable against top-level attacking talent. While alterations to rules and the emphasis on attacking meant this was arguably a problem across all professional football, many nations could cope due to one or two outstanding defenders. Brazil, for example, could deal with the inconsistencies of David Luiz because they had the magnificent Thiago Silva and Dani Alves. Italy wrested World Cup and European Championship wins on the twin rocks of Giorgio Chiellini and Leonardo Bonucci. Argentina had no comparable players so coaches had to decide whether to risk playing to the team's attacking strengths, leaving the defence exposed, or balance the team and place a huge burden on the likes of Messi and Di María to create something in the few opportunities they were given.

The attritional nature of the European football season, with league games, domestic cup games and lengthy Champions League campaigns, meant many players limped into summer carrying niggles, injuries and generally in need of rest. Messi was a good case in point. He never looked to be operating at maximum efficiency at any World Cup after 2010. Instead, he was tired, playing with a knock, shepherding himself. The results would be a decade and a half of mounting frustration for player and country, during which his relationship with the Argentinian public – and his comparative stature when assessed alongside Maradona – would shift and evolve.

Qualification for the 2010 World Cup had begun well. With Basile still at the helm and the side from the 2007 Copa América still largely in place, Argentina brushed aside Chile, Venezuela and Bolivia in the first three games. Riquelme was still assured, combining with Messi and Tevez, while the likes of Milito and Agüero made important contributions. But a defeat to Colombia in November 2007 seemed to shake Argentine confidence and the team's form was rocky thereafter, with desperate draws against Ecuador, Brazil and Paraguay in the next three games.

Brazil were at a similarly low ebb and the way Messi and Riquelme were cheered for their determination to play football against their own destructive, utilitarian side by Brazil fans in Belo Horizonte was surreal and indicative of the way many football fans were beginning to regard Messi. But the media in Argentina were persistently hostile to Basile for his inability to properly utilise the glittering array of talent at his disposal. When Argentina did win, they were not convincing, not fluid, not attractive, not dominant, not good enough.

One of his biggest critics was the player whose failed drugs test had sunk Basile's first attempt to win a World Cup in 1994, Diego Maradona, who was always asked for his opinion on Argentina. Regarding any player linked with the squad, results or performances, his comments were generally quotable and emotional but rarely showed any understanding of tactical nuance. The issue with Basile did not seem to be tactical, however. He set out his side the same way Batista had at the Olympics, a way that should have guaranteed good football and results. He let Riquelme dictate with Mascherano behind. He had the likes of Gago and Cambiasso to link the two, then Messi and Agüero or Higuaín up front.

The ageing defence was an issue, but those attacking players could generally be relied on to offset any goals against. That suited Basile; he was from the Menotti school of football romanticism, playing a high-speed form of la nuestra, moving the ball and allowing players to express themselves. He had been part of Menotti's coaching team in 1978 and that was the problem; there was a huge generational gap in the Argentina set-up. Basile struggled to understand the kids who were suddenly massive international superstars, with their smartphones and social media and video-game tournaments. His inability to galvanise players began to leak out to the media after some of his coaching staff began to feel similarly alienated by his old-school approach.

For all that, Basile was a legend and had won Argentina's last two international trophies – the 1991 and 1993 Copa América triumphs – but this new generation had enjoyed playing under the younger Batista at the Olympics and their grumbling leaked to the scandal-hungry Argentine football press as Maradona and other ex-players sniped from the sidelines. Riquelme suffered too. There were reports the younger players resented his influence and many in the media agreed, finding the team far too reliant on him.

There were so many alternatives to Basile. Argentina exported not only players but coaches across the Americas and into European football, and some had become legends for their success in Argentina. Already the likes of Diego Simeone were being discussed as future Argentina coaches but Basile's fate would be decided by another iconic Argentine coach as he brought his side to Santiago to play Marcelo Bielsa's young Chile team in October 2008.

Bielsa had taken a break following his resignation as Argentina boss but that experience and his studies since had only hardened his belief in his own principles of how football should be played. His ideas were becoming increasingly influential. Pep Guardiola adapted Bielsa's approach with an added touch of Johan Cruyff, while a whole generation of Argentine coaches would use Bielsa's work as a launch pad.

Bielsa had taken a generation of Chilean footballers and instilled his football philosophy into their approach with gratifying success – they played thrilling, aggressive, attack-minded, versatile football based around a few really talented players. That night in Santiago, Chile overwhelmed an Argentina side missing Riquelme, their 1-0 win flattering the visitors. Again, many of the young Argentina players were disappointing. Messi was anonymous, Agüero invisible, and Bielsa's proactive, dynamic style made Basile look out of touch. The Argentinian press went nuclear. Argentina had never lost a competitive game to Chile before and Basile was hammered. He resigned, shocked by the hostility.

Messi claimed change had been required for some time and it looked as though Batista would be handed the job, something Messi and his friends in the squad evidently favoured. Instead, the AFA went for a media-friendly appointment and gave Maradona the role. It was time for Messi to learn at the feet of his predecessor, or so it seemed.

The CONMEBOL qualification system is a marathon, and unforgivably brutal. Maradona took over an Argentina side that had won one game in its last seven and he tried to do what he had when he was a player – harness his emotions and turn them into football success.

It worked, at first. His first game was a 4-0 hammering of traditional South American whipping boys Venezuela at the Monumental. Messi opened the scoring in what seemed a symbolic moment, wearing the sacred number 10 shirt for the first time, with further goals from Tevez, Maxi Rodríguez and Agüero.

Riquelme had quarrelled with Maradona in the press so Messi could take his place as the leader of the side, just as

Maradona had done. But Messi was not Maradona. There were similarities but Messi had emerged at a Barcelona where the systems all functioned smoothly, where the team played to a regimented pattern in which players knew their roles and filled them with skill and dedication. Argentina – especially an Argentina under the volatile Maradona – was not remotely like that.

Maradona selected 38 players during the remainder of the qualifiers. He changed and tweaked his tactics constantly, with panicky half-time substitutions revealing his insecurity about the project. Despite that, the expectation was that Messi would perform. He would produce magic when he had the ball, no matter how chaotic the team and squad around him had become. Maradona as a player would have loved that, he thrived off emotional energy and chaos as long as he had responsibility. Messi – to some extent – retreated into himself but it is testament to his immense gifts that he still produced and was able to find those magic moments as often as he did, given how different Argentina was to his usual environment at Barcelona.

Maradona's second game was against Bolivia, at altitude in La Paz. The advantage altitude gave the Bolivians was tackled differently by South American rivals. Some arrived early and tried to acclimatise, others wore oxygen masks in the build-up. Some got in and out as swiftly as possible, as if hoping the players' systems would fail to notice. No approach consistently worked – and things certainly didn't work for Argentina as Bolivia hammered them 6-1. Messi was sub-par, as was the rest of the side.

The next game was a cagey 1-0 win over Colombia followed by successive defeats, away to Ecuador and at home to Brazil. Maradona was changing his team like a kid playing a video game – any Argentina player experiencing a spell of good form was likely to feature alongside ever-presents Messi and Mascherano. Messi, predictably, never looked entirely comfortable.

Argentina needed to win their last two games – against Peru and Uruguay – and desperate late goals saw them qualify for the World Cup. Surely now, with the pressure off, Maradona would get the best out of Messi? The two famously met in Barcelona before the tournament to discuss their approach. Maradona toured Europe, visiting his leading players at their clubs and getting his picture taken at half the training grounds on the continent with a generation of players awed by him. The maestro spoke of how 'emotional' his chat with Messi was and his willingness to change his tactics to unlock Messi's gifts. Messi and Maradona had an obvious rapport, and there was a hope they could use that to win together.

Despite their recent struggles, Argentina entered the 2010 World Cup in South Africa among the favourites. Messi alone – at a ridiculously high point in his club form – would have guaranteed that but the whole squad was full of quality, even if Maradona had bafflingly chosen some sentimental favourites over more obvious candidates. An ageing Palermo was in the squad as was Mario Bolatti, both apparently on the basis their goals had been the match-winners that guaranteed qualification rather than any merit or tactical reasoning. That left the likes of Gago, Banega and Ezequiel Lavezzi bemused at their exclusions.

Maradona did change his tactics for Messi. He allowed him to play in a more conventional number ten role behind two strikers, with Mascherano behind and either Verón, Bolatti or Maxi Rodríguez linking. That worked well against humdrum group-stage opposition and Messi looked inspired, creating chances and finding space in wins over Nigeria and South Korea. The 2-0 win over a very limited Greece suggested Messi and Verón were on the same wavelength, and they looked a class above the rest of the players. Verón set a new record for passes completed in a World Cup game with his metronomic precision. He and Messi were seemingly engaged in a personal mission to complete as many one-twos as possible.

But Maradona tinkered with the team before the round-of-16 game against Germany. His continued love of Tevez demanded that he played up front and he dropped Verón in favour of Maxi Rodríguez, who tended to play higher up the pitch. That meant Mascherano was isolated and overwhelmed at the base of midfield, unable to both defend and work the ball forward to the attacking players.

Messi could not influence the game when he did not have the ball, and without Verón there was nobody to give it to him, with Di María and Rodríguez both playing as wingers. Had Gago or Banega been in the squad, they would have filled the same role as Verón but Bolatti was a far more limited player and, when Maradona did make substitutions, they were bizarre and desperate. He introduced playmaker Javier Pastore for centre-back Otamendi and replaced winger Di María with another striker in the form of Agüero as his side sought to claw their way back into the game.

Germany were rampant and beat a broken-backed Argentina 4-0. Maradona took a lot of flak but Messi was harshly criticised in Argentina too. The expectation on him was immense and he had failed to deliver. Not only that, his Argentina form was in stark contrast to his Barcelona efforts. Now the perception of him as 'Catalan' was aired loudly in the media for the first time. People claimed he cared more about club than country. His reserved, dispassionate aura did not help.

AFA boss Julio Grondona had shown great foresight when he negotiated Maradona's contract; it ended after the World Cup. That allowed him to dispense with Maradona's services without sacking him. Batista came in, as Messi and his generation had wanted for some time. Batista embraced youth, and the players he knew from the underage teams – the likes of Banega, Lavezzi, Gago, Lucas Biglia and Pastore – all returned to the squad. Batista also set about replicating conditions at Barcelona to harness Messi's ability, playing him as a 'false nine'.

In the friendlies under his watch, Argentina were sensational. They thrashed the seemingly unbeatable world champions Spain 4-1, with Messi central to the attacking play. He also scored the only goal in a 1-0 win against Brazil, Argentina's first victory over their eternal rivals in five years. That was great preparation for the 2011 Copa América held in Argentina but, unfortunately, at that point the issue of Tevez versus Messi came to a head.

Tevez was the favourite of Argentina fans thanks to his stardom at Boca, his origins in the slums of Buenos Aires, and his passion and personality. He was seen as everything Messi was not. The two got along well and had combined a few times for the national team but they could not play together naturally enough to sustain a run in the same side.

In the first two games of the Copa, Argentina drew 1-1 with Bolivia and 0-0 with Colombia. Messi was faltering, with Tevez little better. Making Argentina like Barcelona was not working. Argentina fans cheered Tevez and were cold towards Messi, the distant 'European' superstar who did not reflect Argentina's image of itself. Batista and his staff could see the issue – Messi should not have to play around a lesser talent or be second choice for passes into the forward lines. So Tevez was sacrificed, Gago introduced, and Messi pulled closer to midfield behind a young front line of Agüero, Higuaín and Di María.

After two draws, Argentina needed to beat an U23 Costa Rica side to avoid sliding out of the competition, something that would be deemed a disaster for the hosts. Messi finally showed the Argentine public why he had won the Ballon d'Or, with a brilliant exhibition of his exquisite ability. Movement, dribbling, passing, touch; here was the Messi many expected to see in an Argentina shirt but rarely glimpsed. It didn't last long, though. In the next game Argentina came up against a formidable, tactically disciplined Uruguay side sporting their own golden generation. The team that had reached the World Cup semi-finals featured Diego Forlán, Luis Suárez, Edinson Cavani and the best defence in South American football. Argentina were beaten on penalties despite Uruguay having ten men for more than an hour. In the acrimony afterwards, Batista was dismissed.

That was a rare approach by the AFA. In the past it had been reluctant to sack coaches, allowing them to see out their contracts or encouraging them to step down. But it had been 18 years since Argentina last won a title and desperation was a constant, with short-term thinking the new reality. They had Messi, and they needed to be winning trophies while he was in his prime.

* * *

The next coach on the merry-go-round was another former number ten who had proven himself an astute coach of well-organised teams. Alejandro Sabella had managed Estudiantes de La Plata since 2009, utilising the fading ability of Verón to win a Copa Libertadores and a Primera title, no small thing in an era when the former competition was dominated by more traditional Argentine and Brazilian clubs.

Estudiantes had been Sabella's first head coach job but he had been assistant to the legendary Daniel Passarella for years, following him from River Plate and the national team to Uruguay as well as jobs in Brazil, Italy and Mexico. Only Passarella's retirement allowed Sabella to step into the limelight. He was an intelligent coach and recognised that, to be successful, he needed to make Messi happy, although that went against his natural instincts to some extent.

Argentine football is broadly split between schools of thought dictated by the country's two World Cup-winning coaches – 'Menottistas', attack-minded coaches in the romantic mould of César Luis Menotti, vie with 'Bilardistas', more pragmatic, defensive coaches influenced by Carlos Bilardo. While Basile and Batista had definitely been under the spell of Menotti, Sabella was a Bilardo man, prizing hard work and organisation above fluidity and beauty.

Sabella struggled through his first year or so in charge to balance the resources at his disposal, just as his predecessors had done. The central question was how best to deploy Messi without disastrously unbalancing the team. His first move was to drop Tevez, with the aim of establishing a great team spirit and a happy camp. Although his popularity had made Tevez close to undroppable for years, the fact he missed a penalty in the shoot-out loss to Uruguay in the Copa América gave Sabella an opportunity to get rid of him.

Sabella took his chance – Tevez would never feature consistently for his country again – but it was also a message to Messi: you are the man now. Sabella underlined it by making Messi captain. Mascherano remained the most vocal, tactical voice on the pitch and in the dressing room but Messi was the star, and the team could not win without him. It became clear that something had shifted at the heart of the Argentina team. Making Messi feel comfortable and happy was now the priority. The notion was that if he could produce, Argentina would thrive.

Argentina came first in CONMEBOL qualifying after a faltering start. The players Sabella selected in attack and midfield seemed to understand that their roles included a lot of hard work and defensive responsibilities, allowing Messi to do what he could to hurt the opposition from a free role on the right. It worked, although Argentina never looked defensively stable. Messi's goalscoring rate surged with 25 goals in 32 games under Sabella.

Messi needed a functioning collective of the type Sabella provided; as long as the defence and midfield could avoid Argentina conceding too many, he could create enough at the other end for them to win the game. Sabella also fostered a relaxed atmosphere of respect and camaraderie – he was modest and lacked the ego of many of the giants who had come before him. He had none of the stubbornness of Bilardo, Menotti or Bielsa, nor was he as emotional and unpredictable as Maradona. Instead, he was popular with his players, thoughtful and well prepared.

At the 2014 World Cup in Brazil, Sabella's style came close to working for Argentina all the way to the trophy itself. Sabella had never seemed comfortable with the fragility of his side in defence. All the way through qualifying, Argentina lived on their nerves, one last-ditch covering run from Mascherano or a Garay clearance away from defeat.

In the first game at the World Cup, he opted for a defensive 5-3-2 formation against Bosnia and Herzegovina. Argentina took an early lead thanks to a fortuitous own goal, but they were awful. At half-time, many of the players spoke out – Messi most vocally – and Sabella quietly abandoned the formation, reverting to the 4-3-3 the team had used for the qualifying campaign. Argentina were efficient after that, doing just enough and allowing Messi to provide one or two moments a game. Messi responded, scoring once in that opener, a last-minute golazo that proved the winner against a defensive Iran, and two against Nigeria to win the group.

In the round-of-16 game, Argentina struggled against a dogged, talented Switzerland but never conceded. During extra time and heading for a penalty shoot-out, Messi ran at the heart of the Swiss defence, drawing players towards him before slipping a ball across for Di María to sidefoot into the far corner.

By now Argentina had momentum but with injuries robbing them of Agüero, and Higuaín and his understudies Rodrigo Palacio and Lavezzi all in fitful form in front of goal, there was even more pressure on a plainly exhausted Messi to deliver. Thousands of Argentinians had travelled north to Brazil and the team enjoyed deafening, passionate support everywhere they went. They beat Belgium 1-0 with a nervy performance in the quarter-finals and, when hosts Brazil were stunned by a 7-1 defeat by Germany, they became the last South American team in the competition. It seemed this could be their year, 21 years on from the last Argentine success in international competition.

Louis van Gaal had strategised his Netherlands team to the semi-finals with a combination of ageing but enduring beaten 2010 finalists and some exciting youngsters. His team had counter-attacked brilliantly throughout the tournament but, against Argentina, Van Gaal seemingly had only one idea – stop Messi. His team stifled Argentina's attacking players by packing the zones around their own box but sacrificed any attacking instincts. It worked to an extent, Messi didn't get a sniff in the game with one shot and only a couple of chances created, but the Netherlands were equally uninspired and Argentina held their nerve better in the shoot-out.

Messi was under extraordinary pressure heading into that 2014 final. A popular sentiment was that he needed to win a World Cup to be considered the equal of Maradona. The wonders he consistently performed at Barcelona had become routine, the public now expected Messi to perform wonders on a daily basis. But a World Cup Final? That was something else.

That German side was excellent – strong in virtually every position, dominant in midfield, tactically astute. The destruction of Brazil was an ominous watch for Sabella and his side.

In the final, Messi was again stifled. Germany controlled the centre of the park and he remained strangely peripheral. He had a few fine moments, though, and while Germany were certainly the stronger team, Argentina had by far the better chances. Higuaín, in particular, has never been forgiven in Argentina for the handful of opportunities he missed in normal time and the idea that Agüero's injury cost the team remains a compelling one.

It wasn't only Higuaín who was culpable, though. Palacio missed a chance and Messi missed a few, sending one shot past Manuel Neuer but also past the post. When Agüero was eventually introduced, he was clearly not 100 per cent fit and had little effect on the game.

Messi also missed his old attacking partner, Angel Di María, who was absent through injury. Di María and Messi had played together so much over the years that Messi had a habit of hitting blind passes into the channel where he knew Di María would be lurking. It would be effective right up to the 2022 World Cup but, in this final, Messi had no comparable partner.

Nevertheless, Argentina remained as hard to beat as they had been all tournament. Mascherano was magnificent, refusing to allow his team to concede. The game went to extra time but German substitute Mario Götze scored a fine winner in the 113th minute. Messi looked devastated. World Cup finals are a one-off for most footballers and he must have thought about the turmoil he had experienced with Argentina over the years and wondered whether he would ever get another chance. As a small consolation, Messi won the Golden Ball as player of the tournament, a move that met criticism due to his muted performances in the knockout phase of the competition.

* * *

For Messi, winning trophies had become habitual. It was a disaster for Barcelona to go a season without a trophy and his Argentina struggles must have been difficult to comprehend. The AFA understood that to some extent and realised Argentina would be paid handsomely to play friendlies across the world if Messi played. As at Barça, Messi remained a tourist attraction, a marquee name worth seeing in his own right. So the efforts to keep Messi happy intensified.

When Sabella resigned after the World Cup – his efforts finally appreciated to some extent in his homeland – he was replaced by Gerardo Martino, a known quantity for Messi. He was from Rosario and instead of Menotti or Bilardo, he was a 'Bielsista', a disciple of Bielsa. As a player, he was the attacking midfielder in Bielsa's legendary Newell's Old Boys side, and Bielsa's influence on his coaching ideas was obvious. His sides played hard-running, high-pressing attacking football. He had coached at a sprinkling of smaller Argentinian clubs as well as finding great success with Paraguayan giants Libertad before he took the job as Paraguay coach and revolutionised the side. He coached Paraguay to a World Cup in 2010, reaching the quarter-finals with a more pragmatic adaptation of Bielsa's style as Martino had no qualms about grinding out a result if he needed to.

He did even better at the 2011 Copa América, reaching the final only to lose to the same Uruguay team that had eliminated Batista's Argentina. Then it was back to Rosario and Newell's, where he saved the languishing club from relegation before winning a Primera title in 2013. Martino followed that with a barnstorming run at the Copa Libertadores, where his side lost a two-legged semi-final on penalties to Atlético Mineiro. That attracted Barcelona and Martino's star-studded team played fine football during his single year in Spain. Messi seemed happy and was his usual productive, inspired self but Barcelona lost out on the La Liga title on the last day of the season to Simeone's Atlético Madrid, and Martino resigned.

That meant he came to the Argentina job as someone who had worked with Messi, who understood him and who Messi liked. By that point, that was half the battle for an Argentina coach. The other half was making it all work on the field.

Martino tinkered during a year of friendlies, bringing back a calmer Tevez, who must have accepted his role as just another water carrier for Messi, and rejigging his midfield to make it more attacking in nature in the space between Messi and Mascherano. That was the approach entering the 2015 Copa América in Chile. Argentina had a fine squad, perhaps the best Messi had played in since 2006. Martino had pushed Messi into the front three where he was free to roam and create. He also played Di María as part of that forward line, with either Higuaín – enjoying a remarkable goalscoring run in Serie A at the time – or Agüero as the centre-forward. Javier Pastore played as something between a number ten and an Argentine number eight, linking productively with Messi and Di María, with either Banega or Biglia behind the ever-present, indestructible Mascherano.

Argentina stuttered to some degree in the group stage – creating bags of chances but not scoring as many goals as their football deserved. Messi again looked exhausted, his Barcelona efforts evidently not leaving much in the tank. He was also ageing and still learning how to efficiently use his energy in a game as his body changed. Where, as a youngster, he had been explosive, now he tended to be inactive for long periods of games, walking in small areas, watching the play. This was when he 'downloaded' the game – the patterns of play, the areas where there were spaces, the players he could target. Then he would come to life with short bursts of devastating productivity. As he grew older and his pace and stamina waned, Messi would perfect the ability to pace himself that way but, in 2015, he was just beginning to learn how to effectively manage his own energies. Nobody in their 30s can charge around all game.

Having topped the group, Argentina battered Colombia for 120 minutes but were forced by excellent goalkeeping to win on penalties. The team finally exploded against Paraguay in the semi-final, obliterating them 6-1 with a blistering attacking display. Messi pulled strings, threaded through balls, and rolled off dribbles and passes around players. He made playing exhausted look remarkably easy and created three of Argentina's goals in the game. Argentina looked to be enjoying themselves, something that was rare given the pressure the side always seemed to be under.

Martino's team faced Jorge Sampaoli's Chile in the final. Sampaoli was another Bielsista and his Universidad de Chile team had been a fabulously exciting and successful example of Bielsa's ideas in motion, winning three Chilean titles and the Copa Sudamericana.

Sampaoli's Chile side was constructed around a mixture of players he had coached at La U and those Bielsa had led to the 2010 World Cup. Classical enganche Jorge Valdívia and Messi's Barcelona team-mate Alexis Sánchez were the stars but there was a rock-solid foundation of quality players around them, ranging from the combative Arturo Vidal and

Gary Medel to the cerebral central midfield promptings of Marcelo Díaz, the energy of Charles Aránguiz, and the more exciting and creative Eduardo Vargas and Mati Fernández. It was Chile's greatest generation of players and they were determined to win a Copa América before they were too old.

In the final they singled out Messi for rough treatment as the teams cancelled one another out. Messi was relatively quiet and, again, Argentina faced a penalty shoot-out. Messi scored his penalty but when the unfortunate, seemingly cursed Higuaín missed his, followed by another miss from Banega, Chile were champions and Messi had missed out again.

In the aftermath, he refused to accept a player of the tournament award as criticism for his role in the defeat mounted from the Argentine media and fans online. The same old accusations were aired – he cared more about Barcelona, he wasn't really an Argentinian player in his approach or passion – but he had changed during the tournament, becoming more vocal, more of a leader. There were younger players emerging now and Messi was an experienced pro who they looked to for guidance and leadership. Those facets of his character were beginning to emerge just as he played his 100th game for his country in the group match against Jamaica.

Messi had another chance at a trophy with Argentina just a year later when the Copa América Centenario was held in the US. The 16-team tournament was a collaboration between the football confederations CONMEBOL and CONCACAF. Argentina would again reach the final – their third in succession – a demonstration of the Messi effect but also the enduring quality of their footballers.

The last time Argentina had reached successive finals had been in the early 1990s. Of course, few people in Argentina appreciated the achievement. All they saw was the fact none of those finals resulted in Argentina winning a trophy. Messi showed some rare emotion when questioned about it on Argentine TV. He knew about the criticism and people questioning his love for his country – and it angered him.

With every tournament came articles and TV pieces claiming this was Messi's 'last chance' to win something with Argentina, his 'last chance' to show he was the equal of Maradona. The pressure on him was extraordinary. Messi started the tournament with a back injury and missed the opening game, a 2-1 win over Chile. At that point he was also embroiled in a trial in Spain following accusations of tax evasion, which meant he had to fly back and forth across the Atlantic to attend court and join in with training, just another example of his commitment to the Argentinian cause.

He returned to the side rampant, scoring a hat-trick against an outmatched Panama in a 5-0 victory. The side was much the same as in the Copa América – Lavezzi was in for Tevez and Erik Lamela played more of a role – but the stalwarts of the past decade or so remained.

Argentina crushed an improving Venezuela in the quarter-finals, then swept USA aside in the semis. Higuaín scored a brace in each game, with Messi adding another two goals as part of five he scored in the competition overall. His goal against the USA lifted him above Gabriel Batistuta as Argentina's highest goalscorer, just another record broken in a lifetime of breaking records.

He also fashioned four assists in the tournament and, heading into a revenge-style final against Chile, it looked as though he might finally win a trophy for his country. But the final was a repeat of the Copa América a year before. Chile won on penalties after a bad-tempered, niggly game. Messi stepped up to take his penalty and hit it high over the bar. It seemed all the pressure had taken a toll after all. He was distraught on the pitch as Chile celebrated. Here was the passion and emotion Argentina fans had questioned. He cared, he put himself under more pressure than anyone, and he could barely cope.

His emotional response to the loss immediately after the game also suggested the pressure had become too much when he announced his international retirement. He had done his best, he said, reaching four finals, but he felt it would be best for everyone if he called it a day as it was obviously not meant to be. If ever Messi resembled Maradona, it was now; an emotional, impulsive decision taken in the heat of a painful defeat and delivered directly and honestly to a media hungry for any scrap he threw their way.

Argentina reeled at the news and, perhaps for the first time, the country began to realise what life would be like after Messi. Almost immediately a campaign began to convince him to stay. Mauricio Macri, president of Argentina and former chairman of Boca Juniors, appealed to him; fans begged him online and in person; and thousands gathered in Buenos Aires as part of an organised campaign.

Martino had resigned after the Copa defeat and Argentina appointed Edgardo Bauza to take over. Bauza found himself in a tricky position. The qualifiers for the 2018 World Cup began in September and he had taken on a team whose morale had been crushed by their series of near misses. Some key players were near the end of their careers and in definite decline and, as Batista had warned when his young side won Olympic gold in 2008, the Argentinian production line of talent was not what it once was. In a few years, a clutch of clubs would step up and donate some key players – notably River Plate, Boca Juniors and Vélez Sarsfield – but for a year or two it seemed as though the well had run dry.

Bauza, something of a journeyman in South American football, had been in Carlos Bilardo's 1990 World Cup squad and his football had some Bilardismo to it. Defensively solid and well organised, he had taken Ecuador's LDU Quito to a shock Copa Libertadores win in 2008.

He emphasised collective effort above star players and won the Libertadores by capitalising on the advantage playing at altitude gave his side in home games and a willingness to play a game based on aggressive wingers and physical strength.

That success eventually led him to San Lorenzo, one of Argentinian football's five 'grandes'. There he broke a curse that had been eternally used to taunt San Lorenzo fans when he won a Copa Libertadores in 2014. Again his side were pragmatic and unflashy, controlling midfield with something of a double pivot, using an old-school enganche in the form of Leandro Romagnoli to knit moves together and focusing attacks down the flanks. It worked, and when Martino went, Bauza's appointment made sense. He was, it is important to note, also from Rosario.

When Bauza journeyed to Europe in pre-season he visited Messi and Mascherano at Barcelona, seeking to persuade the number ten to return to the Argentina fold. Messi eventually agreed, announcing he loved his country and the shirt too much to stay away.

He would miss the first match of the qualifiers for the 2018 World Cup with a knee injury so Agüero wore the number 10 shirt against Ecuador in his stead. But Bauza, it appeared, was destined to be an unlucky Argentina coach. Agüero lasted 20 minutes before injury forced him off. Tevez replaced him and Argentina dominated possession for the majority of the game but, without their main creator, they were toothless and as defensively suspect as they had been for the past decade or so.

Garay and Otamendi played at the centre of defence and were probably the first-choice pairing. But Garay was starting to miss more and more games through injury, meaning the ageing Martín Demichelis was still in the squad alongside erratic youngster Rogelio Funes Mori and the equally unpredictable Marcos Rojo. When teams went at Argentina, even with Garay and Otamendi in tandem, they struggled.

Ecuador held on while Argentina controlled the ball, then hammered them on the break late in the game for a smash-and-grab 2-0 win. The Argentine media noted it all with its usual hypercritical hysteria. Was this how dependent on Messi Argentina had become? Could they even win without him any more? Bauza also came under increased scrutiny and all the uncertainties about his appointment became minutely articulated doubts and questions. He had never coached at this level before. Could he really command the respect of players of this calibre? Could he create a tactical plan convincing enough to improve them as a team? There were serious doubts that if he failed to stop Ecuador from scoring twice, he stood no chance against the likes of Neymar, Jesus and Firmino when Argentina encountered Brazil.

Messi returned to the team for Argentina's fifth game in the qualification process. In his absence they had endured laborious draws with Paraguay and Brazil and fortuitously beaten Colombia 1-0 in Barranquilla. Bauza's position was already being openly questioned by the Argentine media. Faced with a brewing crisis after that opening defeat to Ecuador, Bauza had gone back to basics – he set up his team to be solid and hard to beat, sacrificing attacking flair – but Argentina lacked the defensive strength to play an entirely defensive game. Inviting opponents on to them only loaded pressure into areas unable to withstand it and, without Messi, the team was unlikely to nick too many goals through moments of genius.

The problems remained even with Messi's return, however. The defence could not push up too high for fear of a lack of pace being exploited. Mascherano and his central midfield accomplice – usually Biglia at this point – were overworked, and even Messi had too much distance to cover when he dropped deep for the ball. Bauza's team was a mess, with or without Messi. The players still had great quality, though, and sometimes that would be enough. They beat Chile 2-1 on Messi's return and there followed an upswing in fortunes with wins over Bolivia and Uruguay in Buenos Aires. But it never really convinced.

When Messi was again injured for a game against Venezuela in Mérida in September 2016, Banega wore the number 10 shirt. With Biglia alongside, he was his usual impressive self, showcasing his orchestral range of passing, but Argentina could not turn their control of possession into control of the game and were reliant on a late Otamendi equaliser to rescue a point with a 2-2 draw.

That was followed by another 2-2 draw, this time against Peru. By that point, young star Paulo Dybala was filling the Messi role, with Agüero wearing the number 10 shirt – but Dybala was nowhere near ready and Agüero had never been a number ten. Just a few days later, things became worse – Argentina lost 1-0 in front of their own fans in Córdoba. Bauza's constant tinkering with his side was exacerbated by injuries to Otamendi, Funes Mori and Zabaleta. Perennial prospect Nicolás Gaitán replaced Messi, while Higuaín and Agüero both missed chances, Agüero even putting a penalty over the bar. The defeat left Argentina fifth in the table, outside the automatic qualification places.

Their next game was in Belo Horizonte against Tite's exciting Brazil side, who were top of the table. Bauza again went for a cautious, defensive plan in the hopes of protecting the soft underbelly the team possessed in place of a defence. He basically set two banks of four across the pitch, with an increasingly less-mobile Higuaín foraging up front and Messi behind him, expected to create whatever he could. Messi almost managed it too, showing flashes of his menacing speed and imagination early on. But once Neymar and Philippe Coutinho got at the Argentina defence, the game was over. Brazil ran out convincing 3-0 winners.

Unthinkably, Argentina looked in danger of not qualifying, slipping to sixth in the table, below the fifth spot that assured a play-off. Bauza again changed his team for the crucial game against Colombia. Old-fashioned number nine journeyman Lucas Pratto had featured in squads of late, and he started up front. Messi responded to the pressure and the raucous fans in San Juan, opening the scoring with a beautiful free kick. He then looped a lovely cross towards Pratto, and the target man buried a header into the corner. Argentine TV cut to Higuaín, looking mildly uncomfortable on the bench. Di María added a third to make it a lot more comfortable than anyone had expected.

The next game was a nervy 1-0 win over bogey team Chile, with Messi avenging his penalty miss by scoring the only goal, from the spot. Argentina moved back into the qualifying positions with that win, but they could not stay there. Without a suspended Messi, they looked toothless in a 2-0 loss to Bolivia in La Paz in March 2017, and dropped back to fifth place.

* * *

The AFA sacked Bauza a month later. The possibility that Argentina might fail to qualify was just too great and Bauza's record was even worse than Maradona's – his eight games had resulted in three wins, two draws and three defeats. Even worse, the football was frequently turgid, especially considering the talent in the squad, with more goals conceded than scored – nine for with ten against. It looked as though it would be the last World Cup for most of Messi's generation who had won that Olympic medal in 2008 – missing it entirely would be a disaster.

The AFA turned to Jorge Sampaoli to rescue qualification. Sampaoli's reputation was on a high at the time. After a peripatetic start to his coaching career, taking in roles at a dozen clubs across the continent, his success with Universidad de Chile had been stunning. He then led the Chile national team to a Copa América, perfecting the high press Bielsa had introduced and beating Argentina in the final along the way.

Omar Sivori, a perfect example of the scurrying, fearless 'pibe' who starred for River Plate and eventually played for Italy instead of Argentina.

Rene 'El loco' Houseman, star of the legendary Huracán team of the early 1970s and the Argentina side who won the 1978 World Cup. He foreshadowed Maradona in both talent and self-destructiveness.

Diego Maradona, already a star for Argentinos Juniors in 1980.

Maradona scores the 'Goal of the Century' against England on 22 June 1986 at the Azteca in Mexico City.

Serie A was full of brilliant playmakers in the 1980s and '90s, but even an artist like Platini admitted Maradona's greatness.

Claudio Borghi during his brief, ill-fated spell at AC Milan, 1987.

Ariel Ortega, River Plate icon, 2010.

Juan Román Riquelme toys with Real Madrid in the Toyota Cup.

Riquelme was sublime in the group stage of the 2006 World Cup.

Unlike so many others, Pablo Aimar made a success of a move to Europe at Valencia and then Benfica.

Carlos Marinelli wasn't ready for the Premier League.

Dario Conca, a pioneer in China.

Lionel Messi, breaking records at Barcelona.

Carlos Tevez, the 'player of the people', especially beloved by fans of Boca Juniors.

Messi equals Maradona's achievement with Argentina, December 2022.

Di Maria and Agüero, on opposing sides in the Manchester derby.

Diego Valeri's huge success at Portland Timbers opened up a path to the MLS for Argentine playmakers.

A move to Sevilla in La Liga had resulted in some dazzling football and inconsistent results but Sampaoli had shown he could deal with big egos and big stars. Messi knew of him and was said to approve of the appointment. Sampaoli was a dogmatic coach, wedded to one idea – inspired by Bielsa – of high-energy, high-press football that strangled the opposition in their own half and transitioned into attack with blinding speed.

Without that he could look a little lost, and Argentina did not have the players to execute the plan. The squad was ageing and incapable of the athletic feats the approach demanded so Sampaoli turned to what youth there was available. Dybala and exciting striker Mauro Icardi started his first qualifier against Uruguay but the same problems remained – there were no strong defenders emerging and the glut of talent in forward positions made it hard to find a system that brought the best out of Messi. Icardi and Dybala made no impression against Uruguay in a game typical of Argentina in that era – absolute control of possession, few viable goalscoring opportunities.

Messi looked frustrated. The contrast could not have been greater for him – he had played in a Barcelona side where there was a philosophy for more than a decade. Results came and went but the team always knew what they were doing, even with personnel changes. With Argentina, even when there was an idea, they did not have the players to make it work.

Sampaoli's second game was another atrocious draw, this time 1-1 with Venezuela in Buenos Aires. He changed his side yet again, showing that, like Bauza, he was struggling to solve the riddle of strengthening his side defensively. He dropped Mascherano back into defence, where he had been playing at Barcelona, and replaced him with Guido Pizarro alongside Banega in the middle. Messi, meanwhile, struggled to find any chemistry with Dybala and Icardi and another draw followed, 0-0 against an improving Peru at La Bombonera.

It all came down to a game in Quito against Ecuador in October 2017. Ecuador's win in Argentina had started the crisis, the worst period Messi had experienced with the national team. He had been persuaded to return only to witness a chaotic shambles of a qualifying campaign, and it came down to this last game. If Argentina failed to win, they would not qualify and presumably Messi would retire from the national team for good.

Sampaoli changed his team again. Darío Benedetto started up front but the defence was still the problem. Sampaoli played a back three with wing-backs – still desperate to press the opposition – but Ecuador took the lead inside the first minute when the diminutive Mascherano was beaten in the air by strapping striker Roberto Ordóñez and Romario Ibarra buried the knock-down.

The time had come for Messi to put in the kind of performance only genuinely great players can. Sampaoli's tinkering helped for once; his wing-backs allowed Messi and Di María freedom of the attacking areas of the pitch and they began to link the way they had been doing regularly since they were in youth teams together. Messi scored a hat-trick, two of the goals before half-time and the third coming after a tactical reorganisation designed to help Argentina see out the game, and the effects of altitude gave him a single opportunity in the second half. Messi was justifiably celebrated.

This was why he had returned to the international fold – the glory of success with Argentina – but that would have to wait.

The 2018 World Cup in Russia was the messiest Argentina had seen since Maradona's campaign in 2010. Sampaoli kept tweaking his side but nothing worked. Argentina were dreadful in an opening draw with minnows and World Cup debutants Iceland. Messi looked unhappy and stressed, and he performed fitfully.

Worse was to come. Croatia convincingly beat Argentina 3-0 in the second game. Too many players were underperforming, while a handful were not really up to the standards of an Argentina shirt. The main problem, however, was Sampaoli. His insistence on pressing left the old, slow defence exposed. After the game, Messi and Mascherano reportedly sat him down and told him how they wanted to play. Keeping things simple, going back to basics.

For the last group game, Argentina returned to a familiar 4-3-3 and ground out a 2-1 win over Nigeria to escape the group. Messi had apparently insisted Banega was included, understanding he had a range of vision and passing beyond anyone else in the squad, and so he was restored in midfield alongside Mascherano.

Banega had always enjoyed an understanding with fellow Rosario native Messi and they combined in exhilarating, superb fashion for the first goal. Banega picked out a precise, arcing long pass that Messi somehow took down on his thigh before placing a drive on the half-volley across the goalkeeper into the top corner. Messi was ecstatic in celebration. He was under so much pressure in that tournament, leading a creaking, anxious squad. The

TV cameras cut to a wild-eyed Maradona in the stands as he celebrated in a trance-like state.

Victor Moses equalised early in the second half to make it more painful – it always was with Argentina – but a late Marcos Rojo volley secured the win. Their reward was a game against an ominously strong France side containing the talents of Antoine Griezmann, Paul Pogba and young starlet Kylian Mbappé, already being spoken of as the player most likely to take on Messi's mantle as the world's best.

Sampaoli changed the team again, introducing the pace of Cristian Pavón, and the sides produced the game of the tournament with a surging, oscillating 4-3 win by France. Mbappé scored twice so the stock media line was that he had outshone Messi but it was more a case of France coach Didier Deschamps outwitting Sampaoli. The Argentina coach was experimenting by playing Messi alone up front but he found himself isolated and hampered by Blaise Matuidi, who Deschamps had tasked with pressuring the number ten. Even when he decided to drop into his more natural position and Agüero was introduced, France devoted a lot of energy to shutting Messi down.

Deschamps also allowed Argentina's defence to carry the ball upfield and encouraged his team to exploit the space that created with quick passes towards the insanely pacy Mbappé. His direct running terrified the Argentine defence, causing Rojo to concede a penalty early on and enabling him to score two later on to effectively win the game. Messi still had moments, his clipped pass for Agüero's late header was perfectly placed and weighted, but his team had lost. Another World Cup was gone and he was not the equal of Maradona, it seemed.

* * *

Nevertheless, his Barcelona successes continued. While the team was struggling under coach Ernesto Valverde, Messi had learned how to carry his side. His influence was frankly ridiculous in 2018/19. He scored 51 goals in 49 games that season, winning his sixth Golden Shoe. He also contributed 13 assists and was the dominant player in Barcelona's misfiring forward line in which Coutinho flopped and Dembélé was rarely fit. At the end of the season, Messi won another Ballon d'Or.

Messi had avoided the World Cup fallout as the Argentinian press and public had learned not to blame him and it was obvious he had been struggling with the tactics and personnel around him as much as he had with the opposition. Instead, Sampaoli was castigated. Mascherano retired, exhausted from years of trying to protect a fragile defence, and the generation Messi had grown up with was starting to fall away. The issue for the AFA was that Sampaoli had been given a lucrative five-year contract and sacking him after a year could cost them as much as £7m. Negotiations began instead and Sampaoli agreed to step down 'by mutual consent', accepting a £1m pay-off.

Messi had stated he would not play in Argentina's September friendlies and doubted he would play again for the national team in 2018. Rumours and conjecture began that he was planning his international retirement again. César Luis Menotti – in his strange role as a sort of executive at the top of the Argentina international set-up – said he felt Messi just needed a break and would be back. In the meantime, Argentina were without a coach.

Candidates with immense domestic success such as Marcelo Gallardo were mooted, as were Argentinians thriving abroad – the likes of Simeone and Mauricio Pochettino at Champions League clubs. But the cash-strapped AFA could not really afford any of those options. Instead, they delved into the youth-team coaching staff to pick Lionel Scaloni, who had played with Messi in that 2006 side.

Scaloni had been Sampaoli's assistant at Sevilla and with the national team, while also coaching the U20 team where he and his friend and assistant Pablo Aimar became acquainted with the next generation of talent awaiting their chance to make the first team. Scaloni and Aimar were given the Argentina job on a caretaker basis, a move much criticised by the country's media. Scaloni's lack of experience was the main objection, although there was recognition that he was cheap and could do no worse than Sampaoli.

Initially Scaloni had a series of friendlies to oversee and without Messi he could look at strengthening his midfield and, crucially, his defence. He immediately set about transfusing some young blood into his squad. Higuaín was dropped, while midfielders Leandro Paredes, Rodrigo De Paul and Gio Lo Celso were introduced alongside Lautaro Martínez up front. But the defence remained problematic and it would not be until the 2021 Copa América that Scaloni seemed confident in the unit he had formed. By then, young players had emerged who would be the basis of the defence at the 2022 World Cup in Qatar.

Scaloni's most important job was to convince Messi to return and he did that via a Zoom call in early 2019, when he and Aimar outlined their vision and plans. Scaloni has since claimed the key to their success was the fact Aimar was Messi's boyhood idol. True or not, it can't have done any harm. Messi demonstrated his commitment over the next few years, sticking with Scaloni as his club career transformed. Indeed, during a turbulent period in Europe it seemed as though Argentina had become a refuge. In this young team he had some trusted old friends alongside him – Agüero, Otamendi and Di María most notably – and a dressing room full of young players who were awestruck by him, lived and died by his respect in training, and just wanted to make him happy.

* * *

Messi captained Argentina in the 2019 Copa América in Brazil but Scaloni was still working out his best side and the defence was still an issue that would cost them. An opening defeat to an exciting Colombia was followed by a draw with Eduardo Berizzo's tough, Bielsista Paraguay team. Argentina needed a Messi penalty to rescue that one.

At the ripe old age of 31, Messi was more voluble and emotional than he had been with the national team before, perhaps reflecting the way things were going at Barcelona, where he was increasingly unhappy. It felt like – perhaps for the first time in his long, incredible career – Argentina had become the priority. He was much more obviously a leader, handling more press duties than before, protective of and encouraging the younger players in the squad.

In terms of on the pitch, Messi had started to understand how to play in bursts. He no longer pressed or defended; he strolled, watched and waited. He liked the ball played to his feet, which meant Scaloni's preferred 'vertical' football was hampered by his best player. But even then, Messi had the tactical intelligence to use the ball to make up for his decreased pace and energy. He could play accurate one-touch passes to maintain the speed of a break. His dribbling was still mesmeric; he could get beyond a man but was unable to keep ahead of them so he tended to slow opponents, befuddle them with a feint, and then use the ball in the instant he had created.

Argentina needed to beat Copa guests Qatar to qualify from the group stage, and they did that with goals from Martínez and Agüero. That sent them into a quarter-final against Venezuela where another early Martínez goal settled nerves and a late second from Lo Celso sealed the game.

The semi-final was a huge clash with Brazil, who had a much more settled squad and a more experienced coach in Tite. But Argentina acquitted themselves well, even as they lost 2-0. Messi was handed a suspension and was fined for an uncharacteristic swipe at refereeing decisions he claimed had gone Brazil's way but even this seemed a positive. Messi was engaged and passionate, just as the fickle football public had always wanted him to be.

In the aftermath of the tournament, Scaloni was given a contract upgrade. He was no longer a caretaker coach and continued to blood young talent in friendlies, building towards the 2021 Copa América with the aim to filter some into the squad during the qualifiers for the 2022 World Cup, which were due to begin in October 2020. The Covid-19 pandemic would change all that.

* * *

Barcelona were already in crisis mode when coronavirus struck, with countries and industries closing across the globe. Suddenly the club had no gate money for Camp Nou's 80,000 seats, no sales to tourists from their club shop or hugely profitable tours of the stadium itself. It was the same across European football. Only the wealthiest clubs had insulation but Barcelona had spent wildly for years and, as football returned with games played in eerily empty stadiums, the extent of the crisis became clear.

Messi was already unhappy and made it clear through the media. He had not agreed with some footballing decisions – the departure of his friend Luis Suárez for one – while his contract discussions were dragging on. For the first time, it looked as though he might leave Barcelona. Eventually it came down to the fact that, given their financial crisis and new La Liga rules, Barça could not afford to renew Messi's contract and pay him the immense wages he had become accustomed to. 'Sources' justified the move with claims he was not the same player and that he needed to be moved on to build a new side. In truth, Messi had made the decision easy for Barcelona, complaining about decisions taken by president Josep María Bartomeu, sending the club a document in summer 2020 explaining his desire to leave, and complaining that La Liga had enforced a contract stipulation.

Against this backdrop Messi made his way back and forth to South America for Argentina's qualifying games in 2020 and 2021. By now, Scaloni was more assured and his team understood what was expected of them. They were efficient as the youngsters settled in and there were even some new central defenders emerging. Cristian Romero and Lisandro Martínez looked a likely centre-back pairing for the next decade but the progress of Lucas Martínez Quarta and Marcos Senesi suggested there was also depth below them, while Otamendi remained a big presence in the side.

The team used Messi the way he dictated; he chose when he would burst into life. Qualification was relatively serene, lacking any of the habitual nasty shocks. Instead, they won most games in impressive fashion and drew a few as Scaloni tested different players before the Copa América and the World Cup itself.

The 2021 Copa América was the latest in a long line of 'last chance' competitions for Messi. This was a trophy Maradona had never won, of course, but by now the comparisons between the players rang hollow anyway. Maradona had died of a heart attack on 25 November 2020. An outpouring of love for him and all he had represented swept the football world, and Messi paid his own tribute, peeling off his Barcelona jersey while celebrating a goal against Osasuna to reveal a vintage Adidas Newell's Old Boys shirt beneath and bearing Diego's number ten on the back. On that day, his trademark two fingers pointing to the sky gesture was for both his grandmother and his predecessor as the world's greatest player.

Messi's longevity and consistency were staggering compared with Maradona's career but in that he was supported by what football had become in the modern era. Everything had been fine-tuned to allow a footballer to fulfil his or her potential. It was the perfect time to play football. The game had changed so much with nutrition, sports science, playing surfaces, boots, balls, training methods, tactical awareness and, most crucially, the way referees protected players all advancing massively.

That means comparisons are fundamentally flawed. Messi had been playing at an elite level for 14 years or so, with few perceptible dips, while Maradona managed perhaps five years at a similar level. Yet, until Messi managed to win an international trophy with Argentina, that comparison would always be held up to put him in his place. Maradona carried Argentina to a World Cup, why couldn't you?

With Scaloni's help, Messi looked to rectify that by leading Argentina to their first Copa América since 1993. By now, the team had adapted to Messi and what he needed at this late stage in his career. He was surrounded by players who complemented him and allowed him to play in devastating bursts. If the rest of the team did their jobs and prevented the opposition from scoring, Messi was likely to score or create a goal or two.

He had a strong midfield behind him now. Paredes was cultured and controlling with his passing, while De Paul was more an iron-lunged enforcer who was also progressive in possession. Di María was still around and his understanding with Messi stretched back 15 years and often appeared telepathic. Agüero was more of an impact sub at this stage, his movement still excellent around the box, his finishing better than it had ever been. All three of those old team-mates were 33 years of age at the start of the tournament, as was Alejandro 'Papu' Gómez, a gifted playmaker who had broken into the squad late, on the back of his sustained excellence for Atalanta's superb Serie A form. But there was youth too. River Plate's phenomenal young talent Julián Álvarez and Stuttgart's Nico Domínguez were both knocking on the door of the first team, alongside the new blood in defence.

There was also a new goalkeeper, which would ultimately prove crucial. Emiliano Martínez had been in English football since he left Independiente for Arsenal at the age of 17. But he had never settled anywhere, going on loan season after season to clubs across the English divisions plus a spell at Getafe. However, an injury to Arsenal's first-choice keeper Bernd Leno saw Martínez called into action for the run-in and he played in the FA Cup Final, performing heroics. A transfer to Aston Villa followed, where Martínez's performances were commanding and consistent. He was rewarded with a spot in the Argentina first team, and his surprised delight made him hugely popular on social media.

These players had grown up idolising Messi and were desperate to win a trophy for him. Argentina were professional and smooth in their progress through the tournament. Scaloni and his backroom staff created a calm atmosphere and a strong team spirit, which meant the side overcame hurdles with an understated confidence. For all their individual talent, Argentina felt like a team without stars. Yes, they had the biggest star of all, but Messi never acted like one. He mucked in, joked with the boys and obviously prized being part of the collective.

Covid restrictions led to Argentina training in Buenos Aires before flying to Brazil for each Copa América game and then jetting straight back home. It was less than ideal preparation but Argentina seemed to thrive on it, forging a siege mentality and togetherness that Messi loved. He scored their only goal in the opening 1-1 draw with Chile, then assisted the only goal in their 1-0 win over Uruguay. That featured a trademark shimmy to evade a defender followed by a pinpoint cross for Guido Rodríguez to head high into the net. Fellow veterans Di María and Gómez then combined with Messi for the winner against Paraguay in another almost restrained Argentina performance. Di

María slipped a threaded pass into the box, where Papu finished on the turn.

A lack of drama in the camp and the consistency the team was displaying looked promising. Messi appeared happier on national duty than he had been for years, as if the confidence of knowing he was playing in an Argentina side that was unusually solid had taken a weight from his shoulders. A video emerged during the tournament of a group of Messi's team-mates entering his room at night and giving him presents, singing 'happy birthday' to him and generally larking about. Messi seemed to love all of it, and that was reflected in his form. He could be quiet for long periods of games now but, when he came to life, he always made a difference, always made things happen.

Messi had a hand in every one of Argentina's 11 goals on their march to the final. He would float, receive the ball, and then head towards goal, sometimes via a one-two, sometimes with a dribble or a misdirected shimmy. His team-mates made runs off and around him, confident he would pick the right pass. Opposition defenders were wary of tackling him. Messi had always ridden challenges well so, if a tackle was less than perfect, he would evade it and be in position to do damage or accept the foul and the promising free kick it created.

In the quarter-finals, Argentina blew Ecuador away 3-0. Messi assisted the first two, sweeping a first-time pass to De Paul to finish after a mix-up in the Ecuadorian defence and feeding Lautaro Martínez after Di María had won the ball on the edge of the box. Messi finished the game himself with a deft free kick in stoppage time. After each goal, the team ran to Messi to celebrate.

The semi-final was a 1-1 draw with Colombia that led to the dreaded penalties. Messi's generation had been here before and could be forgiven for suffering nerves but in 'Dibu' Martínez they had a goalkeeper who loved penalty shoot-outs, who thrived on the gamesmanship and was imposing and dynamic enough to make saves unless the penalty kick was perfectly placed. He barracked Colombians, ostentatiously celebrated saves and misses, and despite De Paul miscuing his effort, Martínez's heroics meant Argentina won the shoot-out 3-2, with Colombia missing three penalties. Messi labelled Dibu a 'phenomenon'.

The final was another clash with Brazil. Argentina were on top early on and Di María scored after 22 minutes, taking a long, quarterback-style pass from De Paul on the bounce and chipping Ederson for a lovely goal. After that, Argentina were happy to concede possession while looking to catch Brazil on the counter, mimicking what Brazil had been doing to them for the past decade or so. The game became fractious and niggly as the sides traded chances, including a couple for Messi, but Argentina held on to win that elusive trophy.

Celebrations in the squad and in Argentina were unrestrained and joyous. Messi had finally done it. The rest of the football world celebrated on Messi's behalf, too, feeling he had deserved and earned it. The Copa Final was Argentina's 20th unbeaten game in a row and they looked serious contenders to add the World Cup in Qatar to their trophy cabinet.

* * *

Messi returned to Europe and the newfound chaos of his club career. He was now officially a free agent as his

Barcelona contract had expired. Negotiations were ongoing and it was plain that Messi hoped Barça would blink first and give him what he asked for. However, he eventually agreed to a huge pay cut of up to 50% to make it easier for the club – but even that amount of money wasn't there. Messi must have sensed Barcelona's executives were starting to plan for life without him so he joined Paris Saint-Germain on 10 August 2021 on a free transfer.

PSG were bankrolled by gulf state Qatar and Messi reportedly earned more than £80m from the move but that didn't prevent a tearful exit at a Barcelona press conference when he called them the 'club of my life'. His children had been born and raised in Catalonia and he had lived there longer than he had in Argentina. Messi must also have realised he might not be the top man in a team where Neymar and Mbappé were already battling for supremacy and coaches were rarely given more than a season to develop a style before being dismissed.

Unsurprisingly, his first season was difficult. PSG were almost guaranteed to win the Ligue 1 title – traditional contenders such as Marseille and Lyon had been dwarfed by their financial might and left scrapping for second and third place. Champions League success had become PSG's main focus. Messi had been bought partly for the stardust but also for his huge Champions League experience. Despite their seemingly unlimited funds, PSG had struggled in Champions League knockout ties, losing their nerve and choking in a series of winnable games.

Messi struggled for form all season, though, picking up knocks, suffering from Covid-19 and failing to gel with Neymar and Mbappé, but there was optimism heading into the round of 16. The PSG side Messi lined up with had more galácticos than the youthful Real Madrid they were facing. The legendary midfield of Modrić, Kroos and Casemiro was ageing and could be controlled by Paredes, Verratti and Danilo. Neymar, not fully fit, was on the bench, but his replacement was Di María, who would work harder and combine better with Messi and Mbappé than the egotistical Brazilian.

PSG dominated the first leg at the Parc des Princes in Paris and should have scored four or five. They only managed one, when Mbappé squeezed between two defenders after a lovely backheel from substitute Neymar to score a 94th-minute winner. Earlier, Messi had a penalty saved by Thibaut Courtois. In Madrid, PSG choked once more. Mbappé had given them a 1-0 lead at half-time, putting them two goals up on aggregate, but Madrid came roaring back, three Benzema goals swinging the tie their way and eliminating the French club.

The league all but won already, PSG fans were quick to blame Messi and Neymar for another Champions League failure. The South Americans were booed in their next game and Messi admitted his first season in France had not lived up to his expectations but he knew his second would be better. During that time Messi was periodically returning to the Argentina squad to help extend his nation's unbeaten record. Their progress through the World Cup qualifiers was serene. Buoyed by the confidence they earned with the Copa América win and the unity within the squad, this was a side that rarely thrilled the way some previous Argentina teams had but always did enough to get a result.

In September 2021, Messi scored a hat-trick against Bolivia at the Monumental in a neat show of where he stood in the football of his homeland at that moment. The first was wonderful; he turned outside the Bolivia box, almost dead centre between the goalposts, nutmegged a defender and curled a finish inside the post from outside the area. The Monumental celebrated with deafening noise, while his team-mates swamped him. Argentina loved Lionel Messi these days. His second involved an exchange of one-twos with Lautaro Martínez, a neat little dribble away from a defender, and a simple finish. The third was a poacher's goal, pouncing on a deflected shot.

Argentina looked more assured and secure for the first time since the Pékerman era. The nickname 'La Scaloneta', in recognition of the job the coach had done, became more popular as the team grew in stature. The team put together a 36-game unbeaten run through the qualifiers and heading into the World Cup.

Scaloni had some selection problems before that tournament. Agüero had been forced to retire in 2021 after he had a heart condition diagnosed following his arrival at Barcelona so Julián Álvarez came in as a centre-forward option. Copa América stalwart Gio Lo Celso was injured, so to reinforce his midfield Scaloni brought in young Enzo Fernández, controlling and composed at Benfica after moving from Gallardo's River, and Alexis Mac Allister, thriving as a playmaker in the Premier League for Brighton and Hove Albion after a move from Boca. Both would become crucial pieces of the Argentina team that would compete in Qatar.

And this was it – winning the Copa América was amazing but Messi wanted the World Cup. He knew it would be huge for his legacy. The two players commonly regarded as the greatest in history, Pelé and Maradona, were both defined by winning the trophy. Was Zinedine Zidane a better player than Michel Platini? Probably not, but he had won a World Cup with France and that made a compelling argument in his favour. Qatar was probably Messi's last tournament but he was the happiest he had been with Argentina and they went into the World Cup among the favourites as usual. Of course the gods of football would have something to say about that.

* * *

Argentina began with a game against traditional minnows Saudi Arabia and, for all that the hysterical reports claimed otherwise, Argentina battered them. Messi scored a tenth-minute penalty to give them the lead and they probed and pushed thereafter, with the Saudis hanging on and hoping to hit them on the counter. Argentina dominated possession and had 20 shots on goal but looked relatively out of sorts. De Paul was off form and he, Paredes and Papu Gómez looked an awkward trio in midfield, lacking the security provided by Lo Celso's mix of drive and guile. Lautaro Martínez was also in the middle of a poor run and his confidence looked shot in the forward positions beside Messi. When he had a chance, it never felt certain that he would score.

Saudi Arabia were rapid when they broke forward and exposed Argentina twice in five second-half minutes to turn the game around. The Argentinians were frantic in their attempts to respond but it was not enough; they had lost their opening game 2-1 in what was instantly one of the greatest shocks in tournament history. That made the second game against old rivals Mexico a must-win. Scaloni uncharacteristically overreacted to the Saudi

Arabia defeat and made a string of changes in an effort to find the balance suddenly missing from his team. Guido Rodríguez and Mac Allister joined Lo Celso in midfield, while Lisandro Martínez replaced Romero at centre-back. Unsurprisingly the team played like strangers and the first half was a grind for both teams, with midfield deadlock and little imagination on display. Messi flickered in patches.

The balance only shifted with the introduction of Enzo Fernández after 57 minutes. He is in the mould of a Gago or Redondo; moving gracefully around the pitch and establishing a rhythm with his varied, excellent passing but not above snatching up a loose ball or crunching into a tackle when the need arises. With his arrival, Argentina suddenly clicked; Mac Allister and De Paul looked liberated, and Argentina began to flow. Álvarez had replaced Lautaro too, and his running and sharpness occupied the Mexican defence and gave Messi more space to work in.

The first goal had a familiar look. Messi took a pass from Di María on the edge of the area and placed a shot low inside the post before going bananas in front of the raucous Argentina fans. The second was a formal announcement of Enzo Fernández's arrival on the World Cup stage. He jinked past a player into the box, opened his body and curled a shot inside the far post.

Scaloni was a shrewd coach and noticed the effect Fernández had on the team. He started the third game, against Poland, as did Álvarez up front. Argentina were a joy to watch against an outgunned Poland. The midfield trio of De Paul, Mac Allister and Fernández were fluid, tough and indefatigable. Messi did what he did these days; prompting, beating players, creating moves out of nothing. The team also showed its growth.

When Messi had a first-half penalty saved by Wojciech Szczęsny, the others came through. First Mac Allister fizzed a skimming shot along the ground and in off a post, then the two youngsters who had played together under Gallardo at River combined when Enzo played in Álvarez for a fine finish. The game finished 2-0, but Argentina could have scored many more.

They were growing into the tournament with no danger of peaking early. Scaloni's side faced a well-organised and dogged Australia in the round of 16. It was the 1,000th game of Messi's career and he opened the scoring with a trademark one-two played off Mac Allister before a firm finish. The reception to the goal was interesting; nobody was surprised. Messi was playing with such authority it appeared he could force the issue whenever he wanted. When this team needed him, he responded.

In the second half Álvarez and De Paul combined to press the Australian goalkeeper and Álvarez capitalised with another goal. Desperate, Australia threw everything at Argentina and pulled a goal back after a horrific deflection off Enzo in the 77th minute. Argentina wobbled but did not concede. They would face the Netherlands in the quarter-finals.

That game proved a classic. Argentina began on the front foot and Messi showed his genius early on. His dribbling had been different at this tournament. He ran at defences and toyed with defenders, the ball hovering beneath his body while he was on his toes like a penguin with an egg. He could still shimmy but his feints and shifts of weight were sublime pieces of theatre now, making opponents wobble, lose their bearings and commit themselves. Sometimes he made them back off, afraid that if they got too close some piece of trickery would outwit them.

Messi ran at the Dutch defence in the 35th minute, heading towards the penalty area in a diagonal line from the right wing. He slowed, shifted pace and surged again. Nathan Aké, unsure of how hard to press him and which direction to cover, gave him just a fraction too much space. Messi had already seen the beginning of a run by Argentina right-back Nahuel Molina; they had shared a flank for much of the tournament and Messi had come to understand his patterns of play and how to find him. Still, there were six Netherlands players in two loose lines of three between Messi and the goal, Molina's run right in the middle of the cluster. Messi delayed a beat, took a touch away from goal, then somehow found Molina with one of the great World Cup assists. He played the pass blind, a sharp little swing of his left foot guiding it on to Molina who took one touch with his left to shift the ball on to his right before prodding in his first goal for his country.

Argentina were in control after that, Messi adding another goal from the penalty spot in the 73rd minute. As the Australians had done, the Netherlands went for broke. Coach Louis van Gaal introduced enormous striker Wout Weghorst and went route one, sending long passes and crosses towards him at every opportunity. It worked. Argentina panicked, dropped deep, and Weghorst pulled one back in the 83rd minute, then snatched an equaliser in the 11th minute of added time from a clever free-kick routine.

In extra time, Argentina recovered their poise and had several excellent chances to score a winner, Fernández hitting the post with a drive from distance in the last minute, but it went to penalties. Dibu Martínez was in his element as the Dutch and Argentine players tried to distract and wind each other up. The first two Netherlands kicks were saved, with Messi coolly scoring his in between. Lautaro, whose confidence still seemed an issue, was the player who scored the winning penalty.

Argentina celebrated with even more glee and energy than usual. Messi ran to the Dutch bench to cup his ears in front of Van Gaal and the coaching staff. Many in Argentina read this as Messi referencing Van Gaal's treatment of Messi's old team-mate Riquelme when they were at Barcelona. To follow that, Messi interrupted an interview with Argentine TV to aggressively dismiss and insult a Dutch player, seemingly a starstruck Weghorst wanting a Messi shirt. The Argentinian public loved it, their talisman playing with such machismo and fire. They loved hearing his Rosario accent in that moment but, more than that, they loved seeing him play like this, winning in a young team.

Argentina swept Croatia aside in the semi-final. Messi scored a 34th-minute penalty before two Álvarez goals in the second half made the result safe. Álvarez's first goal was a long run at the heart of the Croatia defence from halfway, scoring with a half-volley when the ball rebounded to him off the foot of a defender. Messi seemed to be enjoying himself. Joško Gvardiol had been one of the standout defenders at the tournament but it was as if Messi decided to break him in this game.

In the first half he shrugged Gvardiol off, shifted away while dismissing the bigger man's efforts to outmuscle him, and rifled a shot at goal. Then, in the 69th minute, he went on a long run from the right. He beat Gvardiol once, turning first one way and then the other at speed. Gvardiol had pace and stayed with Messi, constantly throwing an arm at his chest, trying to tag him, jostle him. Messi slowed, shifted gears again, stopped and turned, then beat Gvardiol once more at the touchline. Free for an instant, he found Álvarez, who scored with a one-touch finish.

Croatia offered little real resistance and it felt as though Argentina were playing within themselves, just waiting for the final. That game, on 18 December, would be against France, who had eliminated Argentina in 2018 and were defending champions. Again, it was billed as Messi vs Mbappé, the old master versus the young apprentice. Both men played superbly in what turned into a classic final, perhaps the most dramatic in history.

Argentina were in control for an hour or so, creating a string of chances. France looked sluggish and casual – there was speculation a respiratory virus was still circulating through the squad as their passivity was otherwise baffling. Messi was elusive and deadly, Mbappé isolated and not in the game. The Argentinian midfield had a stranglehold on the game, creating their passing triangles, nicking the ball off French players, and controlling the centre of the pitch.

An electric Di María was tripped in the area by an uncomfortable, otherwise-anonymous Ousmane Dembélé in the 23rd minute and Messi stepped up to score the resulting penalty. Di María added a second after 36 minutes, finishing a beautifully sweeping Argentina move that involved a Messi flick and a lovely pass into space by Mac Allister.

France coach Deschamps saw what was happening and made two substitutions before half-time, replacing the invisible Dembélé and Giroud with the youth and pace of

Randal Kolo Muani and Marcus Thuram. It didn't change much; Di María and Messi's continual links in attack had the French permanently on the back foot. It was only when a shattered Di María was replaced by Marcos Acuña after an hour that the momentum shifted. Messi's reliable attacking partner was gone, and Deschamps capitalised when he introduced more youthful energy in the form of Kingsley Coman and Eduardo Camavinga.

France had nothing to lose and began to drive forward, their passing crisper, players fresher. They started to win second balls and make effective interceptions. But still Argentina kept them at arm's length, without a shot on goal until Muani was fouled by Otamendi in the 80th minute and Mbappé scored the resulting penalty. Less than two minutes later, Mbappé scored a wonderful second to level the game.

Argentina re-established control but now France were in the game, finally looking for Mbappé and his pace to stretch Argentina. Messi had a rasping long-distance shot saved by Lloris in the dying seconds before the game moved into extra time. In the 108th minute, Messi scored again, a close-range scramble after Lloris had only been able to bounce a Lautaro shot away. But France equalised once more, a contentious penalty given for a handball against Gonzalo Montiel. Martínez saved a Muani shot with a brilliantly outstretched foot in the last seconds and the game went to penalties.

Messi scored his kick, cool and casual. Mbappé also scored his, seemingly immune to Martínez's mind games. His young team-mates were more susceptible, however. Martínez saved from Coman; then, after Dybala had scored, kicked the ball away in the lead-up to Aurélien

Tchouaméni's effort. Tchouaméni put his shot wide, and Argentina had the advantage. The deciding penalty went to Montiel, who had been so unlucky with the handball decision. He buried it, and Argentina and Messi were finally world champions.

In the aftermath, during the wash of acclaim for Argentina and Scaloni, an almost universal love for Messi was evident. The football world had wanted this for him; it removed any asterisk beside his name, any doubt about his status alongside or even above Maradona.

He won his second Golden Ball for player of the tournament, while Martínez and Fernández won goalkeeper and young player awards, just to emphasise that this was a victory for Scaloni's collective ethos.

Argentina celebrated as millions took to the streets to join in parades and parties. Oddly enough, supporters from their traditional rivals Brazil and Uruguay had been supporting Argentina in the latter stages of the competition, too. They wanted a South American nation to win. If football had long been tilting towards the Old World because of European money, this showed that the Americas could still compete. It was the continent's first World Cup since Brazil's win in 2002.

Messi was a figure right at the heart of those issues. Defiantly Argentine, with his love of yerba maté, his Rosario accent and his commitment to the national team, he had been forced to accept he needed that European money early on in his career. He was a blend of two footballing cultures – his essence was that uncoachable pibe of Argentine legend most associated with Maradona. He dribbled, invented, deceived. He was uncatchable, almost unstoppable; a genius at the gambeta. But he had been moulded in the academy at a European superclub where players were coached incessantly, where patterns of play were encoded, where systems removed some of the magic and spontaneity from this most improvisational of games.

Messi needed those systems – they provided the platform for his sorcery to be possible, they allowed him to invent. And sometimes with Argentina they had let him down. But not at this late stage in his career after it had looked as though it might never happen. It was notable, too, how his build and style stood out against opponents. The French and Dutch teams were filled with super-athletes; huge, muscular, powerful and technically adept. That was also the case with England and Germany and was the norm in European football, where more diminutive players such as Phil Foden and some of the Spanish squad were the exceptions to the rule.

Even those smaller players – lauded for their technique and imagination – had been coached to play in systems, and lacked the sheer creativity and magic of the kind of players who had worn the Argentina number 10 shirt over the decades. Many of them looked decidedly average when removed from the systems they knew, just as Messi had done at points during his long history with Argentina. But he had learned to adapt, and he had been patient.

The question of whether he was better than Maradona had not really been answered. It was more that Messi, through his consistency and undeniable genius, had rendered the question irrelevant. He was Messi. From now on, Argentinian players would not only be compared to Maradona, they would be compared to him.

TEN

Ezequiel Lavezzi, 'El Pocho'
Angel Di María, 'Fideo'
Sergio Agüero, 'Kun'

OTHER PLAYERS from Messi's generation were named as possible new Maradonas as they developed. They all emerged in Argentina, while Messi's European trajectory meant his eventual arrival fully formed in the Argentine consciousness meant he was like a total eclipse; all other 'new Maradonas' were suddenly obscured by the enormity of his talent. Most of those other emerging stars had fascinating careers of their own, however, intersecting with the legend of Maradona and the career of their peer Messi along the way.

Ezequiel Lavezzi hails from Villa Gobernador Gálvez in Greater Rosario, making him another Rosarino in the group surrounding Messi in Argentina squads. He was raised by a single mother and his older brothers in what he has characterised as a 'hard-scrabble setting'.

Lavezzi played seven-a-side football for Sol Naciente from the age of four, then from the age of 12 for Coronel

Aguirre, where his pace and quick feet marked him out as special. His nickname 'El Pocho' (the chubby one) came not only from his build but also from a dog he had as a child, although he had the classic stocky power and pace of generations of Argentinian attackers.

His quality quickly attracted European attention and Italian Serie C side Fermana flew him to Italy for trials, where he impressed. However, at the time, it was against European Union law for a Serie C side to sign an underage citizen of a non-EU country. On his return to Argentina, Lavezzi was taken in by Boca Juniors' huge youth system, but they declined to offer him a contract after almost eight months in their sides.

Lavezzi briefly quit football before Club Atlético Estudiantes of Buenos Aires offered him a contract. He spent three years there, graduating into the first team, where his blistering single season as an 18-year-old resulted in 17 goals from 39 games, mostly in the Primera B Metropolitana.

Lavezzi could play across the attack. Probably best suited to old-fashioned wing play, he was pacy and aggressive, full of trickery and imagination, and never stopped running. Those qualities transferred well to a position as second striker, where his sharpness on the ball created space and a goal threat. Best of all, he had some of the fire and rage Argentinians love; he was mischievous, provocative and loved winning.

His success for Estudiantes again attracted European interest. In 2004, Genoa, a famous old Italian club that had enjoyed some success with Argentinian imports, bought him for €1m. He was immediately loaned back to Argentina, this time to Buenos Aires giants San Lorenzo.

There, he proved he could handle the Primera, scoring eight goals in his first season.

The idea had been that Lavezzi would return to Italy after a year in Argentina but a match-fixing scandal meant Genoa were demoted to Serie C and, in dire financial straights, they sold Lavezzi outright to San Lorenzo for €1.3m. He took up the number 10 shirt and, now used to the pace and technical level of the league, set about tearing up Argentinian football.

He was never quite a classic number ten, however, the 'pausa' was never part of his game, which was more dependent on energy and ceaseless motion. He would score 25 goals in 84 games at San Lorenzo and, in his final season, the club won the Argentinian title for the first time in six years, under legendary coach Ramón Díaz.

There was no talk of Lavezzi as the new Maradona at this stage – his progress had been too faltering and his game more one-dimensional – but his move back to Europe guaranteed those comparisons would be made.

* * *

Napoli had been in the doldrums since the Maradona era ended. Relegation, bankruptcy and years of massive underachievement were erased, however, when they climbed back to Serie A in 2007. Extrovert film producer Aurelio De Laurentiis was the club's chairman and he wanted some statement signings to ensure Napoli stayed in the top division where they belonged.

He signed exciting Slovak attacking midfielder Marek Hamšík from Brescia, where he had impressed, then turned to South America, adding Uruguayans Walter Gargano and Marcelo Zalayeta to Lavezzi, who cost €6m. The new Napoli squad was competitive and ended the season in eighth place, with Lavezzi proving a fans' favourite and attracting those inevitable Maradona comparisons from an excitable Italian football press. That showed the power of the Maradona myth extended far beyond Argentina – perhaps nowhere quite as forcefully as in Naples. Lavezzi's performances were nowhere near Maradona's level, in truth, but he was short, loved a dribble, direct, and extremely passionate. When he was good, he was very good – scoring the first hat-trick by a Napoli player in years, against Pisa in the Coppa Italia. His finishing wasn't consistent enough – something that would be an issue throughout his career – but he still scored eight goals in 35 games that season.

Lavezzi himself dismissed the Maradona talk, instead comparing himself to Tevez, who had a similarity in terms of competitive spirit and energy. He would remain at Napoli for five years, a key presence as the club established itself as a genuine force in Italian football and returned to European competition. Once Edinson Cavani was signed from Palermo, Lavezzi had a genuinely world-class strike partner, and Napoli recruited wisely as they built on that first season back in Serie A. The likes of Hugo Campagnaro and Goran Pandev added experience and quality.

In 2012, the club won their first trophy in years when they defeated Juventus 2-0 to win the Coppa Italia. After that, Lavezzi was off to France via a big-money transfer to PSG. He had scored 48 goals in 118 Napoli appearances and established himself in the national team during his time there.

His Argentina debut came in 2007, while he was still at San Lorenzo, although he had played and roomed with

Messi for the U20s before that. After his debut, Lavezzi suffered from a glut of players in his position. He had the favour of certain coaches but not others. Batista liked him – he had been used regularly during the 2008 Olympic tournament and only really became established for the Albiceleste once Batista was made coach.

Basile and Maradona both preferred others but Batista was loyal to the players who had succeeded for him at youth level, so Lavezzi played at the 2011 Copa América. Sabella also liked his hard work and commitment – and his closeness with Messi, often still isolated with the national team – and he played in six games at the 2014 World Cup, snatching two assists but no goals.

Martino saw something in him too, including him in the squads for the 2015 Copa América and the Centenario the year after. Lavezzi started that tournament showing his best form for his country, with two goals in the first five games. After scoring against the USA, Lavezzi was hugely unlucky when he fell backwards over an advertising hoarding while chesting a high ball. He broke his elbow on landing and missed the final, where Argentina lost to Chile on penalties. He only appeared for his country a handful of times after that and, once he had chased the money offered by Chinese football, it was as if he had unofficially retired from the national team.

That China move came after four seasons at PSG, from 2012 to 2016. PSG had paid Napoli €30m for his signature and Lavezzi joined a team already full of talent and expectant of success. Lavezzi had not necessarily wanted to leave Naples, he just wanted more money. De Laurentiis was infuriated and accused him of a lack of professionalism. Lavezzi's love life was fodder for Argentine trash media, meanwhile, as he had a penchant for dating models and a Maradona-esque love of the high life.

In Paris, Lavezzi was consistent on the pitch, if perhaps not as spectacular as Parisian fans had hoped. Alongside the flamboyant Javier Pastore and charismatic Zlatan Ibrahimović, his 11 goals in 42 games that season helped PSG to the French title. He was soon joined by his Napoli striker partner Cavani, and the French side won two more titles in the next two seasons as Lavezzi scored 21 goals in 93 games.

In 2015/16, he played less, partly due to the arrival of his international colleague Angel Di María, and in February 2016 he signed for Hebei China Fortune in Langfang, who played in the Chinese Super League. The move would reportedly net Lavezzi £10m a year and, at the age of 31, increasingly injury-prone and decreasingly effective, it made sense. He was there for four seasons and gave his all, with 35 goals in 75 games before announcing his retirement in November 2019.

* * *

If it was not for the existence of Lionel Messi, there is a very good chance Angel Di María would be regarded as the greatest Argentinian player of his generation. Like Messi and Lavezzi, Di María hails from Rosario. His father made charcoal bricks in the back garden and money was always a struggle for the family – Di María remembers his mother fixing his boots with glue because they could not afford to buy new ones.

He started playing football at the age of four after a doctor told his mother the sport could help with his hyperactivity. After only a year at local club Torito, Rosario

Central came calling. Di María's father was a Newell's fan and not keen on the move, emphasising they could not get their son to the Rosario Central training ground without a car, but his mother was a 'canalla', or Rosario Central die-hard, and cycled him the nine miles there and back, carrying him on the bike with his little sister.

Angel was a spindly boy – hence his nickname 'Fideo' (the noodle) – and slow to develop but he was athletic, hardworking, and astoundingly talented. He could beat a man, especially on his left side; had pace to surge by people; could shoot; was excellent with set pieces; imaginative; and creative with his passing. He could play on the wing or as the enganche.

After toiling for years in Central's youth teams, always a little smaller and skinnier than his peers, a sudden growth spurt allied with his accustomed ability to grind made a difference to his performance level. Di María made his debut for Rosario Central in December 2005 at the age of 18, and his progress over the next year and a half was startling enough that he was called up to the Argentina squad for the U20 World Cup in Canada in 2007. There, he would play alongside young men who would be his team-mates for the next 15 years – Sergio Agüero, Éver Banega, Papu Gómez and goalkeeper Sergio Romero.

Argentina won the tournament, with Di María one of the stars of the team, scoring three goals from the left wing. In July that year, Portuguese giants Benfica bought him for €8m. Acquired to replace departing star Simao, Di María didn't settle straight away and it was only in his second and especially third seasons that the Benfica faithful saw what he was capable of. Then, he was stronger and more accustomed to the demands of European football, and his directness and skill allowed him to dominate matches and destroy opposition teams.

Any Maradona comparisons were made on the basis of Di María on one of his better days – when he was in the mood, he was unplayable. He was courageous, tough and repeatedly ran defenders ragged; ceaselessly dribbling, playing in team-mates, shooting from all angles. He seemed to have it all. But he had frequent off-days too, days when his decision-making was awful, where he made silly tackles, gave the ball away, and ran about like a headless chicken. He had a knack for scoring and performing when it mattered most, though. He was a big-game player.

That wasn't quite evident in his first year at Benfica, however. Then, he was mostly on the bench and used as a substitute when his pace and ball carrying could torment tired teams. When he was called up to the squad for the 2008 Olympic tournament, he played alongside Messi for the first time. Di María has spoken about their on-field connection as feeling like magic. He could make a run to find Messi had somehow put the ball at his feet. That relationship would be a constant for Argentina all the way to the 2022 World Cup Final. In 2008, Di María showed his clutch qualities by scoring the winner in extra time during the quarter-final against the Netherlands from a Messi pass. Then he scored the only goal in the final against Nigeria with a deft chip over the goalkeeper.

* * *

His third season at Benfica was his breakout year in Europe. The unplayable version of Di María showed up more and more, with ten goals in 45 appearances. In summer

2010, Real Madrid came calling, wanting to add him to their incredible roster of galácticos. José Mourinho was assembling a team fit to take on Guardiola's all-conquering Barcelona, and he built a team around the defensive rocks of Sergio Ramos and Pepe, with Xabi Alonso in midfield and Cristiano Ronaldo and Karim Benzema leading the forward line. Di María joined a small group of Argentines he would have known from youth teams: Gago, Garay and Higuaín.

Mourinho also added exciting young Germans Sami Khedira and Mesut Özil to an overstuffed squad that still featured Brazilians Marcelo and Kaká. Di María fitted right in and Mourinho appreciated his work ethic and Argentine fighting spirit. He was also willing to learn and became more defensively aware than ever before. Di María made 53 appearances that season, scoring nine goals, as Madrid were beaten to the La Liga title by Barça by four points and eliminated from the Champions League by the same team in a momentous semi-final.

Di María stayed at Madrid for the next four seasons, winning a league title and the 'Decima' – the club's tenth Champions League. Although his quality was not quite so breathtaking in a side also containing Ronaldo, Gareth Bale and Modrić, Di María retained his ability to come good in the biggest games, winning man of the match in the 2014 Champions League Final.

He was also a fine team player, leading the La Liga statistics for assists, especially after coach Carlo Ancelotti moved him into a more traditional number ten role. This was a good chance to assess the short-lived Maradona comparisons of old and, beyond some skills, Di María had more of a resemblance to his old Rosario Central idol, Kily

González. His years as an out-and-out winger had changed his game and made him more direct and more vertical in approach.

Madrid fans loved him but the club is a complex organism and he was never quite as marketable or essential as some of his team-mates. The emergence of Colombian attacking midfielder James Rodríguez drew covetous eyes from the Bernabéu and adding him would have given the club three top-quality attacking midfielders competing for one position, with young Spaniard Isco still developing. While Di María was at the 2014 World Cup, he received a letter from Madrid telling him he must not play in the final. He had picked up an injury and they wanted to protect their property as they needed a big-money sale to enable them to purchase Rodríguez. It turned out Di María was not fit enough to play anyway but it was the breaking point in his relationship with the club.

* * *

Madrid sold him to Manchester United in August 2014 for a then-British-record £59.7m. Di María did not want to go and nor did his wife, who later criticised more or less every aspect of British life in an interview. Once the summer ebbed away, they hated the British climate but the money was incredible and United were one of the few clubs big enough for a player of Di María's stature. He was not the new Maradona or anywhere near, but he was one of the best players of his generation.

United were in the middle of a long period of seemingly endless transition at the time, still recovering from the retirement of Sir Alex Ferguson and searching for an identity. Each coach that came in bought and sold players, resulting in a patchwork squad full of talent but without any coherent vision for how they could play together.

Louis van Gaal started that season with a bold attacking idea – he wanted to play with a midfield diamond, which had worked for him at other places in his long career. But he misused players to make it work and the Premier League is not the place to experiment with player roles. Van Gaal repurposed Daley Blind as a midfield screen, tried the versatile Ander Herrera as a linking player, and Di María? Well, Van Gaal could not seem to work out how to use Di María.

He was given the sacred number 7 shirt at the club, previously worn by legends such as Bryan Robson, Eric Cantona, David Beckham and Cristiano Ronaldo. This was some hint to the expectations – United assumed he would be their next great player. He started off incredibly well, too, establishing an immediate understanding with the likes of Wayne Rooney and Juan Mata in the first weeks of the season. But a game against Leicester in September 2014 changed everything.

Di María scored early with a beautiful lob and United were on the front foot and looking as though they might score with every attack but Van Gaal had neglected to prepare his defence accordingly and, although United scored three, they conceded five. After that, Van Gaal became much more cagey and controlling in his tactics. He moved Di María around, playing him in six different positions during the season, but Di María struggled, as so many have, with the physicality of the British game, its ferocity and relentless pace.

For lazy journalists and fans, he seemed not to fancy the weather or conditions – the occasionally ugly beauty of English football. People remembered he had written a message to Madrid fans on social media when his transfer was confirmed, pleading that he had never wanted to leave Madrid and blaming politics at the club. In February 2015, his house was burgled. With young children and an unhappy wife, it seemed as though he had already decided the UK was not for him.

He left United – labelled a huge flop – for PSG in August 2015 for a fee of £44m. There he would return to the form seen at Madrid over seven impressive seasons. In a team filled with talent, his hard work and spirit stood out and made him a fan favourite. He would go on to score 92 goals and record 112 assists in 295 games for the French club, winning five league titles and nine domestic cups. In July 2022, at the age of 34, he left Paris for Juventus on a free transfer.

For all his enduring success as a club player, Di María will perhaps be better remembered for his heroics with Argentina. There, he became Messi's most dependable wingman, scoring crucial goals, providing stylish assists, always adding energy and a winning mentality, even if it was often not quite enough. He played alongside Messi in every World Cup between 2010 and 2022 and every Copa América in the same period. He was generally a key player in the Argentina team at those tournaments, stationed on the left, stretching the attack across the pitch while Messi came in from the right.

He was reliably excellent – that unplayable Di María was far more likely to show up in a big game for Argentina than in any for his clubs. He also retained the ability to perform when it was most needed. He scored the winner in the final of the 2021 Copa América against Brazil with a fine chip.

In the 2022 World Cup Final he was sensational; winning a penalty and scoring a goal before he was substituted, plainly exhausted. France had been unable to contain him for an hour and his brilliance gave Messi more time and space to shine. Di María's substitution allowed France to get back into the game, and his subsequent dramatic agonies on the bench as he watched extra time and the penalty shoot-out went viral online and made him resemble a fan suffering like everybody else.

He was too distinctive and too individual for the Maradona comparisons to have ever made sense, but his career was outstanding, a quite thorough expression of his talent over almost two decades of football.

* * *

While the likes of Di María earned a 'new Maradona' tag because of his quality on the pitch and his dribbling ability, and Lavezzi got it because of his move to Napoli, Sergio Agüero qualified under several criteria. First, he broke a record set by Maradona when he made his debut for Independiente on 5 July 2003. At the age of 15 years and 35 days, he became the youngest player to play in the Primera, breaking a 27-year record.

Like Maradona, Agüero emerged from a hugely impoverished background in Buenos Aires. His mother and father had moved to the capital from Tucumán as teenagers and he was born within months of their arrival. His father struggled for work and the family suffered the effects of a huge flood and the looting that followed. They were also subjected to robbery and extortion during the early years of his life.

They eventually left the tough district of Gonzalez Catan and moved to Florencio Varela, where their house was next door to a 'potrero', one of the rough informal football pitches that have contributed so many players to Argentinian football culture. Agüero has spoken of playing football constantly, of playing with older boys and adjusting. As many of his childhood friends fell into lives of criminality, Agüero only grew more obsessed with football. He was playing from the age of four and in that period he picked up his nickname. 'Kun' came from his favourite Japanese cartoon, an anime entitled *Wanpaku Omukashi Kumu Kumu*. It followed the adventures of a Stone Age family with a mischievous little boy, and it was reportedly toddler Sergio's attempts to pronounce the name that earned him the nickname from a neighbour, although other stories say it was because of his resemblance to his favourite character.

His potential on the pitch was obvious, even as a five-year-old, and over the next few years his father took him all over Buenos Aires for training and games with his youth teams, Los Primos and Loma Alegre. His story then becomes familiar; little Agüero was already a different class to his peers. He scored bags of goals and beat players at will. He was short and squat but had searing pace. He was obviously special and was poached by Independiente in 1997 at the age of nine.

Lanús and Quilmes had been interested in signing him but both clubs demanded that anybody in youth negotiations had to be a club member and the Agüero family, with seven children and still living in relative poverty, could not afford the fees. That benefited Independiente, who had no such rules, but a couple of other giants were hovering – Boca and River both made offers. What swayed Agüero's father to Los Rojos, however, was the fact local businessman Samuel

Liberman had started investing in Independiente's best young prospects.

Uruguayan striker Diego Forlán had gone through that process and now Liberman legally acquired 100 per cent of the economic rights to Agüero for the next ten years. In exchange, he bought the family a bigger house in a better area, paid for Sergio to attend a private school and made regular monthly payments. Agüero's father even got a part-time job as a kitman at the club. That again showed similarities between Agüero and Maradona – the legendary pibe from the barrio whose football excellence lifts his family out of poverty – but he had his own, distinct personality. Smiling, charming and warmly charismatic, Agüero was hard for even opponents to dislike.

It was his finishing that really set Agüero apart. He was intelligent enough and possessed an instinctive ability to find space in the most crowded of penalty boxes, most likely honed in the crowded, hectic potreros of his childhood. It was then-Independiente coach César Luis Menotti, legendary 1978 Argentina coach and iconoclast, who noted the player Agüero really resembled was the Brazilian Romário. They were similar in stature, gait, sharpness, movement, and their way of making even tap-ins move with venom. But it is also the reason the 'new Maradona' talk died quickly in his case – he was not a number ten.

Agüero did drop into the hole on occasion, could play in team-mates with his intelligent use of space and was a good team player. He was a tousled-haired, mischievous pibe, alright, but he wasn't a playmaker – he was a number nine, a goalscorer, a finisher.

His favourite European player growing up was Michael Owen, the English phenomenon whose pace and cold-blooded precision were lethal before injuries undid him. And Agüero had similarities to Owen as well as Romário; he could burn off defenders through sheer acceleration, while his shooting was ice cold.

After his early Independiente debut, Agüero didn't feature much for a year or so, instead playing in youth teams. But when he was ready and graduated to the senior team, between 2004 and 2006, he scored 23 goals in 56 games, a sensational record for a teenager.

The financial realities of Argentine football being what they were meant Independiente could never hope to keep this exciting young star and he was snapped up by Atlético Madrid in May 2006 for €20m.

In Spain, he was eased in with many appearances off the bench in his first season, with Fernando Torres as first-choice striker. With the sale of Torres to Liverpool in 2007, Agüero was reunited with Forlán from Independiente. His finishing was as precise as ever – he scored 27 goals in 50 appearances that season and more or less matched that rate from then on, with 101 goals for Atlético in 234 games. He won the Europa League in 2010 when Atlético beat Fulham in the final but injuries had started to affect his progress and, like many players with such a stunning change of pace, Agüero's hamstrings would be a problem throughout his career, a problem that started in his early 20s in Madrid.

* * *

Nevertheless, his development was fantastic and bigger, richer clubs than Atléti were circling. Most notable were the newly wealthy Manchester City. Financed by an Abu Dhabi company whose majority shareholder was Sheikh

Mansour bin Zayed Al Nahyan, a politician, businessman and member of Abu Dhabi's ruling family, City were determined to make themselves one of the top clubs in European football. Agüero, understandably, went where he had the best chance of winning trophies and where he would be best paid. Both things happened for him in Manchester after his £35m transfer.

At that point the 'new Maradona' label should have evaporated – even his new coach Roberto Mancini noted Agüero's resemblance to Romário – but Agüero had married Maradona's youngest daughter, Giannina, in 2008 after meeting her in Madrid. Their marriage produced a son, Benjamin, in February 2009 and football fans were already excited about the potential talent a boy with a mix of Maradona and Agüero's DNA might possess. The marriage only lasted four years but it tied Agüero's name to Maradona's forever. Not that he needed that association in order to be celebrated. At City, he broke records and made history. During ten seasons and 390 games, he scored 260 goals, won five league titles, six EFL Cups and an FA Cup as City made themselves part of England's new 'Big Six' and established themselves as part of the European elite. He also became City's all-time top goalscorer and made himself immortal on 13 May 2012 when he scored a 94th-minute winner to beat QPR 3-2 to seal City's first league title of the modern era, providing a platform for further success.

After a terrific decade in Manchester, Agüero found himself playing less in 2019 and 2020. He had never really been a Pep Guardiola favourite. The Catalan tactician could not ignore his effectiveness but there was always tension between them and the feeling that Guardiola would have preferred a forward who was more tactically flexible. The caricature of Guardiola is of someone who is such a tactical purist, he only really wants to win one way – and Agüero's goals were not really that way.

Guardiola publicly professed his love for Agüero but, when the striker started to lose a step due to age and injury, Guardiola was quick to bench him. The Argentine, so used to being the star man, was not going to accept that for long and, as City brought in new players in every transfer window, the situation was only going to worsen. In summer 2021, he moved to Barcelona on a free transfer.

* * *

For all his success at club level, Agüero has never hidden the fact that the Argentina national team is where his heart truly lies. He was selected for the youth sides and tasted success young, too, then spent most of his senior career as part of a heralded generation, seeking to recapture that glory. He finally got there in his last tournament.

As a teenager, he played in and won two consecutive FIFA World Youth Championships. In 2005, he was in a squad alongside Gago, Garay, Biglia, Zabaleta and Messi, which was where the two became room-mates and lifelong friends. Later, this would become a problem; they were so close there was talk that Messi only spoke to Agüero on away trips.

In 2007, he was an old head alongside Banega, Di María, Romero and Gómez. He would be the top scorer and breakout star of that tournament, winning both the Golden Boot and the Golden Ball as best player while captaining the side to glory. He must have assumed that playing for Argentina was easy – a non-stop parade of success, surrounded by great players.

The 2008 Olympics would have only emphasised this – another win, another medal, playing alongside the likes of Messi and Riquelme, scoring more goals. But Agüero's Argentina career was never quite what it might have been. Although he became the third-highest goalscorer in Argentina's history, behind only Messi and Batistuta, with 41 goals in 101 games, he played in three World Cups but failed to score a goal in the tournament until his first game in Russia in 2018, when he found the net against Iceland in a 1-1 draw.

Like Messi, he often carried knocks and niggles into summer tournaments and, even when he was fit, the draining demands of a season at a European club competing in multiple competitions had an impact on his body – he often looked fatigued, and his performances were not at his usual level. However, he was talented enough and intelligent enough to still score, assist and make an impact in games.

In 2014, a fit Agüero would surely have scored one of the chances missed in the final against Germany. Those chances mostly fell to Higuaín, who was often Agüero's strike partner for Argentina, but some coaches felt that in a system that utilised Messi best, only one of the two forwards could play. Higuaín was taller, better in the air and a more obvious physical presence than Agüero, and he was often favoured.

The Copa América was a similar story. Agüero played in four tournaments as well as the Centenario and although his scoring rate was better than at World Cups – albeit against a lower standard of opposition – again he underperformed due to tiredness and injuries.

He was part of the squad that finally won a senior trophy, however, under Lionel Scaloni in Brazil in 2021.

By now, Higuaín had departed the international scene but Lautaro Martínez had emerged as the preferred option at centre-forward. Players such as Nicolás González and Julián Álvarez waited in the wings but Agüero could still perform when asked; he assisted a goal for his friend Messi in Argentina's 4-1 win against Bolivia.

Agüero would have been part of the squad for the 2022 World Cup in Qatar. His 'dream' move to Barcelona had shown promise; with the team in transition his experience would be useful and he scored his first goal in a defeat against Real Madrid. But he felt chest pains during a 1-1 draw with Alavés in October and was taken to hospital. There he was diagnosed with cardiac arrhythmia, an irregular heartbeat. Doctors advised him to quit football and fitted him with a chip to monitor his heart. Agüero announced his retirement during an emotional press conference in December.

During the Covid lockdowns, he had opened up a new career for himself – streaming his marathon online gaming sessions on the Twitch platform. He had always had a warm and engaging personality, and he quickly garnered more than a million followers. He rang Messi live during one session and in another answered questions and spoke candidly about his condition and retirement.

He had been part of the Argentina national team for 16 years before he retired and Scaloni recognised how big a hole he left – not only on the pitch but in the group dynamic – so he went along to the 2022 World Cup as part of Argentina's staff; not as a coach, just part of the group. He was there to give Messi a man-of-the-match award in the group stages and was there, celebrating on the pitch with the victorious players, after the final.

Messi sat on Agüero's shoulders, World Cup trophy in his hands. Not many begrudged Agüero his involvement – a player who had given as much as he had. Not the new Maradona or even, really, the new Romário, but a legend in his own right.

ELEVEN

Javier Pastore, 'El Flaco' Maximiliano Moralez, 'Frasquito'

ON 5 July 2009, Vélez Sarsfield played Huracán at the José Amalfitani Stadium in the last game of the 2009 Clausura. It was a decider, basically, with Huracán in first place, ahead of second-placed Vélez by a single point. It felt, however, like there was more at stake than just the league title – both clubs were contenders for the unofficial title of the 'sixth Grande'.

Argentina's 'Big Five' are established by history, popularity, cultural impact and success. Boca Juniors and River Plate stand slightly apart, while San Lorenzo, Independiente and Racing Club are the other established, acknowledged giants.

Beyond those there are another five clubs vying to be regarded as the sixth club alongside the generally accepted list. All the clubs have heritage, big fanbases and were included on FIFA's list of the 11 'classic' Argentinian football clubs alongside small-but-influential Argentinos Juniors. There are the two Rosario giants in the form of Newell's Old Boys and Rosario Central; Estudiantes from

La Plata; and only two other clubs from Buenos Aires – Huracán and Vélez.

In 2009, Huracán were looking to win their first title since Menotti had taken their swashbuckling, stylish side to triumph in 1973. The club had established itself with a series of trophies in the 1920s and remained one of the biggest in Buenos Aires, forming a traditional rivalry with San Lorenzo, even if they were always in the shadow of that club and the rest of the 'grandes'.

Menotti's team gave 'El Globo' an identity it has maintained to varying degrees ever since – a club that tries to play stylish football. Perhaps the truest, closest expression of that idea came in the 2000s when Angel Cappa took charge.

Cappa was a middling player who learned at Menotti's feet as an assistant coach at Barcelona. He then became a journeyman coach across Argentinian and Spanish football, rarely lasting more than a season anywhere as he worked at the likes of Banfield, Las Palmas and Racing Club. He had already endured a disappointing season at Huracán in 1988, when they were labouring in Nacional B, before a league title in Peru with Universitario gave his résumé some sparkle.

When he returned to Huracán, little was expected of him or the club besides mid-table mediocrity as his team was composed of youngsters and rejects from other clubs. Yet Cappa chanced upon the purest expression of la nuestra Argentina had seen in years, with a beautiful short-passing, ceaselessly offensive team that was a joy to watch. And that joy centred around a few revelatory young talents who seemed destined for great things. Chief among them was Javier Pastore.

Vélez Sarsfield had a very different profile. Although they are another of the old clubs of Buenos Aires, their first success came with a league title in 1968, and they really flourished from the 1990s onwards. In the modern era they have been one of the best-run clubs in Argentina, combining an ability to consistently produce and sell young players with the knack of creating winning sides and avoiding too many messy transitional seasons. Since 1993, Vélez have won nine league titles, a Copa Libertadores and four other South American trophies. That and their infamous barra bravas mean they have been going toe-to-toe with the Big Five for the past two decades.

In 2009 they were coached by Ricardo Gareca, a club legend as a player and the man whose goal had ensured Argentina qualified for the 1986 World Cup, although Bilardo left him out of the squad for the tournament. They were built on a tremendously solid defence, marshalled by the young Nicolás Otamendi, but also had a powerful attack. That was focused around a classic enganche and Argentina youth-team star in the form of Maxi Moralez, who was surrounded by the power and presence of Uruguayan target man Santiago Silva and the pace and trickery of Juan Manuel Martínez.

While Huracán received all the plaudits from the media and neutrals for the beauty of their play – particularly after a 4-0 destruction of River Plate – Vélez had put together a long run of strong results to keep them in the hunt for the title. Going into that last match, Vélez needed a win but Huracán would win the title with a draw, always an odd position to be in for a team who played their best football going forward. The game itself was far from a classic, but its drama and repercussions give it a resonance within Argentinian football.

'La Final Bastarda' was played in front of a rabid crowd of 'El Fortin' fans and Vélez responded to the backing by dominating most of the game. Huracán had started the better, however, and had a goal wrongly ruled out a few minutes in after the linesman judged Eduardo Domínguez was offside when he headed into an empty net. That decision was so evidently bad, their bench and players became distracted and a sense of injustice began to fester.

Despite that, Huracán stayed on the front foot until the match was suspended after an apocalyptic hailstorm. It appeared that the game would be abandoned, but referee Gabriel Brazenas led the players back out on to a pitch covered with hailstones the size of tennis balls. The surface didn't help Huracán's sophisticated short-passing game in any way, and they started to falter.

Vélez were awarded a penalty soon after the restart but Hernán Rodrigo López Mora's shot was saved by Gastón Monzón, who was destined to become a key figure in the outcome of the game. Vélez settled in, dominating possession and space, with Huracán finding a couple of great chances on the break in the first half. Pastore and Moralez both flickered, with Huracán's other young creator, the 'new Messi' Matías Defederico, a more obvious threat with his direct dribbling into channels.

In the second half, Otamendi handled in the box. Already on a yellow card, he should have been sent off but was not and the few Huracán fans in the stadium and Cappa's coaching staff were incensed. Seven minutes from time, it got worse.

Joaquín Larrivey was a product of Huracán's youth system but was back in Argentina with Vélez after a year on the bench in Italy at Cagliari. He and Monzón both darted towards a header from López Mora and, when the ball bounced between them, Larrivey seemed to leave his foot in on the goalkeeper, who writhed in the box as the ball broke loose. Moralez swept it home, Monzón still on the ground, then wheeled away to celebrate maniacally, tearing off his shirt to earn himself a second booking and a sending off.

It took Brazenas almost two minutes to actually issue that red card such was the chaos that erupted after the goal. Huracán's players and bench all protested, minor scuffles broke out, and once it was all cleared up the referee had to play 13 minutes of stoppage time. Even against ten men, a clearly rattled Huracán failed to break through and their best late chance was cleared off the line.

Pastore and Defederico had found themselves swamped by the battle and, when Vélez celebrated their victory and the title, it was seen in many quarters as a match that said something important about Argentinian football. In the aftermath, Huracán fans protested outside AFA headquarters, while Brazenas never refereed another game, claiming he was retiring due to physical problems. That game was to follow him around, however, and he would be accosted by a Huracán fan while watching Argentina at the 2018 World Cup in Russia nine years later.

Cappa stayed at Huracán for another season but Pastore, Defederico and eventually classy defensive midfielder Mario Bolatti were all sold, ripping the heart from the team and sowing the seeds of the club's relegation just two years later, in 2011. Huracán's inability to win the title that many believed they deserved seemed to be symptomatic of the death of something poetic and magical in Argentine club football – Cappa and his acolytes sold that idea in interviews and articles. Vélez and their football were painted as cynical, even agricultural, which does players such as Moralez, Martínez and Emiliano Papa a disservice.

Moralez might have beaten Pastore in that game but they were to have radically different careers, both interesting examples of the way international football was beginning to regard the phenomenon of the Argentine number ten a decade after Maradona's retirement, with Riquelme near his peak and Messi suggesting he might be the greatest player of his generation. Pastore and Moralez were a tier or two below those players but were still talented footballers, and their contrasting paths were fascinating.

* * *

Javier Pastore was born in Córdoba in June 1989 and grew up in a comfortable middle-class family. His nickname, 'El Flaco' (skinny one), comes from his days in schoolboy football, at which point his skill and athleticism was already evident. He signed for Talleres in 2007 and made his debut for the first team at the age of 17, under Gareca in the Nacional B.

He was primarily a substitute that year and moved to Huracán in 2008. His explosion there was sudden and unequivocal; he was seen as perhaps the greatest talent Argentina had produced since Messi emerged a few years before. Pastore spoke of his adoration of Riquelme, and that was evident in his style. He drifted into pockets of space and played some sublime passes between the lines. He seemed to possess the preternatural vision of the born number ten, slipping balls along invisible lines into the paths of team-mates.

But there were also comparisons to the Brazilian Kaká. Pastore was dynamic and energetic – his stringy legs gave him a surprising burst of pace, and he was a brilliant dribbler. He pulled off caños and roulettes, drew players towards him as Riquelme did, then used trickery to slip by them and play a devastating pass. He was the standout player in Cappa's thrilling side, orchestrating attacks with the maturity of a veteran, his every touch a sumptuous display of skill and talent. He scored seven goals in that campaign, with three assists.

Big European clubs were interested but Pastore was of Italian stock and, advised by his family, he reportedly turned down Manchester United, Barcelona, Porto and Chelsea to sign for Palermo in a €4.7m deal. There he found himself in a team stuffed with talented young attacking players such as Uruguayan youngster Abel Hernández and, in his second season, the Slovenian Josip Iličić. Pastore was soon the first-choice playmaker, though, behind the deadly strike partnership of Edinson Cavani and Fabrizio Miccoli. After needing a few months to settle, Pastore had clearly adapted to European football and his full arsenal of tricks and plays was evident. He helped Palermo to a fifth-place finish in Serie A, scoring 14 goals and achieving ten assists in 69 games during his spell there.

Maradona called Pastore up for Argentina for an unofficial 'friendly' against the Catalonia national team in December 2009, but he made his proper debut against Canada in May 2010. Like all other Argentina players in that era, his inclusion would be dependent on his ability to play alongside Messi. But Pastore was an intelligent player and, when they did feature together, he and Messi were beautifully complementary.

Messi always seemed to appreciate a player who was on a similar wavelength – somebody who could receive his passes and give him the ball back. Pastore – alongside the likes of Banega and Gago – was cultured enough to do that to a Barcelona standard in the Argentina squad. Pastore would, however, have a mixed Argentina career in a difficult era. He played at the 2010 World Cup for Maradona, coming on as a sub as a 20-year-old in a couple of wins. He also played in three Copa América tournaments but it was there that the lack of continuity hurt him. He was seen as a bit of a luxury in a team that already had one top-class creative attacking midfielder in the form of Messi. Playing both together from the start of a game was a risk most Argentina coaches were unwilling to take. The likes of Sabella would always opt for the extra insurance of a Biglia or Banega alongside Mascherano rather than Pastore, who played a pass further forward and provided less defensive presence.

* * *

He and Messi were never really given the chance to nurture their understanding. That was partly because Pastore was becoming increasingly injury-prone, with that skinny frame responding to years of high-level sport by repeatedly breaking down. In the 2015 Copa América, Pastore was given a run in the side alongside Messi by coach Gerardo Martino and responded with his best football in an Argentina shirt. His presence against a muscular Uruguay in the group phase allowed Messi to focus on doing damage closer to goal, and Pastore played in every match until the final, notching a goal and an assist in the 6-1 semi-final evisceration of Paraguay.

He was back in the squad for the Copa América Centenario in 2016 but by now the younger Erik Lamela and Nicolás Gaitán had risen above him in Martino's pecking order. For all his talent and the glimpses of magic he showed for his country, in terms of his entire career he was yet another attacking player who seemed to underperform for Argentina.

Most football fans will know Pastore for his role in the rise of Paris Saint-Germain. PSG were only founded in 1970 following the merger of the newly established Paris FC and the much older Stade Saint-Germain, who dated from 1904. The new club struggled to establish itself and earn the support of the huge potential fanbase in the French capital but, by the mid-1990s, PSG had won two league titles and a slew of cup competitions. When the merger first took place, though, they were a typical Ligue 1 club – just as likely to finish mid-table as in the European places. Marseille and Olympique Lyonnais were dependably more successful big clubs, with the history of the likes of Bordeaux and Saint-Étienne meaning they, too, were high in the ranking of French clubs.

In 2011, Qatar Sports Investments (QSI) purchased PSG and instantly set about transforming it into one of Europe's biggest clubs, capable of regularly winning the Champions League. With the financial might of a gulf state to call on, PSG bought more or less a whole new team in the 2011 transfer window in a move perhaps reminiscent of Chelsea or Manchester City.

French internationals Blaise Matuidi and Kevin Gameiro, Pastore's Palermo team-mate Salvatore Sirigu and the Brazilian Maxwell were all picked up. No expense was spared, although most of the players were young and had some resell value. Pastore was the crown jewel of that shopping spree, admired and coveted by clubs across the continent. He cost the club somewhere between €38m and €56m. He was a statement of intent and the record transfer in French football history.

In that season, despite all the money spent, PSG lost out on the title to Montpelier, although Pastore generally performed well, with 13 goals in 33 games amid plenty of stylish football and YouTube-fodder tricks to wow Parisian fans. Considering many big-money players crumbled under pressure, Pastore seemed to love the big stage he found himself on in Paris.

But the pressure he had been under for one season was blown away in the 2012 summer transfer window. In came a host of superstars and suddenly Pastore was no longer the biggest fish in the dressing room. Zlatan Ibrahimović, Thiago Silva, Marco Verratti and Ezequiel Lavezzi all arrived from Serie A. Lucas Moura came from Brazil to compete for the playmaker role. David Beckham arrived from LA Galaxy.

Ibrahimović was key but Pastore kept his place and became more of a creator behind the Swede and his compatriot Lavezzi, with eight assists that season alongside nine goals. Pastore's stated wish to play more like Riquelme had become something of a reality as he added more substance to his elegant, lovely style.

PSG won Ligue 1 by 12 points from Marseille but again strengthened that summer, reuniting Pastore with Cavani. In 2013/14, Pastore suffered a few injuries and his form was affected but the season after was probably the best of his career. He seemed like a mature footballer with a new appreciation for the nature of the game and his own talent. He was consistently influential for the first time after years when he could fade into the background of a game.

In all, Pastore spent seven seasons at Paris Saint-Germain, scoring 45 goals in 269 games. He won five league titles and 11 French cup competitions. He was a focal point in the club's shift from potential giant to actual giant, and his effortlessly stylish football gave the team a gloss of entertainment value and beauty that might have been at odds with the nature of the project.

In his last seasons there, however, he was increasingly dogged by niggling injuries that prevented him having a sustained spell of his best form. He was also overshadowed by bigger stars and their huge egos – starting with Ibrahimović. They had good chemistry on the pitch but as soon as Zlatan had departed, Pastore took his number 10 shirt. It felt like he should have worn it all along.

But he would only have it for a single season. With the arrival of Neymar in summer 2017, Pastore gave up the shirt for the Brazilian to 'make him feel welcome'. It is hard not to feel that this showed an unwelcome amount of humility and passivity from the Argentine. Would his idol Riquelme have been so welcoming? Would Messi? It also showed how much his stock had fallen in Paris. Indeed, that would be his last season in France, with a move to Roma for €24.7m following in June 2018. By then, it felt as though Pastore's time had passed. He was only 29 but he had played his last game for Argentina. He had been eclipsed by younger, brighter stars at PSG. For all his talent, he had never quite become the generational superstar he had threatened to be.

Pastore wasn't adored or respected the way some other Argentina number tens have been. He produced three seasons of slow but unmistakable decline at Roma before mutually terminating his contract and moving to Elche in La Liga in September 2021. There the story was similar. That version of Pastore barely seemed the same player as the one at Huracán, Palermo and PSG. In January 2023, his contract was terminated and he followed the money, signing as a free agent for Qatar SC of Doha.

It was a career going out with a whimper and a talent that had never really been fulfilled. The hope in Córdoba is that he will finally return home for a season or two back at Talleres, where he began, but he is 33 years old now, and time is short. For a peer of Messi's who invited comparison with Riquelme, Pastore's glittering career seems paradoxically not glittering enough for his often sublime gifts. At Huracán, he looked as though he could do anything. European football soon showed the folly of that notion.

* * *

His opponent in the same role for Vélez in 'La Final Bastarda' would also try his luck in Europe, although Maxi Moralez was never quite as beloved as Pastore was. They were almost physical opposites; whereas Pastore was rangy, Moralez was squat. At just 5ft 2in, his nickname 'Frasquito' (small flask) seemed apt but it gave him the low centre of gravity that was crucial to the earliest generations of players performing flashy gambetas in Argentina, and he allied that with an eye for a pass and a goal.

Hailing from Granadero Baigorria, just outside Rosario, Moralez was at Racing Club in Avellaneda from an early age and made his debut in 2005 at 18. His talent and potential were immediately evident: his dribbling was superb, he could play off either foot, and his awareness was brilliantly developed for a young player. Like many young Argentine attackers, he was selfish at that age – running up blind alleys, trying to create chances for himself when passes to team-mates were on, taking on one player too many. But fans will forgive those traits if a player shows grit and flair, and Maxi had both.

He developed steadily over two years in Racing's first team, scoring eight goals in 52 games. His ability was recognised by Argentina's youth system when he was called up for the South American U20 Championship in 2007 alongside the likes of Di María, Banega and Franco Di Santo. Moralez was handed the number 10 shirt in recognition of his singular role and potential influence. The team played well in patches but finished third, never quite gelling as an attacking force. What it missed was a quality striker.

Soon after, Moralez was key to the squad that travelled to Canada for the 2007 FIFA U20 World Cup. That squad was largely the same as the one from the South American Championship, with the addition of Papu Gómez, Mauro Zárate and, in the role of that quality striker, Sergio Agüero.

Although Kun wore the number 10 shirt this time – he was the team's star player – Maxi revelled in the playmaker role and enjoyed a stellar tournament. With Claudio Yacob and Banega offering bite and creativity behind him at the base of midfield, Di María and Zárate buzzing around the box and Agüero his usual mercurial self, Moralez had plenty of the ball and numerous options when in possession. He and Agüero rapidly developed a fine understanding, finding each other consistently with blind passes, flicked one-twos and lofted dinks. Moralez scored four goals to Agüero's six as Argentina won the tournament. He looked every inch the next great number ten from the conveyor belt of Argentinian talent.

European clubs watched that Argentina side in Canada and most of the standout players would soon be playing for clubs on the old continent. Maxi was one of the first to move – too soon, it would turn out – when he joined FC Moscow for €8.7m, including a €3.6m signing-on fee. FC Moscow had only been founded in 2004 and would be dissolved in 2010 but they devoted significant funds to creating a competitive team during their short existence, with Argentine striker Maxi López also joining from Barcelona in that window.

Moralez was only 20 at the time and, aside from the obvious attraction of the money, it was a strange move for a young player of such promise to make. As it turned out, he only lasted six unhappy months in the cold and culture shock of Russia before returning on loan to Argentina and Racing Club. He had only played six games.

Back at Racing and in the number 10 shirt, Moralez was inspired as the club battled to avoid a catastrophic relegation. He scored eight goals in 36 games that season, the best figures in his career so far, but it wasn't enough. Come the end of the season, Racing faced a relegation play-off against Belgrano.

The first leg was a 1-1 draw in Córdoba. In the second leg, at El Cilindro, Maxi scored a fine goal to give Racing a 1-0 win, a 2-1 aggregate victory, and continued top-flight status. His status as a club legend was instantly assured but he was in a strange position – plainly talented enough for

Europe, despite his Russian experience, but too expensive for a perennially cash-strapped Racing Club.

That is where Vélez Sarsfield came in. A famously well-run club, financially stable due to sensible foresight when dealing with players, they could afford to pay Maxi what he felt he was worth, and he joined in January 2009. That season was the one that climaxed in the defining game against Huracán, and Maxi was a key player all season. With pace and power in the players around him, he could flit into spaces, fire off shots from distance, craft opportunities with his astute passing, and scythe through defensive lines with bursts of dribbling.

* * *

El Gráfico magazine wrote a cover story on the new enganches in June that year, with Pastore, Moralez and Lanús' Sebastián Blanco posing together and answering questions such as who was their favourite Argentina number ten, historically and currently; whether they preferred scoring or assisting; and whether number tens were an endangered species.

All three chose Maradona as their favourite historical ten but when it came to contemporary players, Pastore opted for Riquelme, Blanco chose Aimar, and Maxi went for Messi, probably sensing a similarity in their stature and mixture of passing and dribbling.

Moralez remained at Vélez for two years, winning another league title in 2011 and helping the team reach the semi-finals of the 2011 Copa Libertadores. There, they were unlucky to go out on away goals to Uruguayan giants Peñarol, spending the last 20 minutes of the home leg 2-1 up, camped around the opposition box but needing another goal to qualify. It didn't happen, and Moralez was ready for another crack at Europe.

He had matured as a player and a man and, after 72 games and 20 goals at Vélez, he realised the time-honoured route of playing for a smaller team in one of Europe's big leagues was the sensible way to go. In July 2011 he joined Atalanta in Italy for €5.3m. Before the success the club enjoyed in the late 2010s and early 2020s, Atalanta were consistently average. Well supported for a regional team with a solid base of fans in Lombardy, they reached the occasional cup final but were also relegated and promoted on a regular basis.

Maxi did well in Italy, establishing himself as a good Serie A player without ever threatening a move to any of the heavyweight clubs or to another European league. His size definitely counted against him in a football culture where players are bigger, stronger and more athletic – it meant he had to be better. He was better, though. His brain, touch and vision helped him score 18 goals and assist another 20 in 142 Atalanta games and in his last year at the club he was reunited with his old team-mate from Argentinian youth teams, Papu Gómez.

Moralez spoke of wanting to win trophies instead of Atalanta's annual battle to avoid relegation and so, in the January transfer window in 2016, he left Europe to return to the Americas. Like an increasing number of Argentine players, he headed north, to Mexico. Club León of Guanajuato in central Mexico were ambitious, adding Maxi to a roster of Argentines in a variety of positions and with differing levels of quality. Guillermo Burdisso, Mauro Boselli, Germán Cano, Diego Novaretti and Juan Cuevas all became team-mates but Maxi was seen as a big player, one of the most important transfers into Mexican football for a number of seasons.

He spoke of his desire to stay and win things, although the rumours linking him with a return to Racing Club circled back around every transfer window. Maxi did well enough in Liga MX but ended another season without a trophy. There was a feeling that the best years of his career were slipping away without a defining club or statement beyond Argentina. His talent was undeniable, but was he squandering it by choosing the wrong projects and leagues?

* * *

The success of several Argentine playmakers in the MLS in the US – most notably Diego Valeri – had gradually given it a reputation as the perfect place for a certain type of South American talent to thrive. The money was excellent, the lifestyle beyond anything possible in South America in terms of privacy and comfort, and the football was, well, easy. Lacking in the consistent quality of European leagues, the MLS gave a gifted enganche the platform to thrive.

Deciding it was the perfect move for his family and career, Maxi moved to New York City FC as a 'designated player' in February 2017. He replaced departing England legend Frank Lampard and fitted straight into a team alongside a couple of other iconic Europeans in the declining years of their careers, David Villa and Andrea Pirlo. The younger, hungrier Moralez became a key player and would remain in New York for five seasons, making himself a club legend and finally helping them to claim a first MLS Cup. That victory came against Valeri and Blanco, both playing for Portland Timbers, at the Timbers' home ground of Providence Park on 11 December 2021.

Maxi had missed huge swathes of the previous season with the sort of recurrent injuries that increasingly affect an ageing footballer, and his regular return to the side in 2021 was like having a new signing. He sparkled in the final, scoring a crucial penalty in the shoot-out that followed the 1-1 draw.

Maxi spent one last season at NYCFC before the inevitable occurred and he returned to Racing in December 2022 on a free transfer aged 35. His career was an interesting one in terms of how glory and adulation in Argentina can become indifference in other countries. Maxi Moralez was never quite good enough to become a big star in Europe, but he was loved in Argentina and the US.

After his stardom in youth teams, he managed only a single cap for Argentina, and even that is a marker of where his talent placed him on the conveyor belt of ability. He played in a side composed mostly of domestic players for the 4-1 defeat of Venezuela in March 2011.

Selected by Sergio Batista, he played with standout players from the Primera including Valeri; old youth-team colleague Claudio Yacob, who would go on to enjoy a solid career in England with six seasons at West Bromwich Albion guaranteeing him cult status in the West Midlands; Pastore's 'new Messi' Huracán team-mate Defederico; and striker Lisandro Lópe, who, despite years of success in Europe at Porto and Lyon, was rarely given opportunities for the national team.

Moralez played well, but there were just too many abundantly talented players ahead of him in the queue. His role as a number ten from Argentina gave him a certain profile but also a peculiar expectation. Although he had an excellent career by all accounts, he and Pastore were both measured against the other players from their homeland who had worn the same number on the back of their shirts.

Football had changed, even in the few years since Riquelme had thrived as an old-school enganche in La Liga. A playmaker now needed to be faultless if they expected to play in the zone between attack and midfield – there was so little space on a pitch crammed with supremely athletic players and so little time in which a creative ballplayer could operate.

Riquelme had a generational talent, and even he had struggled at times, but for the likes of Pastore and Moralez he was a point of reference and comparison, as was the player many believed was the 'GOAT'. In the age of Lionel Messi, it was hard to stand out.

TWELVE

Franco Di Santo, 'Crespito'
Mauro Zárate, 'El Pibe de Haedo'
Diego Buonanotte, 'El Enano'

AFTER A while, the 'new Maradona' tag became something that could be a weight around a young player's neck, as we have seen in the previous chapters. Few players had the talent or mentality to live up to a comparison with one of the greatest players in history and a player who had transcended the sport in his homeland. But it was also a marketing ploy. If an agent wanted to swing the spotlight on to a young Argentinian player, he could just compare him to Maradona – myth and the media would do the rest.

Argentine football has a very strong sense of its own history and identity – coaches at youth level are encouraged to play their teams in either 4-3-3 or 4-2-3-1 formations because it supports the continuing production of young attacking midfielders, by this point the country's greatest contribution to the global football marketplace. Players were sold and pushed as the new Argentinian playmaking sensation – the new Messi, the new Maradona – and that was even the case when the comparison made no sense whatsoever.

Franco Di Santo was born in Mendoza, Argentina's fourth city, in 1989 but, unusually for an Argentine youngster, he broke through at Audax Italiano in La Florida, a big suburban satellite of Santiago, Chile. Audax regularly crossed the border into the Argentinian towns on the edge of the Andes, and they spotted Di Santo playing in the youth teams of Godoy Cruz, the most consistently successful club in the region.

He signed terms with Audax Italiano in July 2005 and, after a year in their youth system, he made the senior squad. At first he started mostly on the bench but by 2007 he was a precocious target man and goal threat. His performances in the Copa Libertadores – in the club's first-ever campaign – were impressive but it was his improved effectiveness in the area that drew admiring glances. That season he scored 12 goals in 14 games to attract a lot of attention from Europe.

Chile was a good market for European sides – impoverished Chilean clubs were willing to sell at bargain prices – and Chelsea bought Di Santo for £3.4m. Aged just 19, he was a beanpole of a striker; 6ft 4in and skinny. The cliché 'good feet for a big man' was true in his case but he was also deadly in the air. He was a true number nine – a poacher with good movement for his age, and ability to finish with both feet.

The 'new Maradona' tag seemed to emerge when he was playing in Chelsea's reserves, probably from somebody inside the club or their fanbase. It was based on two lazy facts: Di Santo was Argentinian like Maradona and, for a youngster, was incredibly prolific in that period, like

Maradona. He scored 16 goals in 13 games for Chelsea reserves and in the 2008/09 season was included in the first-team squad, which was full of established internationals in every position. In the forward roles, Di Santo was competing with Didier Drogba, Joe Cole, Salomon Kalou and Nicolas Anelka for one of two spots.

He made eight appearances as substitute that season without scoring. The 'new Maradona' tag already looked silly for this rangy centre-forward, who resembled Peter Crouch more than anyone else. His nickname from Chile was more appropriate, even at Chelsea – 'Crespito' meant 'little Crespo' – but he did not possess Crespo's superb movement or his goalscoring record and his career became that of a journeyman, as if it had been designed to showcase the dangers of labelling any young player as the 'new Maradona'.

Chelsea sent him on loan to Blackburn Rovers in 2009/10. He started well and his loan was extended to the second half of the season but his lack of goals at that level was becoming a problem – he got three in 22 that year – and Rovers sent him back to Chelsea.

Chelsea had seen enough. They were a club who always wanted a quick solution – preferring big-money transfers to developing youth players – and Di Santo was sold to Wigan Athletic in August 2010. He stayed there for three seasons, was part of an FA Cup-winning squad, and scored 13 goals in 92 games. He proved himself a good team player in a squad under Spanish coach Roberto Martínez that had a significant Latin American contingent following the success of Ecuadorian star Antonio Valencia, whose performances for the club had earned him a move to Manchester United.

Alongside Di Santo was his compatriot Mauro Boselli, Honduran centre-back Maynor Figueroa and Colombian striker Hugo Rodallega. Di Santo's time in English football had toughened him up and now he was adept at holding the ball up and bringing team-mates into the game. He scored 13 goals in three seasons at Wigan. At the end of the 2012/13 season, Wigan beat Manchester City to win the FA Cup but were relegated from the Premier League. Di Santo had not played in the final and, following Martínez's resignation, Wigan released him.

* * *

After England, Di Santo went to Germany. Two seasons at Werder Bremen led to the best goals-to-games ratio of his career, 18 in 49 appearances. That earned him a move to one of the country's traditional giants, FC Schalke 04, for €6m. He also surprisingly reappeared in the Argentina squad. Sabella had called him up during a patch of good form while he was at Wigan in 2012. He came off the bench late on in a friendly against Saudi Arabia in November and again against Sweden in February 2013. But Di Santo's inclusion in the provisional 30-man squad for the 2014 World Cup was a bit of a shock. He was presumably there as cover for Higuaín, and he was cut when the final squad was announced.

His time at Schalke was not successful, however. In four seasons and 71 games, he only managed five goals and left on a free transfer. That was followed by six games in six months at Rayo Vallecano in La Liga in 2019 that resulted in zero goals. At the age of 30, he returned to South America.

First stop was a season at Atlético Mineiro in Brazil, followed by two years back in Argentina where he did well at San Lorenzo, with ten goals in 33 games. His career was ending the way of so many mid-level professionals, that of a wanderer continually looking for one last season. Now 33, he went wherever he could play – a short spell at Göztepe SK in Izmir, Turkey was followed by five games for Xolos of Tijuana in Mexico.

In December 2022, while some of the Argentina players he had played alongside in youth teams and the senior side were competing for and winning the World Cup in Qatar, Di Santo was returning to where it had all started for him – Chilean football – when he signed for Universidad Católica. The days of being compared to Diego Maradona were far behind him. However, if Di Santo was a wanderer in his career, he does not begin to compare with the nomadic life of Mauro Zárate.

* * *

Zárate came from a football family. His father and brothers were all professionals, although none really made it at the elite end of the game despite playing for the likes of Independiente and Nuremberg. Mauro was born in Haedo, a suburb of Buenos Aires, in 1987. His nickname, 'El Pibe de Haedo' (the kid from Haedo), references his origin while also recalling Maradona's 'pibe' nickname, an indication of the expectations on Zárate from an early age. He was on the books of Vélez Sarsfield as a youngster and had already broken into the first team by the time he was 17 in 2004.

He was part of the team that won the Clausura title in 2005 and his progress was consistent and remarkable. His brother Rolando had been a star at the club almost a decade before but Mauro had significantly more potential. He was an Argentinian number ten, with all the gifts that implies. He could dribble past players and had an arrogance about his own ability that made him try flicks and tricks. His passing was excellent, over long and short range, and he was brilliant with a dead ball. He could play in the hole like a traditional enganche or as a second striker.

In the 2006/07 season, Zárate was a fixture in the Vélez starting line-up and scored a lot of goals, finding the net 19 times to become joint-highest scorer alongside Boca's Rodrigo Palacio. That made Zárate one of the hottest young prospects in Argentina and his multifaceted attacking play and short, stocky stature meant he was compared, of course, to Maradona. But there was another Argentine phenomenon in town, and Zárate was also one of the first players to be compared to Lionel Messi.

Messi's impact was already great enough that players with any resemblance to him might be dubbed 'the new Messi'. But as well as his stupendous longevity and consistency, Messi's career was marked by a lack of drama. No player could hope to emulate both Messi and Maradona – their only real shared traits were nationality, shirt number, and football brilliance. Zárate had the first two and, while he was undoubtedly a brilliant player, he was not quite on the level of his two compatriots. Still, there was time for him to develop further and he showed so much promise. In 2007, he starred in the Argentina youth team and was a key player in the U20 World Cup win, alongside Agüero – who stole most of the limelight – and Di María.

Like those players, Zárate was soon on his way out of Argentine domestic football as a host of European clubs vied for his signature. His brother Sergio was his agent, which might explain Zárate's next decision. Sergio had played for eight clubs during a two-decade career and, while he had featured for Mexico City giants Club América and briefly for German powerhouses Hamburg, he had never had that breakthrough season that established him as a big name or gave him financial security. Instead, he had moved around the world for his career and managed a solitary Argentina cap, in 1992.

Meanwhile, their other brother, Ariel, had played in Spain for most of his career, with nine clubs, peaking during a spell with Málaga. The most gifted of the older three boys was Rolando, who had reached the heights of Real Madrid in 1999/2000, scoring one goal in six La Liga games. Aside from that, he had 13 clubs in his career, with his best spells at Vélez bookending a life of wandering from Spain to Scotland and from Ecuador to Saudi Arabia and Mexico. He won two Argentina caps – in games when an all-domestic team was selected – and a short stint at River Plate but his career, like that of his brothers, must have been a cautionary tale for young Mauro.

Football is a business and players are commodities, so while many young players moving to Europe were thinking about legacy, plotting pathways from one league and club to another, Zárate thought about money. In June 2007 he signed for Al Sadd of Doha in Qatar for £13m and a lucrative personal contract. At a stroke, he had done what none of his brothers had managed – he had secured himself financially – but he had also damaged his career. Zárate would never be the new Maradona or Messi.

Clubs in the Gulf were where Argentine players went as they neared retirement and fancied a hefty payday to cushion that transition. Éver Banega, for example, left Sevilla for Al-Shabab in Riyadh, Saudi Arabia in 2020 at the age of 32, after years in Europe and with the Argentina team. Zárate was still a prospect, however, and it felt as though he was sending his career backwards. He only played six games for Al Sadd, scoring four goals, before he was off to European football on loan. Even then, his choice was unlikely; he signed for Birmingham City, who were struggling badly in the Premier League, in January 2008.

Traditionally, Birmingham's second club behind fierce rivals Aston Villa, City had been bought by Hong Kong businessman Carson Yeung in summer 2007 and showed financial ambition. Zárate's loan deal had an option for a permanent transfer if it went well. It did go well, but not well enough for him to stay at the club. He scored four goals in 14 games and wowed City fans with his flair and vision, but the club were relegated and he was left searching for another loan deal.

* * *

He found it at Lazio, where he signed up to a similar loan with an option to extend, and his football that season was probably the best of his career. Zárate scored 13 goals in 36 games, and many of his goals and best performances came in big games and against hated rivals. He scored in the Coppa Italia Final and the resulting penalty shoot-out against Sampdoria to help secure Lazio's first trophy in four years.

Lazio's ultras loved him and, when his loan was made permanent at the end of a successful season, Lazio buying out his contract for £17m, Zárate was free to show that he loved them too. When he was injured, he attended games with fans. During a loss to Bari, he was photographed giving a fascist salute, and the Italian press did not hold back. Zárate said he was unaware that the gesture had negative connotations and he did not know who Hitler or Mussolini were. In interviews, he never came across as intellectual exactly but such ignorance was barely credible.

His problems at Lazio came in a wave. The first season of his contract started brilliantly but his form deserted him. He scored half as many goals as he had the year before, which would be the case the season after that as well. And then a similarity to Maradona emerged – he responded extremely badly to criticism. He was accused of selfishness and egotism in his play and refusing to adapt his game. He also fell out with coaches – returning to Argentina without permission and criticising tactics and man-management in the media. In addition, Lazio were suddenly forced to pay off Vélez Sarsfield for sums owed after his transfer to Al Sadd.

Zárate might have been worth all that trouble if he had maintained the form he had shown in his season on loan – living up to the billing of Maradona or Messi – but he was misfiring and expensive so Lazio put him up for sale. He would play for 12 clubs over the next 11 years, his career resembling a much better-paid version of the ones experienced by his brothers.

Zárate never played for the senior Argentina side, which is extremely telling. He was never going to play instead of Messi and the host of alternatives who were in and out of the squad were all better than him or a lot less trouble.

He even declared he would play for Chile, based on his father's nationality, but they declined to select him too. Who needed the headache of a Zárate when Chile already had Jorge Valdívia and Matías Fernández? Instead, Zárate played for Inter Milan in 2011/12 followed by a good year back at Vélez before returning to the Premier League to play for West Ham, Queens Park Rangers and Watford between 2014 and 2018, with a year at Fiorentina in the middle. Next came eight games at Al-Nasr in Dubai followed by another spell at Vélez, which prompted Boca Juniors to take him on.

He enjoyed a few good years at Boca but left in 2021 for another nomadic spell. Brief interludes at América Mineiro and Juventude in Brazil preceded another return to Buenos Aires, where he signed for Platense in 2022, still capable of flashes of brilliance at the age of 35 but having failed to fulfil his undoubted potential.

* * *

The confusion over whether Zárate was the 'new Maradona' or the 'new Messi' was not unique to him. While Argentine players such as Juan Iturbe and Matías Defederico were never really compared to Maradona, their size and dribbling did invite comparisons to Messi. But then a whole generation of young creative players across the world was discovering they might be compared to Messi because fans and the press were lazy and unimaginative. Players as disparate as Erik Lamela, Martin Odegaard, Neymar, Sebastian Giovinco, Christian Eriksen and Pedro were all compared to him at one point or another. You just had to be young and extravagantly talented.

Diego Buonanotte was both and he emerged at River Plate, home to several notable 'new Maradona' candidates before him. He was receiving attention from those in the know in Buenos Aires before Messi had broken through at Barcelona, so the Maradona comparisons came first. It was only when he started playing in the first team, in 2006, that he was compared to Messi. In between, he was also dubbed the 'new Aimar' just for good measure.

Buonanotte was born in Santa Fe Province in 1988, and was spotted early by River Plate's scouts. He joined the academy at the age of 13 and his precocity and skill were soon raising eyebrows. Buonanotte was tiny – his nickname 'El Enano' means 'the dwarf' – and at 5ft 3in and with a slight frame, he looked too small to be a footballer. However, he had all the classic gifts of an Argentine number ten. His dribbling was superb. Blessed with the fine balance bestowed by his low centre of gravity, he floated past players and could turn them on either side. He never looked as though he had blinding pace but once he beat a man he was away, surging into space. He would also pause in his running, inviting challenges and pulling defenders towards him so he could either receive a free kick for the inevitable foul, or slip the ball into the path of a team-mate.

Buonanotte possessed a fine variety in his shooting, with surprising power and the ability to curl drives from distance. If you watched him play in his early days at River, the comparisons to a young Messi made perfect sense – he was resilient, dynamic and creative. In a team where he was learning at the feet of veteran Ariel Ortega, he had seemingly limitless potential.

* * *

Buonanotte broke into the senior side at River in 2006/07 but made only a single appearance. In 2007/08 he really arrived, scoring 11 goals in 33 games, playing off either wing or in the centre. The River squad under coach Diego Simeone had an awesome amount of young talent in attack – Buonanotte was playing alongside Radamel Falcao,

Alexis Sánchez and Sebastián Abreu, as another veteran alongside Ortega.

Buonanotte looked perhaps the most promising and was arguably the brightest star in domestic Argentinian football at the time, playing a huge part in River winning the 2008 Apertura title. He was rewarded with a call-up to the 2008 Olympics squad, making his only appearance in the group game against Serbia in which he scored a fine goal with a free kick.

But bad things were around the corner. In December 2009, in the middle of another good season with River, after marking himself out as one of the players of the tournament at Toulon in the summer, Buonanotte was driving his father's car home from a night out when he lost control of the vehicle on the Route 65 freeway in Santa Fe.

It was raining, the road was in a bad condition and, when the car went into a skid, Buonanotte – later confirmed to have had no alcohol or narcotics in his system – could not bring it under control. It hit a tree and all three of Buonanotte's passengers – three of his closest friends – were killed. None of them had been wearing a seat belt.

Buonanotte was badly injured, with a broken collarbone and humerus as well as injuries to his lungs. Doctors said he would be away from football for seven months but he returned to River and the pitch in April. Physically he was healed, but with opposition supporters reminding him of what had happened in the loudest terms possible, it seemed unlikely he would ever truly recover from what happened on that road. Although he was still a game-breaker for River, capable of flashes of brilliance, there is the definite sense that he never lived up to his potential.

Buonanotte inevitably moved to Europe in 2011. Málaga, newly wealthy under Qatari ownership, were set on buying a mix of experienced stars and exciting youngsters, and Buonanotte fitted the latter category. They paid £3.5m for him and he joined experienced pros such as Ruud van Nistelrooy, Júlio Baptista, Jérémy Toulalan and Joaquín alongside other youngsters like Santi Cazorla and Isco. Málaga meant business.

It worked in the short term but Buonanotte failed to force his way into the team, even after the financial picture changed and several stars departed. He only played 35 times in two seasons, many of those appearances as substitute, and managed a mere five goals. This was not the new Messi the world had seen before the accident.

Buonanotte stayed in Europe, moving to another Andalucian club when he joined Granada in January 2013 for €2.3m. His form over two seasons there was similar to his time at Málaga and so, like so many players of his ilk, he entered a journeyman phase.

He went on loan to Pachuca in Mexico and from there back to Buenos Aires for a spell with Quilmes. AEK Athens finally gave him a move with a free transfer in August 2015. He performed well enough there, with nine goals in 27 appearances over two seasons. He also won the Greek cup but again he was mostly used as a substitute and it felt as though that was the extent of his talent in European football. He could come on for a flash of magic but could not consistently make the difference. Too small, too inconsistent.

Buonanotte took the hint and moved back to South America, joining Chile's Universidad Católica in July 2016 on another free transfer. He was only 28, theoretically in his prime. He thrived in Chile, winning three league titles, scoring 26 goals in 136 games and becoming an important player but it still felt as though he had been destined for more, a promise that had been ruined by the car crash.

He was also unfortunate to emerge in an era when Argentina had a glut of players in his position – at least one or more senior caps was expected for the fearless kid roasting veteran defenders alive in 2007 and 2008, but Diego Buonanotte never even got one. He had a fine career by most standards: won trophies in several countries, played for big clubs in massive stadiums, experienced many glorious moments. It is a tribute to his youthful talent that all of that feels somehow insufficient.

THIRTEEN

Paulo Dybala, 'La Joya'
Diego Valeri, 'El Maestro'

PAULO DYBALA may be the last Argentinian footballer to be called the 'new Maradona' the way so many before him had been. The impact of Leo Messi has finally broken that paradigm, and as Messi's career and success stretched over the years, so Maradona's achievements became something historical and ancient.

Football has a short memory and recency bias warps the way supporters and the press view the game – so the next time a little playmaker emerges from Argentina with dribbling skills, vision and goalscoring ability, the likelihood is that he will be compared to Messi and not Maradona.

The Messi comparison will make sense to more people in the modern world, and Messi's 2022 triumph at the Qatar World Cup removed any doubts some might have had about his worthiness in comparison with his predecessor as Argentina number ten and captain. Only in Argentina itself and Naples will the cult of Maradona ensure he is still a point of reference for young stars.

Dybala is a case in point. He is left-footed and possesses many of the skills associated with a classic number ten. When he moved into senior football in Argentina, he set about breaking records and performing feats that should have been beyond a teenager. Then he moved to a club in southern Italy and continued to impress, to the extent he was wanted by Napoli.

That was enough to allow the Maradona comparisons to thrive, that and the fact Messi was still building his own legend while Dybala's career was entering its mature phase in Serie A, and he was taking faltering steps with the Argentina team, competing with several others for a place alongside Messi in the team.

Dybala was also – obviously – compared to Messi once he started to show his ability in European football. Messi would have to retire at some point, and somebody would have to definitively step up to replace him. For a long time, Dybala looked the most realistic candidate but his career didn't quite reach the heights many had expected, and he didn't become the dominant number ten he had threatened to be. At the age of 29, he remains a player with great potential who appears to have missed his big chance to some extent. He was never the 'new Maradona' but then, as we have seen, nobody is. Not even Lionel Messi.

Dybala was born in November 1993 in Laguna Larga, a small town outside Córdoba, Argentina's second-largest city. From a lower-middle-class family with a mix of Polish and Italian roots, his father was dedicated to his son's success, driving him to schoolboy games around Córdoba province to get him noticed.

Córdoba, like most Argentine cities, has numerous football clubs. The two traditional powerhouses in the city are Talleres and Belgrano, with Instituto and Racing typically playing in the second tier of Argentinian football. It was in that second tier –Primera B – that Dybala made his debut in 2011 at the age of 17. He had been playing for Instituto's youth sides from the age of ten. He was a bit taller than the archetypal 'pibe' number ten; at 5ft 10in he was agile and elusive. His hero was not Maradona or Messi but Riquelme, and Dybala possessed something of that player's elegance on the ball, a head-up awareness of what was going on around him.

He started off at Instituto on the wing but his versatility meant he could play anywhere across the attacking zone. He was perhaps best used as a playmaker between the lines or as a support striker, where his eye for a pass made him hard for defenders to handle. In his single year with Instituto's first team, 'La Joya' (the jewel) scored 17 goals in 38 games and broke a handful of records set by Córdoba legend Mario Kempes – youngest player to score for the club, first to score two hat-tricks in a season, and scoring in six consecutive games. It was an auspicious start to his career and Dybala's potential meant he didn't play in Argentina for long.

He joined Sicilian club Palermo in July 2012 for €8.6m, with Palermo chairman Maurizio Zamparini branding him the 'new Agüero', just to confuse everyone further. Dybala would spend three seasons at Palermo and, once he had adjusted to Serie A, proved to be one of the best players in the league.

Playing as a second striker, he could drop into the hole on the edge of the box to control the angles of attack, trick his way into a shooting position, or slip a pass through to his strike partner.

His long-range shooting meant he consistently gave himself highlight-reel goals and, while he did have elements of Riquelme and Messi in his game, Dybala's pace meant he could lead a sharp counter-attack with the ball at his feet, which made him a consistent threat. In reality, the player Dybala most resembled was another Córdoba boy who had thrived at Palermo before moving to a bigger club, Javier Pastore, who was busy winning titles at PSG but missing huge swathes of games through injury.

Palermo were relegated to Serie B in 2013/14 but Dybala stayed there and helped them win promotion back to the top flight. Then, truly acclimatised to the league, he had his best season with 13 goals and ten assists in 35 games.

* * *

Palermo had long been the kind of club South Americans such as Pastore and Edinson Cavani moved to as a springboard to bigger things and Dybala was sold to Juventus in June 2015 for €32m. While clubs had been angling to sign him, Napoli had been strongly linked, and those old Maradona comparisons were briefly revived as if the suggestion he could recreate the effect Maradona had on Naples would turn Dybala's head.

However, Juventus were Italy's biggest club and Dybala went where he had the best chance of winning trophies. He would stay in Turin for seven seasons, winning five Serie A titles and four Coppa Italias. His versatility would ultimately become a problem, though. At Palermo he had worn the number 9 shirt but played in his favourite role, as a second striker. At Juve, he took Andrea Pirlo's number 21 and was generally played in one of the forward roles by coach Massimiliano Allegri. Which one depended on his strike partner and whether the free-roaming, attack-minded central midfielder Paul Pogba was playing behind him, in which case they often occupied the same areas.

Playing that season as a dedicated striker in such a dominant side helped Dybala's goalscoring. He scored 23 goals in 46 games that year and maintained similar numbers for the next three seasons. Gonzalo Higuaín was recruited in 2016 and Dybala played deeper, but the duo found a good understanding as a front two. In summer 2017, Dybala accepted the number 10 shirt at the club, previously worn by legends such as Michel Platini, Liam Brady, Alessandro Del Piero, Roberto Baggio and Omar Sívori.

Juventus were routinely winning Serie A at that point and the Champions League became an all-consuming target for the club. They lost the 2017 final 4-1 to Real Madrid, though, with Dybala turning in an ineffectual performance. To win the trophy, Juventus went for a proven Champions League winner in the transfer market and bought Cristiano Ronaldo in July 2018 for €100m. His arrival changed the dynamic of Juventus as a team; he was a player purely devoted to scoring goals, with no defensive duties or interest in anything beyond getting the ball into the final third as quickly as possible. It worked – Ronaldo's goalscoring for Juventus was stupendous, with 101 goals in 134 games over three seasons – but it also damaged Dybala.

To offset Ronaldo's single-minded pursuit of goals, Allegri generally played Croatian target man Mario Mandžukić as his strike partner. The Croat would do the dirty work for the Portuguese star: running himself into the ground, making dummy runs, occupying defenders, foraging deep and pressuring defensive midfielders when they had the ball. Dybala had always been a defensively aware, hardworking striker but he didn't have Mandžukić's physical strength or quite the same warrior mentality.

That is where the likes of Messi and Maradona stand out and part of what made them so special. Messi would force the issue through pure quality. He was always the best player in his team. That was not true of Dybala, who went through patches of form. He had been the darling of the fans of the 'Old Lady' but, with the arrival of Ronaldo, he was disposable.

Dybala also lacked the assertive personality of Maradona, who was a leader, a provocateur. Maradona would have raged to be deposed as the focus of attack in his team when at his peak. But Dybala had a milder personality, spending his time praising Ronaldo on social media and massaging his own brand.

Juventus were not averse to selling star players if the money was right and, after two consistently underwhelming seasons for Juventus between 2020 and 2022, they bought prolific Serb striker Dušan Vlahović in summer 2022, intending to change their style of attacking football. A playmaker like Dybala was not part of the plan, and he was sold to Roma in July 2022.

Dybala had been on the market for a while but nobody seemed to be in a rush to sign him. Manchester United, Inter Milan and Tottenham Hotspur were consistently linked but his wage demands were huge – another reason Juve were happy to be rid of him. He had shown his tactical inflexibility over the latter half of his Juve stint, too, and he was increasingly injury-prone. He had contracted Covid during the pandemic and seemed more fragile after that, with a series of injuries badly affecting his form in his last two seasons in Turin. Nevertheless, Roma took him on a free transfer and he quickly looked like a shrewd signing.

In Rome he was met by a rapturous reception and assured of his importance. Working with great man-manager José Mourinho, the player seemed reborn. For all his mildness, perhaps Dybala needed to be treated like the talent he was and at Roma he was the big star of the attack in a team that always had a soft spot for a stylish number ten based on a long-time appreciation for the talents of Francesco Totti.

Dybala got off to a flyer in 2022/23, with seven goals in 12 Roma games, looking like the best attacker in Serie A again. He played behind a classic number nine in the form of England striker Tammy Abraham and the space that gave him to thrive as a second striker was greedily accepted, even if Abraham hadn't quite gelled with him yet when the season was paused for the 2022 World Cup.

* * *

Dybala had never played in Argentina's youth teams. He was called up to U17 and U20 sides but missed out through injury or because he had just moved to Sicily. There were numerous talented players in his position throughout the Argentine system and Dybala needed to prove his quality before he could truly compete with the likes of Messi, Agüero, Tevez, Pastore and Higuaín for a role in the attacking positions.

His first senior cap did not arrive until Martino brought him on as a substitute for Tevez – who he had just replaced at Juventus – in a September 2015 World Cup qualifier against Paraguay. After that, he never quite became a key component of the Argentina squad.

The main problem was that Messi was in the way. Dybala could contribute little that Messi did not already provide. He was already being touted as Messi's long-term replacement, but there were doubts about his consistency.

Martino wanted Dybala to play in the U23 team at the 2016 Olympics in Rio but Juventus refused to release him and he failed to make the squad for the Copa América Centenario. Instead, he was in and out of squads for qualifiers and friendlies; always an option off the bench or if Messi was absent but rarely fully convincing.

Dybala made Sampaoli's squad for the 2018 World Cup in Russia but featured only briefly as a substitute in the group-stage defeat to Croatia. In the 2019 Copa América, Scaloni picked him and he registered one goal and one assist in the competition while playing rarely.

Dybala missed the triumph in the 2021 Copa with one of those injuries that had marred his season at Juve, but Scaloni evidently saw his usefulness as an option in the squad as he went to the 2022 World Cup, even though younger players such as Julián Álvarez and Lautaro Martínez were now firmly ahead of him in the pecking order.

Dybala's inclusion was justified in the final when he was brought on in place of full-back Nicolás Tagliafico in the dying seconds of extra time so he could take a penalty in the decisive shoot-out. He scored with a cool rolled finish right down the middle, Lloris diving to his left, and Argentina won a few moments later. For all that his career with the national team had been somewhat disappointing, with 36 caps and three goals in seven years, Dybala was a world champion, and he celebrated accordingly.

There is still time for Dybala – he is only 29 and can still make an impact for Argentina – but nobody sees him as the new Maradona – Pelé said in an interview that he was not good enough for that – or the new Messi. But Messi will retire from international football at some stage and Dybala will be a contender to pick up that storied number 10 shirt, which has a mythic quality these days. Many clubs beyond Argentina have given their number ten an aura denied to other positions; it is the number worn by the most artistic player, the genius, the magician. Beyond Argentina, players such as Cruyff, Pelé, Neymar, Zico, Laudrup, Scifo, Rooney, Zidane, Hagi, Bergkamp, Ronaldinho, Stojković, Rui Costa, Baggio, Valderrama and Platini have all given the shirt some stardust in different countries and at different clubs. But the idea of the Argentinian number ten has become more persistent and exportable.

* * *

In the 2000s and 2010s, the MLS became a new market for Argentine playmakers seeking a nice lifestyle in a football culture that allowed them to express themselves. The unlikely model for that was Guillermo Barros Schelotto.

He had been a winger for Gimnasia La Plata in the 1990s, then moved to Boca Juniors in 1997 and was part of the sensational era of success under Carlos Bianchi. When Juan Román Riquelme emerged as first choice for the number ten role at Boca, Schelotto was versatile enough to play behind Martín Palermo as a second striker, to return to the wing where his dribbling could be devastating, or to replace Riquelme when he was injured.

He was at Boca for a decade and left an absolute legend, having won six titles, four Copa Libertadores, two Copa Sudamericana, two Recopa Sudamericana and two Intercontinental Cups. But he never went to Europe and featured for Argentina only ten times and never in a major tournament.

There is no doubt Schelotto was talented but he was also quite firmly a second-tier creative player, too good for the Argentinian league but not quite good enough to be a big player in Europe. So, in 2007 at the age of 34 when he was surplus to requirements at Boca and looking for a transfer, where could he go? The answer was the MLS.

To attract more recognised international talent to the league the MLS introduced the 'designated player' system in 2007, which helped LA Galaxy bring in David Beckham and all the publicity he could draw to soccer in the US. Designated players (DPs) were allowed wages beyond a club's salary cap and that rule would attract a number of 30-something Argentines over the next few years, including international players such as Marcelo Gallardo and Claudio López.

Schelotto would be the most successful DP in that era, however, after he signed a two-year contract with Columbus Crew. He remained there for three years and, once he had adjusted to the game in America, he made it look effortless. At 34, with his running power and pace significantly lessened, his touch and awareness were still a level above most of the players around him. American players then were extremely athletic and remorselessly coached, but the country had no culture of producing creative players.

Schelotto's ability to find team-mates and create chances made it appear he had more time than anybody else on the pitch. He had a fantastic season in 2008, powering the Crew to the MLS Cup and achieving three assists in their 3-1 victory over New York Red Bulls. He was also voted the league's MVP and scored seven goals with 19 assists.

His success made other MLS clubs realise Argentina – and other South American leagues to some extent – was fertile ground for young talent. Not everybody would get picked up by European vultures and the MLS could offer more money and a better lifestyle than most South American clubs. And so the cult of the Argentine number ten became part of US football culture.

* * *

Probably the greatest beneficiary and example of an Argentinian playmaker in MLS history, however, was not even a number ten – he was naturally a number eight. Nobody ever compared Diego Valeri to Maradona or Lionel Messi but he would make his own contribution to the way Argentinian creative players were regarded in modern football.

Valeri grew up in Lanús, a major industrial satellite of Buenos Aires. He played for the youth sides of big local team Club Atlético Lanús from the age of nine, then worked his way up through the reserves until he made his debut for the senior side in 2003 at the age of 21.

He was an almost perfect example of an Argentinian number eight. Athletic and hard working, he would run and defend but was also extremely creative when in possession. He could dribble and had a strapping, powerful physique but was perhaps better at establishing his passing game, creating a rhythm and exploiting defensive gaps.

The best examples of that type of player tend to go to Europe and flourish. In the athletic, tactical world of European football, the likes of Ossie Ardiles and

Lucho González were both regarded as highly creative playmakers who could also tackle and do the dirty work when necessary. It should have been the same for Valeri. He played a key part in Lanús' first-ever Argentine title triumph, dovetailing with the more classical number ten Sebastián Blanco behind striker José Sand to devastating effect in 2007/08. Valeri scored nine goals in 39 games that season and, as usual, European clubs came knocking.

Valeri went on loan to Porto in 2009/10. The club had proved masterful in its use of a South American scouting network over the previous decade, bringing in young unknowns for low prices, watching them explode in Portuguese football and European competitions, then selling them on at huge profit. Lucho González and Lisandro López were two recent Argentine examples.

Valeri joined a clutch of South Americans at the club including Fernando Belluschi, a talented enganche from River Plate via Olympiacos; Brazilians Hulk and Helton; and Colombian internationals Fredy Guarín and Radamel Falcao. Valeri never quite settled, though. He was mainly used as a substitute and never made enough of an impression for his loan to be extended.

In July 2010 he began another loan spell, this time at Almeria in La Liga. That didn't work out either, with nine uneventful appearances before the loan was cut short in December and he returned to Lanús. Valeri looked to be one of those players who was too good for Argentina but not good enough for Europe.

Over the next year there were enquiries from clubs in the US, including Chicago Fire and Seattle Sounders, and when he was carjacked in Buenos Aires in October 2012, Valeri decided it might be better for his family to get out of Argentina. He spoke to representatives of US clubs, who promised a life without the threat of violence from supporters, a nice house in a safe neighbourhood, a sporting culture designed to maximise player fitness and effectiveness, and very good money. That was crucial in an era when even the wealthiest Argentinian clubs struggled to pay their players on time.

Valeri joined Portland Timbers on a one-year loan in January 2013, with an option to extend. He was the club's designated player and his success in America would permanently change the model of what a DP could and should be. Whereas before Valeri – and after – many clubs went for a European star in the last years of their career, seeking one last payday, he showed that a good DP in their prime could bring results.

At the Timbers, Valeri wore the number eight but played like a number ten, floating at the tip of a midfield three, looking to feed his strikers and marauding full-backs with his acute passing. He was also a serious goal threat, with his shooting from distance and combination play a constant worry for opposition defences. In 262 games for Portland, Valeri scored 86 goals and recorded 91 assists. He became a talisman for the club and his success drew other South Americans to the league and to Portland. When his old Lanús team-mate Seba Blanco was signed from San Lorenzo in 2017, they rekindled their partnership. Valeri dropped deeper and played more as a prompter, while Blanco had a free role around him.

The Timbers Army adored Valeri – their huge tifo with the word 'Troesma' was both a reference to his 'Maestro' nickname and a play on the dialect of Lanús – and he was visibly moved by it. In his nine years in the MLS, Valeri led Portland to the MLS Cup in 2015, was instrumental in them winning the post-lockdown 'MLS Is Back' mini-tournament in 2020, and was MVP in 2017. He made the MLS All-Star team four times, became the Timbers' all-time leading goalscorer, and gained the nickname 'Saint Valeri' for his community and charity work in Portland. All of this from a player who only gained three Argentina caps, all in 2011 friendlies while he was starring for Lanús.

Valeri had shown the MLS the magic of an Argentinian playmaker, and the success of his contemporaries Federico Higuaín at Columbus Crew, Maxi Moralez at New York City FC and Mauro Díaz at Dallas demonstrated that other clubs had taken note. The Timbers coach who recruited Valeri, Caleb Porter, acknowledged that if an MLS club was looking for a creative player to add to their squad, Argentina was the best place to go shopping. In the late 2010s, Argentinians made up the second-biggest demographic of players in the MLS, behind Americans. Valeri was a trailblazer in that regard, and an influential figure.

As he was returning for a final six months at Lanús before retirement, younger Argentines were moving north to the US, which was also beginning to function as a kind of finishing school, polishing youngsters before their inevitable moves to Europe. Paraguayan attacker Miguel Almirón destroyed defences for Atlanta United between spells at Lanús and a lucrative move to Newcastle United, while Atlanta also bought Ezequiel Barco, the most-hyped Argentine youngster of his generation, in 2018, when he was only 19, then returned to the well for 20-year-old playmaker Thiago Almada in 2022.

While playing in the MLS might have harmed the chances of a Valeri or Moralez being selected for the

Argentina squad, by 2022 things had changed. Almada was part of the winning squad at Qatar 2022, playing as a substitute in the final few minutes of the 2-0 win over Poland in the group phase.

The mystique of the Argentine number ten had existed before Diego Maradona, and it had evolved and developed over the decades. In the new world of American soccer culture, it had just as much power as it had ever had. That power was based on quality football and players who delighted in the gambeta and the pausa as well as touch, awareness and passion. In that, for all the successes and failures of dozens of players at clubs across the world, the Argentinian enganche has never really changed.